Michael Smith's
AFTERNOON TEA

The Complete Book of Britain's Tea-time Treats

Michael Smith's AFTERNOON TEA

The Complete Book of Britain's Tea-time Treats

M
MACMILLAN
LONDON

First published 1986 by
MACMILLAN LONDON LIMITED
4 Little Essex Street London WC2R 3LF
and Basingstoke

Associated companies in Auckland, Delhi, Dublin, Gaborone, Hamburg,
Harare, Hong Kong, Johannesburg, Kuala Lumpur, Lagos, Manzini, Melbourne,
Mexico City, Nairobi, New York, Singapore and Tokyo

British Library Cataloguing in Publication Data
Smith, Michael
Afternoon tea.
1. Afternoon teas
I. Title
641.5'3   TX736

ISBN 0–333–43496–X

Designed by Robert Updegraff
Typeset by Wyvern Typesetting Limited, Bristol
Printed in Great Britain by Butler & Tanner Ltd, Frome and London

*Previous page: a seventeenth-century Chinese wine-jug, and a tea-bowl and saucer
from the* Nanking *cargo.*

Contents

ACKNOWLEDGEMENTS

I would like to thank the following people for their invaluable help in the preparation of this book: Michael Bartlett and Hilary Evans, for their elegant line drawings; Pat Brayne, my secretary in London, for typing and patiently retyping the endless pages of manuscript; Elisabeth Smith, for reading the manuscript and suggesting some excellent improvements; Sam Twining, for answering all my questions about tea and for willingly lending me his only surviving copy of *Twinings: Two Hundred and Fifty Years of Tea and Coffee (1706–1956)*; Caroline Young, for translating many of my recipes into Americanese for the American edition and for suggesting certain compromises; Michael Alcock, for his enthusiastic support; Brenda Stephenson, for painstakingly editing the book; Robert Updegraff, for designing it; Tracy Florance, for producing it; and Juliet Brightmore, for her picture research.

Women's organisations, like the Women's Institute, have had a good deal to do with making bakery popular again, as well as with improving its quality. It is in their cake-making competitions that you will find good rich fruit cakes, sponges, cut-and-come-again cakes, parkins, Madeiras and gingerbreads. This, to me, is cake.

This book is for them, and the likes of them.

As you read this book, more than *20 million* cups of tea will be drunk in London alone – TODAY!

Even so, that does not place Great Britain at the top of the tea-drinkers league (we're second). That honour goes to the Republic of Ireland. Third place goes to Tunisia, with New Zealand and Australia bringing up the rear.

PREFACE

I am of a generation old enough to remember afternoon tea being served in my family home, a handsome house in a thriving industrial town set against the backdrop of the Pennine hills in beautiful Yorkshire, land of the Brontës, 'Last of the Summer Wine', cricket, J. B. Priestley and 'All Creatures Great and Small'. The youngest of six children, I was born into a vast Methodist family – over sixty-one cousins at one count! My parents were middling-well-off, which is a Yorkshire expression for middle-middle-class. My father was a textile manufacturer, dyeing and spinning carpet yarns, knitting wools and such-like.

The household consisted of my mother and father, two brothers and three sisters, two live-in maids, a nanny, a charlady and a general factotum. None of these servants were the luxury they may sound to us nowadays; they were a necessity in a household where every stitch of linen was laundered and ironed by the maids and my sisters, and every loaf of bread, every cake and biscuit, pie, pound of jam or marmalade was made by my mother and her helpers. Guests were entertained at our table and not, as is fashionable today, in a local restaurant. We all lived in the mill house – a sturdy, square structure built of huge blocks of cream Yorkshire stone. Nothing too fancy in style, for that went against the Methodist (and industrial northern) ethic, though certainly not against the general Victorian ethic with its tendency to be over-opulent and somewhat frilly at the edges.

My parents were of course Victorians, in every sense. We children were well brought up by today's standards, with a strict discipline and an ingrained sense of guilt! We were never allowed to be idle; we always had to be doing something, and if we had none of our own we were found jobs to do by my mother. We had to walk, never run; talk quietly, never shout; and, worst of all, we were permitted only one piece of cake at tea-time, never two! To have two was considered greedy. 'If you boys are hungry, there's plenty of bread and butter in the kitchen' – my mother's voice echoes in my ears now as I write.

My mother was a kindly woman, an excellent *raconteuse*, almost to the point of hyperbole, and possessed of a chuckling sense of humour, yet we children were constantly being warned not to be 'excessive' in any way. Nothing was ever excessive at home. Enough, yes, and nice, but never abundant.

11

I first learned to be abundant when, as a callow youth of seventeen, I left battle-scarred Britain after the Second World War and headed for the International Hotel School in Lausanne, Switzerland, to start out on my chosen career as an hotelier. There, almost within hours of arrival, I had discovered Mutrux, the choicest tea-room in town. A far cry from Betty's in Harrogate, or Fullers Tea-Rooms in Bradford or Leeds, whose iced walnut cake was renowned throughout the county and the prime reason for everyone's patronage. (I'm happy to say that, as I write, Betty's is enjoying a well-deserved renaissance.) *Le five o'clock tea* was *de rigueur* for the elegant *lausannoises*. Fashionable ladies would teeter into the pretty tea *salon*, cocooned against the icy Swiss weather in black ermine wraps and ocelot muffs, white fox hoods and cashmere stoles – a far cry from the sturdy, heavy worsteds and woollens of wholesome Yorkshire society.

I well recall the interior of Mutrux, decorated in shades of *café au lait*, with a frescoed ceiling, pink quilted cushions on gilt chairs, rosebud china *and*, shock horror, tea in glasses! I'd never seen *that* before – nor had I seen tea in those metal, egg-shaped infusers – nor had I seen tea served so *weak*! I made a mental note of it all, for this couldn't be right; perhaps for foreigners, but not for us Brits.

There were cakes with rich frangipane fillings, fondant-iced tops, and edges coated in crushed pistachio nuts of the palest green. Excess in miniature. But it was not *real* afternoon tea, for where was the toast? Where were the muffins and crumpets? Where were the scones with rich, thick yellow cream and luscious crimson strawberry jam? And, what's more, where, yes *where*, were the potted-meat sandwiches?

Visitors to Europe will find many such famous tea-rooms: Sacher's in Vienna, Rumpelmayer's in Paris, Cova in Milan, The Angleterre in Copenhagen, the exceptionally beautiful Café Luitpol in Munich, and the oldest of them all, Florian's in St Mark's Square in Venice. All still there to be enjoyed, though at a price! Each of these tea-rooms is of the most elegant order, visited only by the *crème de la crème* of society (as Jean Brodie in her prime would say of Mackie's or Jenners in Edinburgh, or of Charles Rennie Mackintosh's tea-rooms in Glasgow) and are certainly not places where you would get afternoon tea in the English manner. Their *chic* is something quite different.

England has always had this strange division between what the 'county' and aristocracy do and what the newly rich prefer. Somehow, on the Continent these two groups blend almost imperceptibly. There people from all the drawers eat in the same place – where the food is good. Not so in Britain, whose self-styled élite will go to whichever restaurant is fashionable.

It was to be five years after going to Lausanne before I encountered my first London tea-room (or café, as they were contrarily called, for one never drank coffee there – certainly not in the afternoon and certainly not if you wished to behave *comme il faut*). I became engaged to my wife-to-be at Gunther's in Curzon Street, right in the middle of London's Mayfair. (My Yorkshire Methodist guilt was already beginning to fade, and I was by then frequenting such fashionable haunts in the name of catering training!) Here was elegance, for Gunther's, along with Fortnum and Mason, the Ritz, Richoux, Floris and many others, was where the British upper-crust took afternoon tea, with sandwiches, hot buttered toast, scones with jam and clotted cream, and cakes. A much better state of affairs than in the Alpine land, I can assure you. No wonder Swiss women didn't get the right to vote until 1971!

Right through the swinging, never-had-it-so-good 1960s these institutions continued to flourish. But all that was to go, as the make-up of our society changed – many would say for the better, but that is open to question. Elegant tea-rooms, tea-shops and cafés were all to disappear, along with waitresses in black frocks and organdie aprons, and, of course, the inevitable string quartet to help the meringues go down. Fast foods and a help-yourself style of service made inroads into our lives, ridding us of that wonderful tradition – and a leisurely, glamorous one at that – of taking tea.

But things have a way of righting themselves. Everyone likes a touch of nostalgia. You only have to look at the huge success, on both sides of the Atlantic, of such British television dramas as 'Upstairs Downstairs', 'The Duchess of Duke Street', 'Edward and Mrs Simpson', to name but a few. Through the small screen we can enjoy, even if vicariously, a taste of the past. And people seem to want to taste it, so we quite rightly and in a timely way have a whole new fashion starting – nay, started; a trip down memory lane in search of such times. Afternoon tea is an essential part of any such trip, and this book is intended to help you make the journey in your own home.

Tea at the Ritz is back; the Waldorf runs a tea-dance; the Inn on the Park, the Inter-Continental and The Dorchester are all on the tea-waggon in the 1980s. You will also find that it is now fashionable to give tea-parties in the home, and to meet people for afternoon tea in town. Afternoon wedding receptions are also becoming stylish again, and this year I will be taking an afternoon-tea picnic to Glyndebourne, shunning dinner during the interval – just for a change, you understand. It will be elaborate and somewhat extended in content, I admit. There will be *foie gras* sandwiches, smoked salmon scones, caviare in wafer-thin brown bread and a scintillating champagne cup. 'Excessive!' I can hear my mother saying from her cloud up in the great beyond. Yes – but fantastic!

Michael Smith
London, 1986

THE
HISTORY
OF
AFTERNOON
TEA

The Story of Afternoon Tea

Had Anna, seventh Duchess of Bedford, not been so incredibly greedy, afternoon tea as we knew it in England, and as we to some extent still know it today, might never have become our national habit.

Legend has it that as the time between breakfast and dinner lengthened in the lighter months of the summer, this august lady, unable to await the immense repast she would surely have enjoyed at her laden dinner table, took herself off to her boudoir mid-afternoon and demanded of her servants slivers of bread spread with 'good sweet butter', upon which, together with 'mackeroons', cheese cakes, tarts, biscuits, small cakes and other niceties, she privately gorged.

It did not take long for her secret to be exposed and, far from ridiculing her (as might well have happened in back-biting eighteenth-century English society), other ladies who also might have enjoyed a clandestine indulgence openly joined her in the habit. Concealing screens were cast aside: teapot and caddy, muffineer and cakestand were revealed for all to enjoy. Afternoon tea became not only an acceptable but also a most fashionable thing of which to partake if you were to remain a lady of status and substance.

Before examining the more appetising side of our afternoon indulgence – for indulgence it is – let us take a brief look at the history of tea-drinking in Britain.

But coffee came first.

THE RISE OF COFFEE

The notion that in the seventeenth century a Cretan should come to study at Oxford University might strike one as odd, but one Nathaniel Canopios did in fact appear at Balliol College in 1637 and apparently introduced coffee-drinking to his fellow students. Before long England's first coffee-house opened in that city of Spires – not, as might well be expected, in our capital. London's first real coffee-house opened in 1652 when Daniel Edwards, a much-travelled merchant, brought back coffee-beans from Smyrna and trained his servant to pound and brew an aromatic drink that was so popular with his City colleagues that it soon became obvious that there was an excellent commercial idea to be exploited. Edwards financed his servant, Pasqua Rosee, in setting up the first recorded coffee-house in London, in St Michael's Alley in the City. However, there were problems, and Rosee's coffee-shop did not enjoy a long life.

Imagine how seductive the aroma of roasting coffee-beans must have been in those narrow City streets and alleys, without doubt overcoming the less pleasant smells emanating from the open sewers bordering every

London street, alley and close. So seductive was it that Pasqua's coffee-shop was packed all day long. But the sweet smell of success, while the best public relations gambit anyone could wish for, did not please the owners of the numerous taverns and alehouses within the City's square mile. They rebelled, complaining to the Lord Mayor that as Pasqua was not a Freeman of the City of London (a necessary qualification for opening a business, or 'going into trade', in those days), he was in no position to run a coffee-house. Daniel Edwards, however, had married well, to the daughter of coffee-drinking Alderman Hodges of the City. Strings were pulled, and a partner was found for Pasqua in the person of Hodges' servant, Bowman. Bowman, however, being of an entrepreneurial nature, soon outwitted Pasqua and opened his own establishment. Pasqua's shop 'went under'.

By the time all this had happened, coffee-drinking had established itself as a City habit, enjoyed by all. (Still for gentlemen only, that is, for no self-respecting lady would be found in such a place.) Male society used the London coffee- and chocolate-houses as centres for political and social intercourse, and for other cultural activity; they were, in due course, to become the foundation for the London clubs of today.

The *London Gazette* for Tuesday, 2 September 1658 carried the announcement of the death of Oliver Cromwell. There also appeared in that issue what is now known to be one of the earliest advertisements for tea, in a promotion for the Sultaness' Head, Cophee House, in Sweetings Rents (buildings) near the Royal Exchange. There is, however, an even earlier reference to coffee in the *Publick Adviser* for 19 May 1657, in which we read what this drink will do for you:

> In Bartholomew Lane on the back side of the Old Exchange, the drink called *cophee*, which is a very wholesom and physical drink, having many excellent vertues, closes the orifice of the stomack, fortifies the heat within, helpeth digestion, quickneth the spirits, maketh the heart lightsom, is good against eye-sores, coughs, or colds, rhumes, consumptions, headach, dropsie, gout, scurvy, king's evil, and many others, is to be sold both in the morning, and at times of the clock in the afternoon.

And there's no answer to that!

Rumour has it that by the mid-seventeenth century there were over 2000 coffee-houses in London alone. York, Norwich, Bristol and other major cities of the day had a goodly choice of their own. So popular had coffee-drinking become that in 1660 the Treasury levied a tax of fourpence on every gallon of coffee brewed – though one wonders just how the authorities were able to keep track of how much was actually sold. The fourpenny tax was followed in 1663 by a £5 fee for a licence to run a coffee-house. Coffee in those days was twopence a 'dish'; it was served in a 'can' – a straight-sided cup – and poured into the dish, or saucer, for drinking. A tip, 'To Insure Promptness', was put into a box, thus starting a habit unpopular the world over to this day.

Coffee-houses were the forerunners of today's gentlemen's clubs: Lloyd's Coffee Room in the Royal Exchange in 1798.

A good deal of business was transacted in these City coffee-houses, if the notices of meetings that ran in the *London Gazette* of those days are any indication. One of them, Edward Lloyd's in Tower Street, was to become particularly famous, for it was here that, around 1688, Lloyd prepared 'ships' lists' for the benefit of seafaring men, ships' captains, merchants, underwriters and the like, and thus built the foundations of what is now the greatest firm of underwriters in the world – Lloyd's of London.

Later, in 1706, one Thomas Twining, then thirty years old, started his own venture by purchasing Tom's Coffee House in Devereux Court, hard by St Clement Dane's Church in the Strand. Twining had chosen his location well. Devereux Court is right in the heart of London's legal land of Temple, Temple Bar, New Court and Inner Temple, all of which lie between the Strand and the north bank of the Thames. Barristers and their clients, physicians, the literati, politicians and men of importance in other fields frequented his establishment. There is evidence of Thomas Twining's signature as witness to important documents drawn up by these lawyers and their clients while they partook of his coffee.

And then came tea.

THE ADVENT OF TEA

The first reference to tea appears in European literature in 1588. Although the Portuguese must have come across it in their trading with China during the early part of the sixteenth century, they did little about it:

18

maybe they didn't like it! It is only with the seventeenth century, after the Dutch made forays into China and in particular to Bantam in Java that we begin to hear about tea, and it was the Dutch who introduced tea-drinking to seventeenth-century Europe (although the first teas used in England appear to have come direct from Java).

When this new drink first reached Britain in 1645 it was called 'cha', the Cantonese slang word for tea. However, when the British moved their Chinese trading base from Canton to Amoy, the name changed to that given in the region to the fragrant tea-leaf: *t'e*. So by the end of the seventeenth century the drink was already popularly known in England as 'tay' or 'tee'.

By 1660 China tea was being sold at prices ranging from fifteen to forty shillings a pound, which is in the region of £812 to £1900 in today's terms. So it was by no means cheap, and this price did not include Parliament's duty of eightpence levied on every gallon brewed. As with coffee, just how this was measured is difficult to establish, but levied it was and money poured into the taxman's coffers.

Nine years later the East India Company, granted a charter by Elizabeth I in 1600, brought back tea in their cargo for the first time: this was from Bantam, and the two lonely canisters carried were treated as a novelty by the directorate of the Company. It was to be another nine years before the Company began regular and serious importation of tea, but from then until 1833 it held the monopoly of tea-shipping (at least from China) and of tea-auctions. (Each time the charter came up for renewal, various independent merchants opposed its granting, but to no avail: the East India Company continued to enjoy its monopoly. There was a break-through in 1813, when some commerce with India was permitted for British ships, but tea was excluded; and it appears that the government of the day would not accept that individual merchants were competent to deal with the wily Chinese at Canton, even though other nations' ships appear to have had little difficulty in bartering with the local merchants. Quarterly auctions went on at East India House, headquarters of the Company in Leadenhall Street.)

To begin with, however, tea-drinking was not fashionable: in fact, it was regarded by many as a filthy habit that was not to be encouraged. There was a good deal of debate, both in Britain and on the Continent, as to whether the drink was harmful or beneficial. The Germans banned it, believing it to be the principal cause of the Orientals' shrivelled appearance!

All that was to change, of course, and what started in a somewhat lethargic fashion soon began to gallop. In Twining's coffee-house, tea-drinking was rapidly gaining in popularity, so much so that by 1717 Twining had opened a second house in order to cope with the increase in trade. This, too, was in Devereux Court and it took the name of The Golden Lion, rather in the way that pubs are named after heraldic beasts.

The sale of tea at Twinings soon exceeded the sale of coffee, and we now find reference to particular types of tea, though in 1715 the records still mention only teas from China, including those bearing such renowned names as Bohea, Pekoe, Imperial, Congo, Green Tea, Gunpowder and Hyson.

While most purchases, particularly refreshments, were paid for in good solid gold, there are nevertheless recorded in Twining's ledgers the names of some 355 customers who were given credit for the purchase of coffee, chocolate, sago, snuff, spa waters and tea. Oranges, tincture of rhubarb, lemons, candles and even hand-made writing paper were also sold at coffee-houses.

In the twentieth century it is the grocer, the speciality shop, or, more commonly, the supermarket that purveys tea and coffee – and, of course, already packaged. It is amusing to recall that in those days these two beverages, enjoyed as much for their stimulating effect as for their taste, also had a sales outlet through such extraordinary channels as milliners and jewellers! It is an amazing thought that tiaras and tea might well have been purchased together!

It can be fairly stated that the history of tea- and coffee-drinking in England, unbroken through twelve reigns, is directly linked to the history of the Twining family, which continues today, in its ninth generation, headed by Sam Twining, director of R. T. Twining and Company Limited. Any reader whose interest leads him to look for more profound information would do well to get sight of the book *Twinings: Two Hundred and Fifty Years of Tea and Coffee (1706–1956)*, by Stephen Twining. It may also interest readers to know that upon application to the firm it is possible to see the ledgers, bills and names of customers of this famous company through the centuries.

By the middle of the eighteenth century, Twinings' teas were being sold abroad: to the Governor in Barbados; to the Consul in Leghorn; to customers in Cadiz and Lisbon; to the British army and navy, which in those days were based in Minorca in the Balearic Islands; to customers in Aix-en-Provence and Rotterdam. And tea was despatched to Governor the Honourable William Shirley in Boston, Massachusetts, where in 1733 the most famous tea-party of them all was held!

The second half of the eighteenth century saw the rise of the pleasure-gardens and tea-gardens, such as Vauxhall, Ranelagh and Marylebone, where fashionable society could go to see and be seen. On payment of a fixed entry fee, customers could drink as much tea and consume as much bread and butter as they liked, in the evening as well as during the day. At the same time they could be entertained by musicians (Handel himself frequently appeared at Vauxhall), jugglers, acrobats and even firework displays. Vauxhall Gardens is known to have been illuminated in the evenings by thousands of candle lamps hung in the trees lining its long avenues.

The King himself, George III, enjoyed tea immensely and his elder son, the Prince Regent (later George IV) was one of the first collectors of teapots. As tea-drinking became more of a ceremony, it began to accumu-

'To see and be seen': fashionable society meets in London's Vauxhall Gardens.

late a whole range of special manners, arts and affectations. For wealthy gentlemen, evening tea would be specially prepared and served in the tea-gardens or the tea-rooms and clubs by attractive young wenches known as 'tea-blenders', who often 'got to know' their employer and his friends in more than one sense!

AFTERNOON TEA IN VICTORIAN AND EDWARDIAN ENGLAND

In contrast to the elegance, orderliness and symmetry of eighteenth-century Britain, the Victorians were opulent and extravagant. Luncheon as the midday meal had by now gained full popularity and had become an important time for ladies and gentlemen to entertain their own sex: the gentlemen in their clubs, the ladies in the comfort of their homes, attended by fleets of servants – an indication to the world that the middle classes could afford things. Dinner in the grander houses was often served as late as 9 p.m., though 8.30 was a more popular time, and the gap between luncheon and dinner had widened, as indeed it had done between breakfast and dinner in the previous century. There was a gap to be filled – and so the Duchess of Bedford's secret munchings began.

The ample time now available to them allowed ladies to create a whole new social rigmarole – the 'At Home'. It provided the upper middle classes and the middle classes with an enjoyable way of passing time as they entertained each other on a daily basis. Inevitably, the ritual became more and more elaborate as delicate finger sandwiches, sausage rolls, patties, 'fancies' and cutting cakes were added to the menu.

21

Weddings, 'at homes' and high and family teas

In Victorian and Edwardian times there were strict rules to follow regarding all these occasions. I have combined extracts from the pens of Mrs Beeton, Agnes Marshall, Florrie White and others to give an amusing account of what went on.

Wedding teas are very much the same thing as 'At Home' teas, but are, as a rule, more crowded and less satisfactory than the latter. People ask so many more guests to a tea party than they would think of inviting to the now old-fashioned wedding breakfast, and the visitors all come together, as the bride has, as a rule, but a very short time to stay. She cuts the cake, or rather makes the first incision, as at a traditional wedding breakfast, but there are no speeches and but little ceremony.

'At Home' teas. Some entertainment is generally provided, usually music, professional singers and pianists being sometimes engaged. When this is the case, the lady of the house does not often ask her amateur friends to give their services; but sometimes these friends contribute the music, and it is well to make a little plan or programme beforehand, arranging who shall be asked to perform, and appraising them of the fact so that they may come prepared. The hostess, even if she be herself musical, has her time taken up very fully with receiving and looking after her guests, and unless she sings the first song, or

'The health of the bride': a country wedding.

plays the first piece, should leave herself free to devote herself to her guests. The instrumental pieces chosen on these occasions should not be long ones, and a good break should be made between each song, solo or recitation for conversation, people going more to these entertainments to meet their friends and have a chat than for the sake of the music. Introductions are not the rule at 'At Homes', but they can be made when there is any necessity. The tea is not served in the drawing-room as at smaller 'At Homes', but at a buffet in the dining-room, where people go during the afternoon, or sometimes as they leave, to partake of the light refreshments provided.

Servants usually do all the work of pouring out tea or handing sandwiches, fruit, ices, etc., unless gentlemen bring refreshments for ladies to where they are seated. At the buffet, people may help themselves or be helped by gentlemen if there are not sufficient attendants.

A weekly 'At Home' tea is served upon small tables, the servant, before bringing it in, seeing that one is placed conveniently near his mistress, who generally dispenses the tea. No plates are given for a tea of this kind, and the servant, after seeing that all is in readiness, leaves the room, the gentlemen of the party doing all the waiting that is necessary.

The tea equipage is usually placed upon a silver salver, the hot water is in a small silver or china kettle on a stand, and the cups are small. Thin bread and butter, cake, petits fours and sometimes fresh fruit are all the eatables given. These are daintily arranged on plates, spread with lace doilies, and placed in a cakestand or on a convenient table.

High Tea. In some houses this is a permanent institution, quite taking the place of late dinner, and to many it is a most enjoyable meal, young people preferring it to dinner, it being a movable feast that can be partaken of at hours which will not interfere with tennis, boating, or other amusements. At the usual High Tea there are probably to be found one or two small hot dishes, cold chickens, or game, tongue or ham, salad, cakes of various kinds, sometimes cold fruit tarts with cream or custard, and fresh fruit. Any supper dish, however, can be introduced, and much more elaborate meals be served, while sometimes the tea and coffee are relegated to the sideboard. In summer it is not unusual to have everything cold at a High Tea.

At *Family Teas*, cake, jam, sardines, potted meats, buttered toast, teacakes and fruit are often provided, in addition to the tea, coffee, and bread and butter. Watercress and radishes are nice accompaniments in summer.

The hours for family teas may vary in many households, but are generally governed by the time of the dinner that has preceded them, and the kind of supper partaken of afterwards. Where this is of a very light character, such as a glass of wine and a slice of cake, or the more

Edwardian ladies enjoy a good gossip over a 'dish' of tea.

homely glass of beer and bread and cheese, a 6 or 7 o'clock tea would not be too late, and a few savouries or eggs would be needed in addition to the bread and butter and cake so generally found; but where a substantial supper is to follow the tea the latter would be of a light description, and should be served about 5 o'clock, or earlier.

Bridge Teas afford a very pleasant afternoon. These generally commence about 3.30 p.m. Punctuality is naturally most essential.

Tennis Teas were customary at many houses during the summer months:

The meal is informal, and usually served out of doors. Iced tea, coffee, claret cup etc. are served, with sandwiches, pastries, cakes and other light viands. The tables are set under shady trees, and members of the family or servants are in attendance at them, the visitors themselves going to the tables for what they want.

This romantic setting would transfer perfectly to present-day entertaining, though the actual tennis match may well have to take place at the local club and I would imagine the actual tea party might well become a free-for-all as manners have changed and servants are, quite rightly, a thing of the past.

Nursery Tea

Until they were old enough to leave home and go to school (which often happened as early as eight years old), the children of well-to-do parents in the Victorian and Edwardian ages were given into the charge of a nurse, only to be returned to their parents at specific times of the day. One of those occasions was tea-time in the nursery, which was often known as Children's Hour.

Nursery tea was a simple affair, typically consisting of such sandwiches as potted meat or fish paste, jam, mashed banana, grated chocolate, a simple spreading of honey, a smear of Marmite, Bovril or some other vegetable extract. A fruit jelly might appear, wobbling tantalisingly until each sandwich crust had been swallowed. Crusts were *never* cut off nursery sandwiches, as they were considered good for the teeth, and this was the cause of more disciplinary action by Nanny than any other misdemeanour. Children made untold efforts not to eat them: crusts were pushed to the side of the plate, hidden inside clothing and even thrown over the fender into the nursery fire. On Sundays a concoction of milk, gelatine, food colour and some synthetic essence appeared as a treat in the form of a 'shape' or 'mould'. Other occasions might see a lightly boiled egg with its attendant toast 'soldiers' as a supplement to the nursery diet, and a good, plain 'cutting cake' would be there at every tea-time. Coconut kisses, jam tarts and buns were considered luxuries to be kept for high days and holidays. Milk was normally the only drink considered fit for children at tea-time, the exception being freshly made lemonade for special celebrations.

To those of us brought up in a very different world, perhaps childhood during this period seems to have been full of prohibitions and over-discipline, yet most British people who survived it think back to nursery days with affection and to nursery tea as their happiest hour.

Le Thé Dansant – The Tea-dance

My first encounter with the tea-dance came when, as a youth, I attended afternoon dances in our local town hall. Evening dances were avoided, particularly in the winter months, because of the ever-present danger of air-raids at night, making the journey home – always on foot, as petrol was rationed, and only to be used for essential journeys – hazardous, especially in the industrial areas. Tea-dances therefore became a common form of entertainment. They were friendly affairs. People would take their own little packs of sandwiches made from meagre wartime rations and pool them together so that everyone could enjoy a taste of something different. A sense of fair play pervaded, preventing any greedy person from claiming more than their share. Often these dances were charity affairs, arranged to raise funds for blankets, bandages and food-parcels for the troops overseas, or for the other good causes that spring up when a country is under siege, as Britain surely was. The organisers would provide a cup of grey tea with a splash of reconstituted dried milk, and a saccharine tablet for the sweet of tooth.

Those who know only the ear-blasting music of present-day disco-dancing have missed one of life's most exciting happenings, for the most exhilarating experience of those far-off days was dancing to the sound of the big bands. Such legendary names as the great Victor Silvester (whose ballroom dancing academy was already on the way to huge success before the Second World War) took their bands on the road to lift the spirits and boost the morale of soldiers, sailors, airmen and civilians. Wherever room could be made on factory floors, in canteens, air-raid shelters or church halls, people would gather to forget the horrors of war, and dance to the sound of those masters of the baton: Joe Loss, Felix Mendelsohn and his Hawaiian Serenaders (!), Ivy Benson with her all-ladies orchestra, or to that magnificent band of the Royal Air Force, The Squadronnaires. The famous bands of the United States were over here too: Tommy Dorsey, Benny Goodman, and the never-to-be-forgotten Glenn Miller all made frequent and dangerous trips across the Atlantic with their musicians to help raise our shattered spirits. Woman danced with woman, with never an eyebrow raised; you made your own fun as and when you could, and out of what was available – and young men were not! Not exactly the sort of tea-dance we think of in our more romantic minds today, you might say, but I doubt if we will ever dance to such wonderful sounds and melodies as those produced by the big bands.

Evidence is scant as to exactly where the tea-dance began on a more elegant social level. The *Supplement* to the *Oxford English Dictionary* says under *dansant* that as early as 1819 there was a *dançant* at 'Old Prince Esterhazy's' in Vienna. In *Punch* of 26 July 1841 there is reference to a tea-dance in London – so Queen Victoria might well have tripped the light fantastic on occasion in the early part of her reign, though I somehow doubt it!

While he was Prince of Wales (and particularly after Queen Victoria retired from public life to become the Widow of Windsor, making only the odd sortie in summer to Osborne House on the Isle of Wight), the future Edward VII led fashionable London society. The Edwardian period, as we think of it, started in the Gay Nineties, before the Queen's death. Dancing-tea, dinner and supper clubs, where dancing was the chief attraction of the afternoon's and evening's entertainment, abounded in London in the Edwardian heyday. Gladys Beattie Crozier, who published *The Tango and How to Dance It* in 1913, tells us that the revival of *le thé dansant* was received with much enthusiasm at Biarritz and all along the Riviera, where British and continental members of the *haute monde* met to dance every single afternoon. French phrases illuminated the talk of the English upper classes of the day, and two dances which were *de rigueur* were the one-step and the outrageous tango. So popular did this second become that tea-dances were often called 'tango-teas' and, according to Mrs Crozier, tango-masters made fortunes.

Soon *le thé dansant*, along with the new dances, slipped across the Channel and was received with such enthusiasm by hostesses in London and in the Shires, that it was to become *the* form of winter entertainment for both the élite and the not-so-élite. It had everything to recommend it; what could have been pleasanter on a dull wintry afternoon at five o'clock or so, when calls and shopping were over, than to drop in to one of the cheery little *thé dansant* clubs which had sprung up all over the West End and throughout the land? Quite one of the most exclusive clubs, organised by Mrs Carl Leyel and a Mrs Fagan, met at the Carlton Hotel. The Four Hundred Club had its venue in Bond Street, and the Public Schools' and Universities' Dance Club had its rendezvous at the Savoy Hotel. The Waldorf, the Boston Club and dozens of other centres were also extremely well patronised, even though subscriptions were high.

The 'tangos' abounded as specialist occasions and could be enjoyed everywhere from London's Hotel Cecil to Jenners' shop in Edinburgh's fashionable Princes Street, and from the Grand Hotel in the elegant spa town of Scarborough to Tilley's Rooms in industrial Newcastle. According to the knowledgeable Mrs Crozier, this last was one of the finest 'galleries' for dancing in the north of England.

In London's exclusive society it was an achievement to get into the club at the Carlton Hotel. Membership was strictly limited to one hundred, subscriptions were often as much as five guineas and election to membership was difficult. Any guest's name had to be submitted to a committee (usually composed of people from a military or county family) by the member introducing them, and the member had to be present to receive and sign in his guest on arrival in the ballroom. No young girl was admitted without a chaperone. Inside the rigidly guarded portals of these emporia, tiny tables crowded the edges of the dance-floor. These were 'set forth' with pretty gold-and-white china, and 'within a moment of one's arrival' a most elaborate and delicious tea was served while the

Intimate talk over the tea-table.

27

assembled company danced to the haunting airs of the tango or to a 'Boston' or even a modest waltz. An hour or two whisked magically by; then at 6.30 it was time to return home to change and sally forth yet again for an engagement at the Royal Opera, a dinner, visit to the theatre, or perhaps an evening at a musical comedy, which was tremendously popular at the time.

At the most exclusive venues, the famous French tango-dancers Les Almanos, hot from Paris, would visit and after tea would demonstrate their latest variations of the Parisian tango. All very heady stuff, when you read that 'their dancing was the most graceful, gay, infectious thing imaginable, and an absolute revelation of the possibilities of the tango . . . for their movements were the very poetry of motion, and no step seemed ever to be repeated twice. . . .' Disco-dancers watch out! If you have ever toiled over the mysteries of the breakdance of the 1980s, I suppose you can imagine yourself trying with the utmost seriousness to master the intricacies of the latest tango variation, the *Maxixe Brésilienne*, 'delicate, spirited and graceful', to music that was 'ravishing, alluring and gay'! It is not difficult to see why the tea-dance, and the tango-tea in particular, was so popular for *le monde qui s'amuse*. What could be more agreeable than dancing in a pleasant bohemian atmosphere starred with fellow-guests who might include royalty, a duke or two, a clutch of well-known peers, and some of the best-known and brightest lights of London's musical-comedy stage?

The First World War saw the end of this national frenzy, though the tea-dance returned in the Roaring Twenties, when 'flappers' enjoyed the Charleston and the sensuous tango slipped in the popularity ratings. Foxtrots and the newer quickstep became the rage, and with the arrival of the great American musical films in the 1930s and 1940s came Cesar Romero and Carmen Miranda with their rumbas and sambas. The cha-cha led gradually to the letting go of our dancing partners for all time, and we began to gyrate alone to the jive, the bop, the twist and the locomotion. Then Bill Haley and his Comets replaced the Big Sound.

Will we ever hold our partners again, I ask? One does wonder. Perhaps some of us will with the rebirth of the tea-dance, for it *is* a pleasant and elegant way of passing an afternoon, and it's an excellent and novel idea for a party in the home, even though your band may be courtesy of the stereo and compact disk.

Varieties of Tea

The Tea-bush

Camellia sinensis, a cousin, though perhaps a distant one, of the garden variety *Camellia japonica* is an evergreen tropical bush, originally (from the British point of view) found growing wild in Assam by eighteenth-century botanists sent out to India by the Royal Horticultural Society. Commercially grown to approximately five feet in height (left wild they have been known to exceed twenty feet), and kept at this height by regular pruning, the bushes are nurtured for five years before they are ready to yield their first pickings. The tea-bush enjoys growing, as does the vine, on a hillside, its feet set in dry, loamy earth. Like the camellia, it prefers the protection of tall trees from the scorching sun; it also likes a lot of rain, but at the right time.

The tea-bush flourishes from near sea-level to heights of up to 6–7000 feet. The higher the plantation, the better the quality of the leaf, because in the cooler air it is slower to mature. 'High-grown' teas are the best and most expensive type used for blending; they are much sought after by those tea merchants in Britain who still prefer to mix their own particular blends.

The actual gathering, or plucking, of the leaves (or, more accurately, the bud together with the top two tiny leaves) is carried out over a period of six months at bi-weekly stages. The first gathering, or the 'new season's tipping', is the best. Subsequent pluckings are referred to in a descending scale as 'first flush', 'second flush', 'quality', 'rains', 'autumnal' and 'end of season' leaves.

As soon as the gatherers, who are paid pro-rata by the weight they have picked, have filled their baskets, these are despatched to the nearby tea-factories and here the leaves are processed into either 'black' or 'green' teas.

Black tea is the type preferred by most Westerners; green tea is nowadays used for consumption in China, Japan and other Eastern countries, and also to an extent in North Africa, though in Britain, with our burgeoning crop of Chinese restaurants and our new preoccupation with health, there has recently been a renaissance of green-tea consumption.

In Britain or the United States it is taken for granted that you will be given milk in your (Indian) tea. If you prefer tea black in this sense, then you ask for tea without milk. But that has nothing to do with what really constitutes black tea!

The manufacturing of tea begins when the freshly gathered green leaves are shrivelled in dry, warm air. They are withered just sufficiently to leave them soft and limp, or 'pliable' as it is called in the tea-making

29

trade. At this stage they are ready for rolling, a mechanical process that releases the unwanted sap or juice. After rolling, the leaf can remain as green tea – the word green meaning fresh or young, as well as referring to the somewhat dingy colour of the leaf – or it can be fermented (oxidised). This fermenting or oxidisation is done on bamboo tables in a humid atmosphere, where, within a period of a few short hours, the leaves turn from green to a bright rust or copper colour. At this stage of partial fermentation, the tea is called *oolong* and can be used in blending. The bulk of it, however, goes through a third stage, during which the leaves are fully fermented by 'firing' – passing trays of the copper-coloured leaves through 'ovens' or hot-air chambers for drying out. The leaf has then become the black leaf known to most of us as regular Indian, Ceylon or China tea.

There then comes the more complicated process of grading. Cutting, tearing and curling is followed by sifting the dried tea through a series of graded meshes from which the leaf emerges in sizes known as Leaf, Broken Leaf, Fannings and Dust.

Leaf, the first quality, is divided into four grades for blending: Orange Pekoe, Pekoe, Broken Orange Pekoe and Broken Orange Pekoe Fannings. Broken Leaf and Fannings are categorised in parallel descending orders of quality, but Dust has only two grades, which are referred to simply as 'one' and 'two'. Dust is the smallest leaf designated for the cheapest packet of tea and, contrary to what you might expect, is not actually the sweepings from the floor. However, it *can* also be the dust of an expensive high-quality tea, and is thus frequently designated for better drinking.

BLENDED TEAS

The bulk of tea drunk in Britain today is blended. In the eighteenth century a hostess would blend her own balance of green and black tea, taking them from her caddy and measuring them with her silver caddy spoon into a crystal mixing bowl. Realising the value of a good sales point, the local grocer often adopted the lady of the manor's blend for others to enjoy. Merchants also created their own blends, which at first were regional if not local, but today are national and even international. It is doubtful that a packet of Earl Grey purchased from your nearest supermarket would bear any resemblance to his Lordship's original mix, but the romantic idea that it does is still an excellent marketing ploy, for we all hanker after a taste of days gone by.

If you care to search around, there remain a few specialist blenders who will make up and hold a recipe peculiar to your particular taste. On the other hand, you could purchase a handsome caddy, buy a variety of green and black teas, settle yourself on a Chippendale chair, summon the butler to bring a kettle of boiling water, and enjoy a unique journey into the past as you personally mix and pour, infuse and sip from a shallow-bowled, baroque-handled Rockingham cup!

How is tea blended?

On leaving the plantation, whether in India, Sri Lanka or China, tea is packed into plywood chests lined with aluminium foil to keep it dry and fresh. Each chest is branded or marked with all the information the British merchants will require when it arrives in dock: the estate name, the grade of leaf, the year it was plucked and fired, the weight of contents and so on. Chests containing one particular type and from one particular grower are known as 'breaks'.

On arrival in the United Kingdom, the tea is stored in warehouses in or around the docks of the port of landing, which could be London, Manchester, Avonmouth or elsewhere. Here samples from each chest are taken and distributed for examination by the various tea-brokers (known as selling or buying brokers) who are going to buy at auction and re-sell the tea to packers and other merchants. Catalogues are compiled by the selling broker giving details of the types and qualities of tea on sale and stating the available quantity of such tea or blend of tea, and where it is warehoused. The smaller buying broker draws his samples from the selling broker so that he in turn can advise his clients (the packers and distributors) and can also assess fairly accurately the probable price each tea will fetch at auction. All this has to be done through the tea clearing house, which deals with the complicated documents of title and the organising of samples of tea to be collected by buyers. Today all this is done by computer.

Stevedores unloading a shipment of tea at London docks. A tea-clipper could hold as many as 8000 chests.

31

When the tea has been auctioned, it is the turn of the manufacturer to make up, or blend, his own brand product for the retail market. This all-important blending is the responsibility of the specialist tea-taster, whose job it is to select a variety of teas from those bought at auction and mix them to the public's known liking. As many as twenty or thirty different teas can go into a popular blend. The taster's blend must match up with previous blends in order to achieve a continuity of flavour, almost in the way that a blended wine must have no recognisable difference from its predecessor. The taster makes copious notes as he works, sipping, smelling, gargling and spitting in order to prepare a final list of the different teas. This is then sent off to the packer's factory, and the requisite teas are drawn from the warehouse where they have been stored. At the factory the bulk blending is done in large revolving drums and the tea is finally sealed into the packets we all recognise.

CHINA AND INDIAN TEA

Most people put teas into two categories: China tea and Indian tea. The former includes Keemuns and Lapsang Souchongs, as well as the various exotic teas such as Gunpowder (so called because sailors thought it resembled gunshot), Formosa Oolong, Formosa Jasmine, and scented Orange Pekoe, all of which are grown from China seed. The latter includes teas from India, Sri Lanka, Africa, Indonesia and Malaysia, all of which are grown from seed from Assam in North India.

China tea

Legend has it that the tea-leaf was discovered in China almost three thousand years ago. It is said that one day in 2737 BC Emperor Shen-Nung was boiling his drinking water to purify it when leaves from the branch of a nearby tea-plant were blown into the cauldron, imparting a delicate flavour which the Emperor found to his liking. Far-fetched? Perhaps . . . but then most legends are. Nevertheless, it is fascinating to know that there had been centuries of tea-drinking going on in China long before the first pound of tea reached the shores of England in 1645.

No one knew who actually grew and manufactured Chinese teas until one Robert Fortune, a collector of plants for the Royal Horticultural Society in London, managed in 1840 and 1848 to penetrate the tea-growing areas of mainland China. Until that time buyers had been kept at arm's length in the township of Canton, dealing only with the merchants. Fortune's second visit to the plantations of the She-Hsien (formerly Hwei Chow) area inland from Shanghai, shows how difficult it was for any foreigner to penetrate mainland China, for it is recorded that he had to adopt a disguise (presumably by colouring his skin and wearing a wig complete with pigtail!). However, he must somehow have endeared himself to the Chinese tea-farmers, for he managed to collect vast quantities of seedlings, which he skilfully packed and shipped off to the East India Company's plantations in the Himalayas.

Gathering the 'fragrant leaf' in a Chinese tea-garden.

In his book *Two Visits to the Tea Countries of China* (John Murray, London, 1857), Fortune describes his journeys and tells how the Chinese, in their crudely constructed cottages in the tea-hills, produced tea for their own families, earning some extra money by selling the surplus to the merchants, as used to happen in the wine-growing areas of Europe. He also tells how they grew, gathered and dried the leaves in iron drying pans set into brick-built furnaces, before hand-rolling them on split bamboo benches or tables. The moisture emitted during this rolling process, he tells us, was of a greenish hue and apparently went to waste. There then followed a second drying process: this time the pliant leaves were exposed to the open air before yet a further session in the iron pans, when the tea was redried and ready for packing.

Tea, in China as well as in Europe, was first drunk as a medicine and stimulant; it was around AD 620 that it began to be enjoyed simply as a pleasant drink. Indication of its popularity in China can be found in a treatise on the subject of tea-growing and drinking: *Cha Ching*, which in the Mandarin language means 'Tea Classic', gives us the first written account of the gathering, bruising and drying, roasting and packing of the fragrant leaves of the tea-plant. It also tells us that by this time other fragrances were already being added to the prepared leaves, for Lu Yu, the author of *Cha Ching*, refers to ginger, orange, peppermint and even onion being used – though I suspect that these additions were originally employed to buck up some particularly weak crop.

33

The importation of tea to Europe followed the natural progress of all things from Ancient China: a procession starting with the Turkish caravans trading on the northern borders of China in and around the fifth century AD, spreading through Asia, Arabia, Persia, Greece, Italy, southern France and Germany, then fanning out to include central Europe, Scandinavia and eventually Great Britain.

From our schooldays we know that it was not until 1497, when the Portuguese mariner Vasco da Gama sailed round the Cape of Good Hope into the Indian Ocean, that trade with the East began to take on any significance. Even then there was little interest in tea, and what interest did exist was limited mostly to verbal reports of the tea-habit in China. More fascination arose from these Eastern men 'sitting at floor level', or at individual tables, drinking rice wine and eating with 'two pieces of wood' than from their drinking 'cha'!

Only when the Portuguese closed their ports to the Dutch in the late sixteenth century did the latter begin to show a serious interest in importing tea. They began to ship the first significant cargoes of green tea from Bantam in Java, using it as a medicine and acclaiming its laxative powers. From the Netherlands, the Dutch traded with France and Italy, where apothecaries also used tea for its strong medicinal qualities.

The link with Britain began when Catherine of Braganza was betrothed and wed to Charles II in 1662. The young Infanta sipped tea in her drawing room at St James's Palace, which naturally popularised it with the ladies and other members of the Court circles.

By now Russia was also well into tea-drinking, being able to trade with China by land, through the back door, so to speak. The Chinese encouraged Russian interest by sending gifts of tea to the Tsar. Controlled by the Tsarist government, tea-caravans travelled a mind-boggling eleven thousand miles, taking up to a year and a half to make the journey from the Chinese border back to western Russia. (It is worth remarking here that the schooners of the East India Company, known as East Indiamen, took as long as four years to complete the round trip by sea from England to China and back.)

In the reign of George III in the late eighteenth century, Britain attempted to form an official trading relationship with China. His Majesty chose an Irishman, Lord Macartney, to make this approach. Macartney was an experienced diplomat, but, friendly though the Chinese were, they were also very guarded, and he was unable to find a way round the restrictive practices in force at the port of Canton – not to mention the language barrier and the fact that 'foreigners' were not allowed to live on mainland China but had to stay in Macao.

What Macartney *was* able to do, however, was to collect seeds from tea-plants, which were eventually cultivated and made to thrive in the botanical gardens in Calcutta. While the Calcutta plants did not yield the quality and quantity of leaves necessary to produce a good tea, they did kindle the first notion that colonial India might be the right place to develop tea-plantations. And, as we shall hear, it was.

In the nineteenth century Britain's tea-importers had to face a strong challenge from the Americans, who had become very competitive since British ports were closed to them following the War of Independence, and, even though British ships were considered the fastest afloat, American skippers were now using new, sleeker and faster vessels in their endeavours to increase their trade with China. They had developed the French-designed clipper, a slimly built boat with three or four sloping masts and concave waterlines. Keels were deepened, and hulls slimmed down to help counteract the vast expanses of canvas needed to catch every gust of wind. The British had to follow suit quickly if we were to stay in business. This we did. A spirit of sportsmanship soon developed between the skippers of the various shipping lines and the legendary clipper races began.

As long as the East India Company enjoyed a trading monopoly, there was no real concern to get shipments of tea back to England quickly, but after the repeal of the Navigation Acts in 1849, an American clipper, the *Oriental*, entered West India Docks in London only ninety-five days after leaving Hong Kong! This was a real shock to the British, and something had to be done to speed things up. So began the legendary clipper races of which the most famous was in 1866, when eleven clippers took part. Having loaded their cargoes at Foochow on 28 May of that year, four of these vast sailing ships, *Ariel, Fiery Cross, Taeping* and *Serica*, were already passing the Western Isles by 29 August. *Ariel*'s Captain Keay was a shrewd navigator and, we are told by observers on land, cleverly blocked *Taeping*'s attempts to hire the first pilot at Dungeness roads, thus taking the lead up the mouth of the Thames estuary. *Ariel* was still in the lead on 7 September. However, *Taeping*'s captain was the first to spot a tug, thereby beating *Ariel* to Gravesend and London Docks. The outcome was a win for *Taeping* by only 20 minutes, earning a bonus for her crew of some ten shillings a ton. (A clipper could carry one million pounds of tea, which is in the region of 500 tons – so it was some bonus!)

The tea-clippers were superseded in 1869 when steam took over from sail and the Suez Canal was opened, cutting the distance between East and West by several thousand miles. Visitors to London can still see a fine example of a clipper in the famous *Cutty Sark*, anchored at Greenwich.

It is interesting to remember that in 1886 the United Kingdom's consumption of China tea was recorded as 170 *million* pounds. This figure dropped dramatically over the next fourteen years to the mere 13 million pounds recorded in 1900, representing but 7 per cent of the total consumption of black tea; presumably loyalties to Empire were of paramount importance. But now China tea-drinking is on the increase again in this country, and it is now enjoyed by a much broader section of the population. Thanks to foreign travel, the British have developed a sophisticated palate as we have learnt and read more about food and drink. Tea without milk has also become an integral part of the régime of the diet-conscious, which means drinking the more delicate China teas.

Indian and Ceylon teas

When the British government abolished the East India Company's China-tea monopoly in 1833, they asked the then Governor General of India, Lord Bentinck, to investigate and put forward proposals to start a tea-planting industry. In the eighteenth century botanists had established that the climate and terrain in Assam, and therefore probably elsewhere in India, was propitious. Five years later, the first Indian teas were sold in the auction rooms in London's Mincing Lane, which had opened in 1834. Twinings, Hornimans, Liptons and other well-known names of today were there bidding.

In Assam, tea-growing burgeoned, though the imported China tea-plants were abandoned in favour of developing the wild bushes native to India. While Indian tea had a flavour totally different from the delicate China teas enjoyed during the previous century, its more robust flavour soon became attractive to the English palate – so much so that it became India's largest export, from which it, and Sri Lanka, still benefit to this day.

The Chinese had ever been secretive about their tea-growing techniques, but not so the Indians or the Singhalese. Of course the reasons for this are obvious. Britain was from the start the sole investor in the Indian development, and could therefore call the tune and control the quality of

Each picker is paid by the basketful: a tea-plantation in India.

the product. They could also eliminate adulteration of shipments, which had been a growing problem in the China trade.

Victorian England was running at a high: the population was growing, industry was booming, the tea-break had begun in the mills and factories of the provinces and tea-drinking had become universal. By the 1890s Britain was importing only one-third of its needs from China. The remainder came from India and Ceylon.

North Indian teas come from the districts of Assam, Dooars, Cachar, Darjeeling and Sylhet (now part of Pakistan) and can be divided roughly into two classes. First, orthodox-manufacture teas, the type of teas that have been seen for most of the present century up to the end of the Second World War. These have black leaves, which sometimes contain golden leaf tips. This type of tea needs a full five to six minutes to infuse in order to elicit its full strength and quality. The second type are those that have a very attractive golden-brown colour in the cup when milk is added. These teas are smaller and browner in leaf than orthodox teas, and their quick infusing also makes them especially valuable for commercial blends. They have a wonderful Muscatel flavour but are rarely strong or colourful.

South Indian Teas are grown in the states of Kerala, Orissa and Mysore, and are somewhat similar in character to Ceylon teas, but seldom equal them in quality or in leaf appearance.

Sri Lanka, or Ceylon as it was known in the days of the Empire, might never have become a tea-growing country had not their coffee crops been struck in 1869 by a killer fungus (*Hemileia vastatrix*). In their efforts to combat almost certain ruin and possible nationwide deprivation, the coffee-planters turned their minds to cultivating the tea-plant. This was to be their salvation.

In his book *100 Years of Ceylon Tea*, D. N. Forrest (1967) refers briefly to Scottish-born James Taylor, whose pioneering work with tea-gardens made him the saviour of the Singhalese people. Taylor, who arrived in Ceylon as a coffee-estate manager in 1852, had already experimented with tea-growing and introduced to Ceylon new technologies, such as machinery for rolling and generally processing the leaves, as well as establishing and building proper factories for the purpose.

Ceylon teas are of orthodox manufacture, but are mostly smaller in leaf than North Indian teas. They vary in flavour and strength according to the district and the elevation at which they are grown. Teas grown high up in the districts of Dimbula, Dikoya and Nuwara Eliya have a very attractive flavour, especially during the two quality plucking periods of spring and autumn. Autumn teas from the Badula district (Uva) also have a very distinctive flavour, as well as good strength and colour. Teas from the lower altitudes have excellent colour and strength but are lacking in real flavour. Except for teas from Dimbula and Nuwara Eliya, Ceylon teas, especially Fannings, infuse quickly, though not as quickly as Assam tea.

The Taste of Tea

How can you describe the taste of tea? It's as impossible a task as it is with wine, yet to write about tea without attempting to give the reader some guide as to what to expect from the different leaves and blends would be to evade the issue. I can, however, convey to you in only the very broadest terms what characteristics to expect.

English Breakfast Tea

A blend of Ceylon and Indian teas, this is a 'brisk' tea with a full-bodied astringent flavour, and is ideal as a 'wake-you-up' tea.

This blend of tea is the one which should also be served when you finally arrive in the breakfast room. It has a good restorative quality about it, leaving you ready to face the day. (It is with this first cup of the day that the 'Rich Tea biscuit' appears alongside the teacup, sitting alone on a tiny plate. 'Rich' is a misnomer if ever there was one, for this ubiquitous biscuit is as plain as they come! Welcomed in the morning as not too challenging, it is good, I am assured, for ladies 'in waiting'.

Russian Caravan Tea

Don't be put off by its name, which sounds like a blend for gypsies! This finely blended tea (originally brought to Russia by the long caravan route) was established by the Empress Elizabeth of Russia in 1735 and is excellent for afternoon drinking.

Yunnan

The deep-toned and golden-hued tea from the western province of Yunnan in China became my favourite during the extensive tasting I did during the writing of this book. Delicately scented, it is ideal for iced-tea, and for the lighter tea-punches.

Jasmine Tea

These teas have only recently been permitted importation to the United Kingdom. As the name implies, the China tea-leaves are scented with dried jasmine petals. It should be drunk weak, with a slice of lemon in each cup, and is good as either a refreshing or a soothing drink.

Darjeeling Tea

Probably the most popular tea at the top end of the market, this is the blend most favoured in London's exclusive clubs, and the Indian tea most likely to be offered to you in any self-respecting country home. It has a delicate yet positive flavour and is Indian tea at its best.

Pure Darjeeling tea is the most costly of the Indian teas and good enough to be drunk unblended: a 'self-drinker', as they call it in the tea-trade, though it is customary to purchase it ready blended. I find its flavour not unlike Muscatel in character, and its colour is a most satisfying deep reddish-brown. Serve it with milk or light cream.

Earl Grey Tea

The name of Charles, the second Earl Grey (1764–1845), Prime Minister of England during the reign of William IV, is probably the best known in the world when it comes to teas. It is a blend of fine China and other exotic oriental teas and it is said that the secret of this delicate, Bergamot-scented blend was passed to Earl Grey 125 years ago by a Chinese mandarin who used it in his own household and eventually had it made up for him by Twinings, who in turn were allowed to sell it to selected purchasers. Sadly for Twinings, they never had the name copyrighted and as a result many tea-merchants today use it, though I consider Twinings' particular blend, with its almost cologne-like scent derived from the oil of Bergamot, to be the best for afternoon drinking and a singularly refreshing beverage on a warm summer's day. Drink it with a slice of lemon, although I often take a weak infusion with the merest drop of milk. If you prefer the scent to be less strong, the tea can be blended with a China Keemun or a good-quality Darjeeling.

Orange Pekoe Tea

This smooth-flavoured blend of specially selected Ceylon teas is excellent for afternoon tea. The word 'orange' refers to the colour of the leaf and not the flavour. Scented Orange Pekoes are always found in an Earl Grey blend.

Lapsang Souchong

This is the tea with the most distinctive flavour of all. Recognisable the instant it is poured, not only by its light greyish-green colour but more particularly by its pungent smoky aroma. 'Souchong' is the generic name of the large leaf of most Congou teas. The true Lapsangs come from a particular district in the Province of Fukien. Chinese Souchong teas are 'positive', rich (too rich for some) and almost syrupy. This tea is never drunk with milk, always either with lemon or totally unadulterated.

Oolong Tea

This tea is manufactured exclusively in China and Formosa (by far the greater part of it in Formosa) and is in reality a cross between green tea and black tea, as it is only partially fermented. Oolong teas, which are principally in demand in the United States and at an élitist level here, have a very delicate, but nonetheless fine, aroma.

Keemun

A north China black Congou tea with a smooth, somewhat sweet, taste and, according to the Chinese, 'the fragrance of an orchid'. Many consider this, along with the slightly smoky I-Chang and Formosa's Oolong, to be among the best connoisseur teas in the world.

All these traditional China teas need a full 5–6 minutes' infusion time.

How to Make a Cup of Tea

While the verb may change, the traditional way of making, infusing, brewing, drawing or mashing tea ought not. The method is as follows:

* Use the finest tea you can afford.
* Warm the teapot either by standing it near the fire or by rinsing it in boiling water.
* Use 1 teaspoonful of tea per person, plus one for the pot.
* Bring freshly drawn water to the boil. Do not allow it to rattle on once it has boiled, as this rids the water of air.
* Take the *pot to the kettle* and pour in the boiling water.
* While the one-for-the-pot rule is known in every house in the land, nowhere are you told how much water to add! You learn this for yourself over the years. I suggest you start off with 1¼ pints of boiling water to each ounce of tea (more water for China tea).
* Stir the mixture well, replace the lid, and allow the tea to infuse, brew, mash or draw (depending on where you live) for 5 minutes.
* Pour the tea into warm cups and add milk and sugar to taste.
* A ceramic pot is best, as it retains the heat well. Aluminium should never be used for a teapot, strainer or tea-ball infuser as it turns the tea black.

In her *Cookery and Household Management* Mrs Beeton gives the best advice I have ever seen in print on making a good pot of tea. How often do you find that the first cup is perfect but that later cups taste stewed and bitter as the pot is left standing – usually complete with a tea-cosy to aid and abet the crime? Mrs Beeton's answer – and a brilliant one, to boot, used by professional tea-tasters the world over – is to use *two* pots! It's as simple as that, yet few people ever do it. Make the tea as instructed. Then, after infusion for 5 minutes, she instructs her readers to *decant off* the freshly made tea through a tea-strainer into a second warm teapot. Hey presto! There you have it: the perfect cuppa to the last drop. Once you have followed this noble lady's advice you'll never revert to your old method, I promise you.

MILK, CREAM, LEMON OR 'BLACK'?

There is probably more debate about whether the addition of milk, cream or lemon makes the best cup of tea than there is on any other food subject in Britain. Those who spurn the addition of milk or cream must be reminded that the Chinese themselves originally made tea by adding boiled milk to their tea, so the argument that the Chinese always drink it in its natural water infusion falls down!

The first European account of milk being used in tea occurred around 1655, when a Dutch ambassador described being given milk with his tea when he first arrived in Canton. There are also references from around that same time to Parisian society taking milk in tea.

The addition of lemon started as an affectation in the Victorian age. Queen Victoria's eldest daughter, the Princess Royal, was the consort of the Emperor of Prussia, where they made tea differently: in fact, it was drunk from a glass in the Russian manner, and served from a samovar, not a teapot. Russians and Prussians were to be seen sucking it through sugar lumps and even stirring in jam! Dear God! How we Brits reacted against this notion! However, the slice of lemon, as served at the Prussian Court, came to us following a short visit by the Queen to her daughter's adoptive country.

Today it is generally accepted in Britain that it is permissible – nay, usual – to add milk or cream to black teas, but it would be tantamount to sacrilege to desecrate green or oolong teas with anything. Not even lemon – and certainly not whisky, which is often added as a comforter to black tea on a winter's eve in Ulster and Scotland!

Sam Twining, Director of R. T. Twining and Company, has this to say on the subject: 'There is no doubt tea is, on the whole, improved by milk. It smooths the taste, and is often referred to as 'creaming', giving a more pleasant, gentler, softer result. Teas like *Gunpowder*, *Green* and *Jasmine*, however are *not* good with milk. Assam type teas cannot be drunk without it.'

Now, whether the milk goes in first or last is a matter for conjecture. In the early days of tea-drinking in England, mugs of silver, pewter or just plain earthenware were used (the same mugs that had hitherto been used for the drinking of ale and porter). The first chinaware was shipped into the country by the East India Company and, ignorant of bone china's great heat-resistant properties, the British thought that pouring scalding-hot tea into the newfangled China tea-bowls would crack the delicate porcelain – so they put the milk in first. Putting it in after the tea has been poured, however, allows each individual to control the amount to his or her taste – so it does seem more sensible.

CLEANING TEAPOTS

Contrary to many old wives' tales, a teapot that is lined with tannin does not make a good cup of tea; it can, and does, make the infusion bitter.

The pot should be meticulously clean, and where a coating of tannin is present this must be removed, either by prolonged soaking or by the use of a cleansing powder, in which case the pot must be well rinsed.

Tea Impedimenta

My mother had a penchant for collecting tea services. If my memory serves me well, she had some ten or twelve different sets of a dozen cups in each. A very pretty one from Minton, with garlands of miniature rosebuds under the gold rims, was *her* favourite. Then there was another delicate fluted white set with simple gold handles from the Belleek factory in County Fermanagh and a third, early nineteenth-century service of handleless tea cans and rimless saucers from the Hilditch pottery, which only existed as a working pottery between 1815 and 1840 and which I now possess. *My* favourite, as a boy, and the one which I always put out if it was my turn to lay the table, was a service from the Royal Worcester pottery given to my mother as a wedding gift in 1908. Its pattern was typical of that period when Art Nouveau was all the rage: the wide shallow cups were in a bright butter-yellow with a deep black band at the rim on which there was a further embellishment of full-blown pink roses. There was then a forbidden-to-touch set in a delicate pale blue, rose-pink and gold pattern, complete with lidded sugar bowl, milk jug and teapot; each of its four cups was footed in a rather fragile shape. This was a gift my father had brought back from the Noritake porcelain factory in Japan, after a business trip he had made to the East. Yet another pattern was from Meissen; but the most valuable of all, with four painted panels of figures and flower garlands on each cup, was from the Sèvres factory in Paris. These last three were my mother's pride and joy and were hardly ever used.

More mundane services, used at weekends and for more ordinary 'At Homes' or to eke out the numbers of cups required when she took it upon herself to entertain large numbers – or, to be more precise, when she wanted to show off to the entire neighbourhood (her attitude to our neighbours was not unlike that of Lucia in E. F. Benson's Mapp and Lucia books) – were from the potteries with such names as Copeland, Mason, Denby or Johnston. I recall a rather tedious blue-and-white printed one. Then there was an ugly 'Green Dragon' pattern; almost every household had *that* one, if not in green, then in blue. There was also a 'modern' pink set with brown polka dots from the hands of the designer Susie Cooper in Staffordshire. Very, very collectable in 1986, though who would have thought that in 1956?

When my mother died I inherited the Hilditch, which I treasure along with a very odd silver tea-service fashioned from what was at one time known as 'Indian' silver and which I think is now more commonly called Britannia metal! It is certainly a curvaceous riot, rococo in style, with bas-relief panels, cabriole feet and asymmetrical knobs and handles. It is also very difficult to clean!

Between 1955 and 1964 I masterminded a series of banquets, buffets and 'At Homes' at Harewood House, near Leeds. In this unbelievably handsome Adam mansion I enjoyed the total freedom of taking from the silver vaults any pieces I chose to use while working in the house. Fashioned by such masters of their craft as Hesther Bateman, Paul de Lamerie and Paul Storr, to name but three, there were vast tea-trays, almost too heavy to carry, tea-kettles, urns, creamers, teapots, strainers, sugar canisters and caddies, each and every one wrought to a rare excellence. It was the experience of working at Harewood House and later at St James's Palace that kindled in me the urge to delve more deeply into the history of English food and domestic life, and which has eventually led to my writing this book on the history of afternoon tea and its impedimenta.

Teapoy

The teapoy is a small pedestal or three-legged table fitted with tea containers, or canisters and mixing bowls. The word derives from an Indian word meaning 'three feet'.

Tea-caddies

The word 'caddy' derives from the Malay word 'kati', meaning one pound – approximately the amount (in fact it was 1.2 lb) held by the small box in which tea was packed for export to England. Canisters, as they were first called, or 'cadies', were unknown in seventeenth-century England, but in the first half of the eighteenth century they became part of

Tea was kept locked away in a teapoy or a tea-caddy, each complete with its own mixing bowl.

43

the silver tea-service so loved as a status symbol by the British from that day to this (though a solid silver service today would cost thousands of pounds). Tea-caddies became objects to which master craftsmen could apply their skills in eighteenth-century England, and plenty of fine examples of the silversmiths' craft survive for us to use.

Caddies come in all sorts of shapes and sizes: plain and elegant, elaborate and ornate, some in silver, most in unusual and pretty inlaid and polished woods. Wooden caddies often had inlaid designs of Chinese scenes and characters, reflecting the origin of tea. Glass canisters were also fairly popular in England from about 1750–1820. Known as 'tea-bottles', they were commonly made of Bristol blue glass, opaque white glass or clear glass, gilded or enamelled with elaborate designs, and often bearing the name of the type of tea they contained. They were usually made in pairs to hold green and black teas. Most had hinged metal lids, some were made with ground glass stoppers, and the more exotic ones might well have had silver or ormolu mounts.

Whatever it was made of, the caddy would be provided with a lock and key to prevent pilfering fingers from removing any of the expensive leaf. Remember, in today's terms, tea in the eighteenth century cost anything between £812 and £1900 per pound! When a hostess did not preside at her own tea-table, the necessary measure and mixture would be taken from the caddy and handed to the servants in a mixing glass, and the caddy would then be locked again. (Ironically, caddies often had sliding bottoms for ease of filling!)

Controversy still reigns as to whether, in the larger three-sectioned caddies, the centre compartment is to hold lump sugar or to contain the cut-glass mixing bowl. Usually there is an obvious solution, for often where a mixing glass is a composite part of the caddy (and the glasses are frequently missing from antique caddies, as they were easily broken), there is a suitably shaped aperture cut out to hold it. Where the centre compartment is a more simple and broader version of its two neighbours, this was probably for sugar; and the mixing glass or bowl would then be a separate article, either with a silver holder or just on its own, depending on the wealth and status of the family. And there were, of course, single caddies for the less well-to-do.

Caddy spoons

The first silver caddy spoons were fashioned in the shape of a shell. Probably this pattern was chosen because in each box they shipped the Chinese used to include a natural scallop shell for scooping out the tea.

Eighteenth-century silversmiths let their imaginations run riot in creating these short-handled spoons to fit inside the caddy when the lid closed. They forged them in every possible shape, from the traditional bowl to hands, leaves, paws and fruits. Many people have fine collections of caddy spoons.

A pretty caddy spoon makes an ideal gift for a christening, coming-of-age or bar mitzvah.

A selection of caddy spoons, a tea-strainer, and a mote spoon, used for removing wayward leaves.

The mote spoon

Rolling, drying and packing teas in the eighteenth century, while remarkably sophisticated even when compared with twentieth-century methods, did have a few problems, one being that 'bastard' leaves and other debris would sometimes escape the eagle eye of the blenders and selectors and would mar the clear golden liquid. But, as usual, the ever-resourceful British had an answer to the problem of unwanted 'floaters' on the top of a filled cup. If these stray leaves escaped the filter (if the teapot was fitted with such a device) or perhaps overflowed the silver strainer placed across the mouth of each cup as it was poured, a mote spoon would be used to scoop up and catch wayward specks of tea dust. These spoons, whose name is taken from the old English word 'mot', which in turn came from the Dutch word of the same spelling meaning dust (we still talk of a 'mote' in the eye), were beautifully wrought and pierced by talented silversmiths in a variety of delightful patterns.

Tea-urns

The tea-urn – often mistakenly referred to as a samovar, which is its Russian cousin – or 'fountain', as it was sometimes called, first appeared in mid-eighteenth-century England to replace the tea-kettle. Its advent was a good sign that tea-drinking was on the increase, as an urn holds considerably more water than a kettle. Almost invariably made of Sheffield plate or japanned metal (sterling silver was generally prohibitive in price, though fine examples do exist), they had a bellied pear- or round-shaped body. Some stand on four feet or curved spindle legs; others have

Filling the teapot from the 'fountain' was a serious business.

a square base with four feet. There was a spigot and tap at the bottom of the urn from which to fill the teapot. Two handles were attached at the sides for ease of handling, and a domed lid with finial finished off the design. Inside there was usually a fixed, hollow, cylindrical compartment, so wrought to receive a thick (1½-inch diameter) red-hot iron rod to keep the water hot.

Tea-kettles

Tea-kettles come in different forms. From the early part of the eighteenth century there are examples of teapots themselves being used as kettles and set over small wick-holders. Usually fashioned with a side handle and with a tiny hinged lid on the tip of the curved spout itself, in addition to the main lid, these were a sign that some people made their tea differently, by putting the tea-leaves in the kettle!

Not much later, there appeared the kettle as we think of it today and of which there are many examples in antique shops. (They are considered an excellent investment. I purchased an early nineteenth-century kettle and lamp in 1969 for £22; today's value is in the region of £800 – an increase of 360 per cent over sixteen years!) The tea-kettle could be made from sterling silver, Sheffield plate or electroplate. As with a teapot, the fixed handle, or 'bail', had an ivory or ebony inset which acted as an insulator. The kettle could be free-standing on its matching trivet complete with spirit lamp; or the kettle could be hinged to the tripod so that all the hostess had to do was to tip it forward to fill her teapot, thus minimising the risk of accidents.

Eighteenth-century carpenters cashed in on the fashion for tea-kettles and created tea-kettle stands. Today these are sometimes taken to be plant or candle stands, for they are small and round with three claw feet; but they are obviously lower in height than the other two pieces of furniture.

Tea-trays

The large oval or oblong tea-tray was made of silver or Sheffield plate (it is said there are more tea-trays made of Sheffield plate than any other item in this medium) and was used in the eighteenth century for serving tea. Four-footed, with two handles for ease of carrying, tea-trays could be up to 22 inches in length. Their edges were moulded or swept in the rococo fashion, and many of the elegant oval ones had a vertical pierced gallery and a slot at each end to act as a hand-hold in place of the more usual extending handles. Their centres would often carry an engraved shield or family monogram.

The tea-tray was designed to hold a kettle (where a separate kettle stand was not in use), a teapot, a sugar canister and tongs, a spoon-tray, a tea caddy and a milk or cream jug (though a matching jug was not considered necessary until late in the eighteenth century; at first a helmet jug or creamer of a different design sufficed). Teacups, saucers and spoons were set out on the tea-table, not on the tray.

Tea-tables

The tea-table was an occasional table with a carved rim that was sometimes made of pierced metal and was to prevent the cups and saucers from sliding off. Later, when afternoon tea was in full flight, extra tables (often in the form of a nest of tables), or a folding table were needed. The late Victorian period also saw the advent of portable free-standing, three-tiered cake stands – an item considered very useful when a variety of cakes and biscuits was to be offered. (It makes an excellent piece of furniture for twentieth-century cocktail parties!)

Teacups and Teapots

During the T'ang Dynasty (AD 620–964), while the Chinese were fast developing their love of tea-drinking, they were at the same time making a type of pottery vastly superior to any seen before – or certainly to any seen in Europe. This pottery became known in Britain as 'china', and it was the Dutch and Portuguese who first introduced it to Europe. What they often brought back were pieces used in Chinese tea-making ceremonies. (Earlier imports had been made of stoneware, and were in fact wine jars, the urn shape of which was eventually to form the basis of the teapot we know today.)

Richard Collins' picture clearly illustrates the different ways of holding a tea-bowl in eighteenth-century England (c. 1730).

The Chinese drank their tea from small bowls, and these became the basic shape for the European teacup, though the handle wasn't added until the mid-eighteenth century – probably because English and European ladies found it uncomfortable to hold the hot, handleless cup with the forefinger on the top rim, the thumb forming the base of a pincer-like grip by supporting the bottom 'under rim' of the bowl. (It is said that this method of holding the tea 'can' or cup gave rise to the 'refained' upward-soaring movement of the little finger to make the grip look elegant. It must also have been more comfortable for jewel-laden fingers!)

The first ceramic teacup was not that different from a coffee or chocolate cup. Coffee cups eventually became straight sided, with one handle, and were known as coffee cans, whereas chocolate cups were given two handles and a lid.

For a time the teacup remained a shallow cup. It had a shallow, rimless saucer, and it was considered quite polite to pour tea into this and drink from the saucer, a habit still in evidence among elderly people in parts of Britain to this day. When it became fashionable to have cups with handles, these tea cans fell into disuse, though many examples can be found in antique shops.

The 'Trembleuse saucer', or teacup stand, the deep recessed or raised rim of which was designed to prevent the cup from sliding about or trembling, was a French design that came in the late eighteenth century.

Early British-made teapots were always wrought and forged from silver or Sheffield plate and were similar in shape to the coffee-pot, with a tapering cylindrical body, a straight spout at an angle of 45 degrees from the body and an ebony or fruitwood handle set at right angles to the spout. The cover, or lid, was dome-shaped with a handsome finial as a knob. Later, the pineapple, a traditional British symbol of hospitality, was a frequent motif for the finials of teapots.

Very early silver teapots were made by cutting down the taller coffee and chocolate pots, and examples of this thrift – and one can't but imagine it was just that – can be seen in the archives of the Goldsmiths Hall in London. There is no logical reason why a teapot should not have been tall, but it did not take long before such eminent silversmiths as Paul de Lamerie, Paul Storr and Hesther Bateman began to modify the shape, using round, polygonal and pear-shaped forms with a moulded foot, the handle and spout (now curvaceous and with a filter set in, welded to the body of the pot) sometimes at right angles to each other, but more usually at opposite sides.

In the last quarter of the eighteenth century, the drum-shaped teapot with a straight spout and flat lid became very fashionable. This was followed in social desirability by the oval, rectangular and multi-faceted boat-shaped pot. Often made with flat bottoms, these pots had matching stands to protect the tops of tea-tables. Stands were often forged as an extra for existing teapots and could well be by a different maker. They were yet another sign of wealth in eighteenth- and nineteenth-century Britain.

By the time tea-drinking became a national habit in the nineteenth century, pots were being made for the common man. These were of pottery and china, the designs for which were originally based on the silver pots of the gentry rather than upon the Chinese wine jug. While many of them were plain in design, most were lavishly ornamented and sculpted in every conceivable form: cauliflowers, rabbits, cottages, human forms, top hats; some even had two spouts. In fact, anything that could be made to hold the golden liquid, tea, was thrown, cast or wrought. Today these pots, for years considered vulgar by the middle and upper classes, are collectors' items of great value, as well as being an excellent social record of times past, as the tea-bag and instant tea make inroads into our busy, servantless lives.

Tea-services

The growth in popularity of tea-drinking and its eventual availability to the middle and lower classes created a whole new business for the pottery industry at Stoke-on-Trent in Staffordshire, and at nearby Derby. Josiah Wedgwood (1730–95), one of the most famous names in the world of pottery, was quick off the mark in introducing machinery to his factory at Burslam. He is perhaps best known for this development of a cream-coloured earthenware that was refined into what is still known today as Queensware (named after its patroness, Queen Charlotte, consort of

King George III). At the bottom end of the trade, so to speak, and alongside his fine china, Wedgwood worked heavily with transfer work as a means of keeping costs down by not having to pay for the hand-painting demanded by china. In about 1767 he developed black basalt, an unglazed black stoneware made from native clay, ironstone, manganese and ochre, which was the basis for the famous Wedgwood vases, busts and relief tablets – and for teapots. Wedgwood's partnership with T. Bentley led to the opening of their well-known Etruria Works in 1769. At first they produced only quality ornamental ware, but soon the demand for domestic ware made great inroads into their production line, at both ends of the scale, for Wedgwood did not forsake the making of exquisite china.

Alongside all this, other potteries at Chelsea, Bow, Worcester and Derby, to name but a few, were jumping on the bandwaggon and fashioning tea-services – or teasets, as they became known – at first using the designs of the silver services as patterns. Soft-paste porcelain, as opposed to the Continental hard-paste porcelain of Meissen and Sèvres, was soon being used to produce the better quality porcelain tea-services that were, and still are, greatly sought after by collectors as well as by buyers who want to use them.

Josiah Spode II (1754–1827) went even further, making porcelain from natural feldspar, a crystalline white mineral. Spode is also credited with the formula for 'bone' china, in which bone-ash is combined with china clay. Much of England's finest and most delicate ware is made from this.

Rockingham, Coalport, Copeland and Minton are other names to conjure with, all equally well known and vying for position as Britain's finest makers of china.

China itself influenced all these famous potters in their designs for many years, giving us the lovely blue-and-white ware known as Delft-ware, which was in itself the Dutch potters' attempt to use tin-glaze to copy earthenware, the Chinese porcelain imported by the Dutch East India Company into Holland in the seventeenth century. The eighteenth-century 'Famille Rose' of the Ch'ung period, and the 'Imari' designs from Japan are two of the most beautiful of the well-known patterns.

Although teasets comprising teapot, sugar bowl and cream jug were probably made before the middle of the eighteenth century, they rarely date from earlier than the reign of George III. In the eighteenth century a tea-service from China would consist of twelve rimless saucers, twelve small handleless teacups, and six small coffee cans, the saucers doubling for both of these cups. A teapot (small, because tea was so costly), milk jug, and sugar and tea canisters completed the set.

It wasn't until the nineteenth century that the hot-water jug became part of the service, along with the slop basin. This slop basin, or slop bowl, appears to have been necessary, as silver strainers were a luxury and stray leaves and other floaters often arrived inadvertently in the cup. Mind you, this gave rise to 'reading the tea-leaves', which superstition prevails to this day.

The large, round, 10-inch diameter bread-and-butter plate was included in early nineteenth-century services, but the small tea-plate did not appear until mid-Victorian times, when a separate utensil for everything became the order of the day. Tea-knives and cake or pastry forks also made their appearance around this time.

And so we get nearer to the whole rigmarole of afternoon tea: all the necessary impedimenta had become available, and every household in the land possessed at least some of the china and silver.

THE TAKING OF TEA

At one time it was usual at breakfast for the lady of the house to sit at one end of the table and supervise the pouring of tea. The eldest daughter, or the mistress of the house's companion, sat at the opposite end of the table, where she was in charge of the serving of coffee and chocolate.

In grander households, a footman or maidservant would carry round and pass the filled cup on a small silver salver to the member of the family or the houseguest who was to receive it. In smaller households, it was passed down the table as we would pass it today. At an afternoon-tea party, the hostess would sit at her tea-table, mixing and infusing the tea. In households where there were many retainers, the black tea would be carried on a small tray with a small creamer, sugar basin and tongs for guests to help themselves.

The Royal Family taking tea at Royal Lodge, Windsor. Detail of A Conversation Piece *by J. Gunn, 1950.*

The most elegant setting for afternoon tea has always been the drawing-room. To me, a fireplace is essential, for where else can you toast muffins, crumpets, pikelets or just plain bread? In a mechanical toaster, you'll say – but that cuts out the romance and pleasure of the occasion. Comfortable armchairs and plenty of small tables are then all that is needed to create the cosy *mise-en-scène* necessary for the ritual to begin.

An elegant Georgian tea-table should be covered with a fine lace or embroidered teacloth and set out with the teacups and saucers, each standing on a tea-plate with an embroidered organdie or linen tea-napkin between the plate and the saucer. An adequate space must be left on the table for a handsome oblong or oval galleried silver tea-tray, which in turn will be the resting place for an elegant silver tea-kettle complete with spirit burner, a sugar basket with a blue Bristol-glass liner, a helmet-shaped creamer, a hot-water jug, a tea-strainer, and the all-necessary 'slop' bowl into which dregs can be poured from each guest's cup before a second cup is proffered. For those households that possess a teapoy, this will take the place of a tea-caddy or canister. A silver muffin dish, complete with hot-water liner and high-domed lid, will be needed to hold freshly toasted *hot* muffins or crisp crumpets, each dripping with good sweet butter, a jam dish and spoon to hold home-made preserves, and a crystal honeypot complete the impedimenta for this part of the tea. A muffineer, not unlike a domed pepperpot (in fact, by some people often mistaken for one) will contain cinnamon, sugar or even salt for gourmets to sprinkle on to their muffins.

For those huddled on the floor by the fireside, an expanding toasting fork will be provided so that each may make his own hot toast, the gentlemen spreading theirs with butter and Gentleman's Relish (see p. 264), the ladies topping theirs with pieces of honeycomb from the local hives, a goodly spoon of preserves or a rich fruit butter (see p. 249).

CHANOYU – THE JAPANESE TEA-CEREMONY

It is impossible to exclude Japan from any book on tea-drinking, not least because most people, when they think of the tea-ceremony, think of this Japanese ritual rather than the social carry-on of the gentlefolk here in Britain.

AD 815 was the year in which the Emperor Saga issued a royal edict that tea should be grown in Japan. However, this initial move suffered a setback of almost 200 years while civil wars preoccupied the Japanese people.

As elsewhere, tea in Japan was originally seen more as a medicine than as a beverage to be enjoyed for its flavour; witness the cure of the Shogun Sanetomo in AD 1203–19. One Yeisai, a Buddhist monk, who had been in no small way responsible for the re-introduction of tea to Japan following the period of unrest, was called upon to attend the sick Shogun. Whatever his illness was, apparently the cure was miraculous, and tea-drinking understandably gained in reputation.

The serious ceremony of tea-drinking in Japan.

Parlour games were not unknown in those far off days, and *tocha*, or tea-tasting, was a popular one introduced into Japan from China. Participants were asked to identify the best tea and say whence it came. Prizes were given and a cult was started. Sixteenth-century Zen Buddhists claimed to be responsible for the elaborate tea-ceremony, which eventually grew out of this early approach to drinking tea.

Special wooden buildings or tea-houses (*sukiya*) are constructed in the corner of a garden for the tea-ceremony, which is overseen by a Tea Master – often, but not always, the host himself. A wealthy host may well employ a professional Tea Master to perform the ritual for him. To arrive in the *sukiya* guests must tread a special path (*roji*) to the door or entrance of the waiting room (*yoritauk*). Meanwhile, in the preparation room (*mizh-ya*) the tea master assembles all the impedimenta needed to perform this four-hour long, spiritually cleansing and socially important ritual. Guests, rarely more than five in number, must prepare their thoughts for the ceremony by walking reverently, and soberly dressed, through the garden to the waiting room. Here they are greeted by their host, who leads them to the tea-room itself. The room is entered by crawling through a low doorway, a ritual seen as a levelling of rank. Much attention is also paid to admiring the painted scroll hanging in a place of prominence. Other observances, such as admiring the quality of the china, vary from ceremony to ceremony.

First of all a light meal (*kaiseki*) is offered, after which the invited guests repair to the garden or waiting room. The sounding of a gong signals them to return to the tea-room, where the scroll in the position of

An example of a tea-ticket: a coupon used in the promotion of tea.

importance has been replaced by a vase of flowers arranged in one of the traditional Japanese ways (*ikebana*): each arrangement has some significance to the particular occasion. A fire is now burning in a low stove, beside which are set a caddy (*cha-ire*), a bamboo tea-whisk (*cha-sen*) a tea-bowl (*cha-wan*) and a scoop (*cha-shakm*), kettle and ladle. (You will notice that the Japanese word for tea, like the Chinese, is *cha*.)

A kettle of water is simmering by the fire. Having cleansed and rinsed all the utensils, in a way Westerners might observe at a Catholic Mass, the Tea Master puts three scoopfuls of green tea (*matcha*) into the bowl and ladles over it a specific amount of hot water from the kettle, handling the ladle in a very precise way. This thick tea is whisked and is then ready. The guest of honour shuffles forwards on his knees and takes up the bowl in the palm of his left hand, supporting it with the fingers of the right. He sips, praises the flavour, then takes two further sips before wiping the rim and passing the bowl to the next guest, who, after partaking, also wipes the rim with a small paper napkin (*kaishi*) which he will have brought with him along with his or her fan. The host or Tea Master then makes a second infusion of thin tea (*usucha*), which is served in individual tea-bowls.

Following this ritual, the host or Tea Master leaves the tea-room, taking all the utensils with him, and the guests either depart or stay on for more social chit-chat and local gossip, as they choose. While there are many subtle variations of the tea-ceremony, such as the mysterious and complex ways of using the tea-ladle, the ritual of taking thick and then thin tea is invariable.

From Then Until Now

So there we have it – the exciting, not to say intriguing, history of the art of taking tea. We have glimpsed its beginning in seventeenth-century Europe, learned a little about the varieties of tea and touched upon some of the innumerable legends and customs that have grown around its drinking. We have learnt the history of the teapot and teacup, not to mention all the other impedimenta of the tea-party.

With the recipes in this book I hope you will make all the traditional tea-party titbits and enjoy many of the newer ideas; and that you will be encouraged to collect the evocative and elegant treasures associated with afternoon tea. But history is a process of evolution. Should we not also build on the past? Learn to mix new blends of the tea leaf? Find new uses for its infusion? Invent new foods to eat with it? Above all, patronise a brilliant new generation of designers and encourage them to produce fine ornaments for the table? France has the exquisite new Monet-inspired yellow and cobalt blue service. Inspired by the work of that great Impressionist, the original is there to be seen at his home at Giverny near Paris, which is now a museum for all to enjoy. In facsimile, this elegant china can be purchased from the shelves of any good store. We in Britain have skilled furniture-makers, silversmiths, embroiderers and lace-makers, whose work we should be collecting so that we can create our own beautiful, up-to-date environment. Given the space-age devices to make preparation of food so easy, we should be building on our know-ledge and experience to create new recipes. The advent of the food processor should alter the look of the tea-table, without any doubt! Nuts ground to powder in a second, added to butter whipped to a white, airy lightness, and eggs beaten to a foam in a trice – all this should mean new, light-as-air cakes. Sandwich fillings take on a new attraction when one can wave the wand of the blender to make fine purées of this and that for more refined eating. Let us, therefore, use our knowledge and imagination to build a whole new era of tea-time delights!

BREADS

SUCCESSFUL BREAD-MAKING

There is nothing more mouthwatering than the smell of freshly baked bread. To achieve a result that tastes and looks as good as it smells, there are a few points to remember.

Yeast is the agent that makes bread rise. This can be bought either fresh – usually from a local bakery – or dried in individual sachets; most supermarkets sell dried yeast.

Fresh yeast should be a creamy colour, smell sweet and crumble readily between the fingers. It will keep in a plastic bag in the refrigerator for up to one month, or in the freezer for one year. If freezing yeast, weigh it in recipe-sized portions before freezing.

Fresh yeast can be added to the flour by any of three methods: (1) blending it with the warm liquid before adding it to the flour; (2) using the batter method in which one-third of the flour is mixed with the yeast liquid and is left in a warm place for 20 minutes until it is frothy, before adding it to the rest of the flour, etc.; (3) blending the yeast with part of the liquid before adding it to the dried ingredients, and then adding the remaining liquid.

Dried yeast is just as good as fresh, and is probably more readily obtainable. It will keep in an air-tight container (or in its foil sachets) for up to six months. Dried yeast also needs sugar and liquid to activate it. The proportion is 1 teaspoon of sugar to 8 fl. oz water. Add the yeast and leave for 10–15 minutes to become frothy, then proceed as for fresh yeast. Dried yeast is more concentrated than fresh, so generally only half as much is needed.

The correct flour is essential in bread-making. 'Strong' white flours have a high gluten content; this helps in the rising of the bread, making a lighter loaf with a more open texture. Wholemeal flour gives a closer texture and a stronger, more distinctive flavour. There are many different flours now on the market besides white and wholemeal – wheatmeal, stone ground, granary and rye, for example.

Salt improves the flavour of bread and also affects the gluten in the flour. Accurate measuring is very important, however, as too much kills the yeast, making the bread heavy and uneven in texture, while too little makes the dough rise too quickly.

The liquid used in bread-making can be water, which gives an even texture and crisp crust, and is especially suitable for plain breads. Milk and water, or milk alone, give a softer texture and help the bread stay soft and fresh longer. The amount of liquid required depends on the absorbency of the flour. The liquid must be hand-hot to speed up the leavening process.

Fats used can be lard, butter, margarine or oil; lard makes the dough softer.

Plain mixtures rise faster than richer ones containing fats, sugar, fruit and eggs.

Here are a few basic steps which should be followed in bread-making:

* If the ingredients and utensils are warm rather than cold, the process will be speeded up somewhat.
* The ingredients must be accurately measured.
* Kneading the dough well is essential as it strengthens the gluten in the flour, giving the dough an elasticity and a better chance to rise well and evenly. To knead well, work on a well-floured work surface, turning the bread towards you with your fingers and then pushing the mass of the dough hard away from you with the heel of your hand (or both hands if you're making a large quantity). Knead the dough for a good 10 minutes, until it is firm, smooth, shiny and no longer sticky.
* The dough should be put in a greased or oiled plastic bag to prevent a skin forming. It needs a warm place to rise in. Extreme temperatures kill the yeast; extreme cold retards its growth. You can leave dough safely to rise in a refrigerator overnight or for up to twenty-four hours. The risen dough should spring back when pressed gently with a floured finger.
* The second kneading, commonly known as 'knocking back', gives the dough its even texture. Knead for 4–5 minutes to knock out any air bubbles.
* Shape the loaves and leave them in prepared tins or on baking trays, either of which should be well greased. Cover with lightly oiled plastic and allow to rise a second time. Make sure tins are only half filled to allow room for rising. This second rising stage is called 'proving'. It is always done in a warm temperature and the dough is left until it rises to the top of the tins or has doubled in volume.
* To keep the tops of loaves needed for sandwiches flat, cover a baking tray with lightly oiled foil and place this, oiled side down, on top of the dough in the tins before the second rising. Place ovenproof weights or small bricks on top and keep the tray in place during baking.
* Glaze and bake in a pre-heated, very hot oven so that the extreme heat will kill the yeast. When cooking time is over, turn each loaf out of its tin and tap the bottom: if it sounds hollow, the bread is cooked. If it is still soft and doughy, return it to the oven without the tin, upside down, for a further 10 minutes.
* The bread should be cooled on a wire rack so that air can circulate around it – otherwise any remaining moisture will make the crisp crust go soft.
* Bread, especially brown bread, is best eaten fresh, but it can be refreshed in the oven by wrapping it in foil and reheating at Gas 8/450°F/230°C for 5–10 minutes, letting it cool before removing the foil. For a more crusty loaf, reheat without foil.
* For a crusty top, brush the dough before baking with 2 teaspoons of salt dissolved in 2 tablespoons of water.
* For a soft, shiny crust, brush with beaten egg or a mixture of egg and milk before baking.

* For a floury crust, lightly sift a little flour over the top before baking.
* For a sticky, shiny glaze, use honey, golden syrup, or sugar-water made by dissolving 2 tablespoons of sugar in 2 tablespoons of water. Brush over the *cooled*, but still warm, loaf.
* For extra crunch, sprinkle before baking with sesame, poppy, caraway, celery or fennel seeds – whichever flavour complements the recipe. Cracked wheat may be used for aesthetic interest.

White Bread

The large cottage loaf is the shape associated with a country farmhouse tea; other shapes are known as plaits, bloomers, cobs or crowns. The dough can also be shaped into individual rolls – knots, plaits, etc.; it makes about eighteen of these. Sprinkle the rolls with sesame or poppy seeds. Alternatively, glaze with egg for a shiny top, salt water for a crusty finish, or dust with flour for a soft roll.

Makes one 2lb or two 1lb loaves

$1\frac{1}{2}$ **lb** strong white flour
2 tsps salt
1 tbsp dried or $\frac{1}{2}$ oz fresh yeast

$\frac{1}{4}$ **tsp** caster sugar
$\frac{3}{4}$ **pint** warm water
1 tsp lard

With a little lard, butter or soya oil, grease one 2lb and one 1lb loaf tin.

Mix the yeast, sugar and water together in a small bowl and leave in a warm place for 10 minutes until frothy.

Sieve the flour and salt into a large bowl and rub in the lard with your fingertips.

Add the yeast liquid and blend together until a firm dough is formed and the sides of the bowl are clean. Turn out on to a lightly floured work surface and knead for about 10 minutes or until the dough is smooth, glossy and elastic: it should spring back when pressed with your forefinger.

Place the kneaded dough in a large, lightly oiled plastic bag and leave in a warm place for about $1\frac{1}{2}$ hours or until the dough has risen and doubled in volume. Punch or knock back the dough, then knead again for 2–3 minutes to knock out any air bubbles. Cut the dough into two pieces, one twice the size of the other. With lightly floured hands, shape the dough to fit the tins. Put the filled tins inside oiled plastic bags and leave in a warm place for 30–40 minutes or until the dough has risen to the top of the tins and doubled in volume.

Pre-heat the oven to Gas 8/450°F/230°C.

Bake in the centre of the oven for 35–40 minutes.

Take the loaves out of their tins and test for doneness. Cool on a wire rack. For really crusty bread, put the loaves on a baking tray and return them to the oven for a further 5 minutes.

Wholemeal Bread

Best eaten either freshly baked or toasted later. This recipe makes two 2lb loaves, four 1lb loaves, or one 2lb plus two 1lb loaves.

1 oz dried or 2 oz fresh yeast	**2 tbsps** caster sugar
1 tsp caster sugar	**2 tbsps** salt
1½ pints warm water	**2 oz** lard
3 lb wholemeal flour	

In a small bowl, mix the yeast and 1 teaspoon of sugar with 8 fl. oz of the measured water and leave in a warm place for 10 minutes until frothy. Sieve the flour, sugar and salt into a large bowl. Rub in the fat with your fingertips.

Pour in the yeast liquid and remaining water and mix to form a firm dough. Turn out on to a lightly floured work surface and knead the dough well for 10 minutes.

Place the dough in a large, lightly oiled plastic bag and leave it in a warm place for 1–1½ hours until it has risen and doubled in volume. Punch down or knock back the dough and knead it again for a further 5 minutes. Divide the dough into the desired sizes and place it in well-greased loaf tins. Put the tins in oiled plastic bags and leave in a warm place until the dough rises almost to the tops of the tins and is virtually doubled in volume.

Pre-heat the oven to Gas 8/450°F/230°C.

For a crusty top, brush the dough with salted water. Sprinkle cracked wheat on the top for an attractive finish.

Bake for 35–40 minutes. Remove from the tin, test for doneness and put on to a wire rack to cool.

Rye Bread

Makes 2 large loaves

2½ lb rye flour, medium milled	**1 pint** warm milk (sour milk is good for this bread)
1 heaped tsp salt	
1 tsp caster sugar	**¼ oz** dried or ½ oz fresh yeast
4 oz lard, melted but not hot	

Mix the flour and salt in a bowl.

Cream the yeast with the sugar in a little of the milk.

Make a well in the flour and salt mixture and pour in the melted lard and the blood-warm milk and yeast mixture. Work into a mass, then knead for 15 minutes or until the dough is springy, smooth and shiny.

Leave the dough to rise, covered with a damp cloth or in a large plastic bag, for 1½–2 hours. Cut the dough into two large or four small pieces. Knead lightly and place in buttered bread tins. The dough should half fill the tins. Leave to prove for 45 minutes, when the loaves should be soft and spongy.

Pre-heat the oven to Gas 7–8/425–450°F/220–230°C.

Bake for 30 minutes, then lower the temperature to Gas 6–7/400–425°F/ 210–220°C for a further 20 minutes.

Turn out, test for doneness and cool on a wire rack.

Skofa Bread

Makes 1 large loaf

Skofa flour can be bought in most health-food shops. If you can't get any, substitute fine wholemeal flour.

1 lb skofa flour or fine wholemeal flour
1 tsp salt
1 oz butter

1 tbsp dried or ½ oz fresh yeast
1 tsp brown sugar
¼ **pint** warm water

Mix the yeast and sugar with ¼ pint of water and leave until frothy. Combine the flour and salt in a large bowl. Rub in the butter. Add the yeast mixture to the flour mixture and add more water until you have a soft but not tacky dough.

Knead the dough on a floured board. Form into a round and place on a greased baking tray.

With a knife, cut a cross about ½ inch deep in the dough. Cover the dough and leave it to rise in a warm place for 30 minutes.

Pre-heat the oven to Gas 6/400°F/200°C.

Bake for 50 minutes. Test for doneness. Cool on a wire rack.

Bridge Rolls

I have never had a hand in bridge, if you'll forgive the pun: but the bridge roll was invented for those who have – which in Britain is a considerable number. So loath are these card-players to leave their velvet-covered tables to partake of afternoon tea, lest their powers of concentration wane, that a minuscule soft, semi-sweet bread roll was thought up that could be eaten at the card table with favourite sandwich fillings, so assuaging any possible hunger pangs!

Makes 18 rolls

1 tbsp dried or ½ oz fresh yeast	**1 tsp** salt
¼ **tsp** caster sugar	**2 oz** butter
3 fl. oz warm milk	1 egg, lightly beaten
8 oz strong white flour	

Mix the yeast and sugar with the milk and leave in a warm place for about 10 minutes until frothy.

Sieve the flour and salt into a large bowl and rub in the butter with your fingertips. Add the yeast mixture and the beaten egg and mix to a soft dough. Turn on to a lightly floured work surface and knead for 10 minutes or until smooth and glossy.

Place the dough in a lightly oiled plastic bag and leave in a warm place for 1½–2 hours until the dough has doubled in volume.

Punch or knock back the dough, then knead it again for 5 minutes. Cut it into eighteen equal pieces. Shape each piece into a roll about 3 inches long. Place the rolls fairly close together in rows on a greased baking tray. Slip the tray into the oiled plastic bag and leave in a warm place for a further 20–30 minutes until the rolls have risen and doubled in volume.

Pre-heat the oven to Gas 7/425°F/220°C.

For a glazed shiny top, brush each roll with a little beaten egg before baking. Bake for about 20 minutes. Test for doneness. Cool on a wire rack.

Sour Cream Bread Cake

This bread cake is best eaten soon after baking.

Serves 4

8 oz self-raising flour	**4 oz** lard
1 level tsp salt	**4 fl. oz** sour cream
1 level tsp baking powder	1 large egg, beaten

Pre-heat the oven to Gas 5/375°F/190°C.

Sieve the self-raising flour, salt and baking powder together. Rub in the lard.

Mix the sour cream and beaten egg together. Using a fork, mix this into the flour mixture to form a soft dough. Turn on to a floured board. Press the dough down and form into a 6–7-inch circle.

Put the dough on to a buttered baking tray. Cut a cross deep into the dough, to about halfway through its depth.

Bake for 35–40 minutes. Cool on a wire rack.

To serve, break the bread cake into four sections. Split each section across and butter it. Eat with damson cheese, honey or a spread of your choice.

Herb and Cheese Bread

Makes two 1lb loaves

1 lb self-raising flour
1 level tsp salt
1 level tsp baking powder
6 oz butter or margarine
4 oz grated Edam cheese or other 'melting' cheese

1 level tbsp mixed dried herbs or 2 tbsps fresh herbs (thyme, chives, parsley, mint)
2 eggs, beaten
milk

Pre-heat the oven to Gas 5/375°F/190°C.

Sieve the flour, salt and baking powder into a bowl. Rub in the butter or margarine until it is the consistency of fine crumbs.

Add the cheese and herbs. Make a well in the mixture and pour in the beaten eggs. Add sufficient milk to make a soft dough.

Divide the dough between two 1lb buttered loaf tins.

Bake for 1½–2 hours. Turn out and cool on a wire rack.

Savoury Herb Bread

Makes 1 loaf

8 oz self-raising flour
1 heaped tsp salt
1 level tsp dry mustard
1 tbsp mixed dried herbs or 1 tsp dried thyme and sage with 1 tbsp freshly chopped parsley

3 oz 'dry' Cheddar cheese, grated
1 egg, beaten
1½ oz butter

Pre-heat the oven to Gas 5/375°F/190°C.

Mix all the dry ingredients together (including the cheese).

Melt the butter and add it to the dry ingredients. Add the beaten egg. Stir until well mixed.

Place the dough in a buttered 1lb loaf tin and bake for 35–40 minutes. Cool before removing from tin.

Nut Bread

This plain nut bread is ideal sliced for sandwiches or cut in chunks for the dinner table.

Makes two 1lb loaves

2 eggs
4 oz dark soft brown sugar
1½ lb strong white flour
4 tsps baking powder

½ tsp salt
¾ pint milk
4 oz mixed hazelnuts and walnuts, finely chopped

Beat the eggs well and add the sugar. Sieve the flour, baking powder and salt together. Add the flour mixture alternately with milk to the egg mixture. Stir in the chopped nuts.

Divide the mixture between two 1lb loaf tins and let it stand for 30 minutes before baking.

Pre-heat the oven to Gas 4/350°F/180°C.

Bake for about 30 minutes until the loaf is firm and risen.

Cool in the tins for 10 minutes before turning out.

Walnut Bread

This delicious bread is very good for making savoury sandwiches. It also makes a pleasant change toasted for breakfast.

Makes one 2lb loaf

1 lb strong white flour
8 oz Muscovado or other soft brown sugar
1 heaped tsp baking powder
1 level tsp salt

1 5-oz packet walnuts, roughly crushed
¾ pint milk
2 large eggs, well beaten
1 level tsp ground mace

Pre-heat the oven to Gas 5/375°F/190°C.

Sieve the flour, mace, baking powder and salt into a large bowl. 'Run' the sugar through this using your fingertips to ensure even mixing.

Mix in the walnuts, then, using a fork, work in the beaten egg, adding enough milk to make a very soft dough.

Spoon or pour the dough into a well-greased 2lb loaf tin, its base lined with buttered greaseproof paper.

Bake for 20 minutes. Lower the temperature to Gas 4/350°F/180°C and bake for a further 30–40 minutes or until the loaf is well risen and leaving the sides of the tin.

Leave to cool in the tin for 10 minutes before turning on to a wire rack.

It is better to cut this loaf when it is a day old.

Croissants

Croissants have won a place at the British tea-table these days. It hardly seems worth making your own, but there are still those people, thank goodness, who set store by effort.

These crescent-shaped pastry-cum-bread buns vary in richness, from very flaky pastry-type affairs to those of a more bread-like consistency. I prefer the latter.

It's the shape that gives the croissant its name. In eighteenth-century England we actually had a native beast like the French croissant: it was called a 'wig'. My recipe is similar.

Makes 6–8 croissants

¾ **pint** milk
½ **oz** brewer's yeast
18 oz fine plain white flour, sieved

½ **oz** salt
4 oz butter
1 egg, beaten, to glaze

Warm 4 fl.oz milk to blood heat (about 100°F/38°C) and pour it into a bowl. Mix in the crumbled yeast and work to a soft dough with 4 oz flour. Leave the dough to rise to double its size in a lightly greased bowl covered with a cloth; this will take up to an hour.

When the dough has risen, add the rest of the milk and sieve in the remaining flour and salt. Knead as for ordinary bread, although you don't need to be quite so forceful – just knead until you have a firm but flexible dough.

Roll the dough into an oblong roughly 14×6 inches and ½ inch thick.

Spread the butter over the whole surface area of the rolled dough. Fold the dough top to middle, bottom over the top, and turn it so that the edges are in the same position as a closed book. Press all the edges together with a rolling pin. Leave the dough in the refrigerator for an hour.

Roll the dough again in a similar way, after which leave it once more to rest for an hour. Repeat again. Lightly dredge the dough with flour and put it in a lightly oiled plastic bag. Leave it overnight in the refrigerator.

Roll out the dough as before, this time approximately 12 inches long, 4–5 inches wide and ¼ inch thick. Cut into 4–5-inch squares. Cut these from corner to corner into two triangles. Roll up the triangles lightly (or somewhat loosely), from the long edge to the point. Seal with a little beaten egg. Form into crescent shapes, nipping and sealing the edges together with a little beaten egg. Leave the croissants to rise again until they have doubled in size.

Pre-heat the oven to Gas 8/450°F/230°C.

Now pull the joined tips slightly apart, brush the croissants with beaten egg and bake for 20–25 minutes.

Brioches

Brioches can be split and served with jam, or, if made as one big oblong loaf, sliced and used as a luxury sandwich bread.

Makes 12–16 brioches

8 **oz** plain white flour	2–3 **tbsps** milk
½ **oz** brewer's yeast	2 large eggs, beaten
2 **tbsps** warm water	3 **oz** unsalted butter, softened to a
1 **level tsp** salt	paste
½ **oz** caster sugar	extra beaten egg, to glaze

Sieve the flour. Put 2 oz into a bowl. Make a well and crumble in the yeast very finely. Add 2 tablespoons of warm water and, using your fingertips, work into a smooth paste. Form this into a small ball.

Take a small pan or bowl of lukewarm water, drop the ball of dough into it to develop and rise in volume (about 8–10 minutes).

Meanwhile, mix the salt and sugar with the remaining flour. Add the milk and eggs. It is quite a messy business to work this into a dough, but you must do so. When you have a workable mass which doesn't stick to the fingers, add the butter and work this into the dough. Don't try adding any extra flour; just persevere.

Remove the risen yeast dough from the water, using your fingers spread out like a fan. Let the dough drain for a minute or so on a clean teatowel. Now knead it lightly but thoroughly with the second dough. Put it into a lightly oiled, floured plastic bag, and leave it to rise and develop for 3–4 hours in a warm part of the kitchen (not on top of the central heating boiler).

Now knock the dough back, but not as laboriously as you would do for bread, put it on a well-greased, floured tray, cover it with a clean floured cloth and leave it in a *cold* place or refrigerator to firm up and take on a manageable consistency.

Knead the dough lightly and form it into small egg-sized balls. Cut off one-third of each ball and form it into a smaller ball with a little point at one end.

Lightly butter your brioche tins. Put in the larger of the two balls. Make a small incision and fit in the pointed end of the smaller ball (this is to give the brioches their mini-cottage-loaf shape when baked).

Leave to prove again for 15 minutes in a warmer place than previously – the top of the boiler or the back of the Aga.

Pre-heat the oven to Gas 7/425°F/220°C.

Brush the top of each brioche with a little beaten egg. Bake for 15 minutes. Turn out on to a wire rack to cool.

SANDWICHES

TRADITIONAL BRITISH SANDWICHES

Although John Montagu, the fourth Earl of Sandwich (1718–92), did not actually invent that device where two pieces of bread enclose fillings such as meat, cheese or salad, it cannot be denied that he popularised and gave his name to this type of food. Legend has it that he was such an ardent gambler that he couldn't bear to leave the gaming tables for long enough to partake of food in a proper manner, so he bade his servants put meat between two slices of bread and bring it to his chair, thus starting a fashion in eating that has been on the increase ever since.

But what has happened to the sandwich since those far-off days? Until the end of the Second World War it was the one way in which every working man in Britain got his midday meal, or 'snap' as it is known in the industrial regions, as it was the only cheap and effective means of transporting food to his place of employment, there being no staff restaurants in those days. At the other end of the social scale, ladies and gentlemen of means nibbled their way through dainty finger sandwiches in their drawing rooms, in fashionable tea-shops and in the lounges of luxury hotels.

Today we meet sandwiches everywhere, usually in an uninteresting and debased form – especially in transport buffets where the caterers' imaginations rarely stretch beyond slices of 'plastic' bread filled with a meagre sliver of 'plastic' ham or 'plastic' cheese, garnished, at best, with a slice of unskinned tomato and a wilted sprig of parsley. Not even the new spate of excellent sandwich shops burgeoning throughout the country, with their goodly selection of imaginative fillings, seems able to shame these public bodies into widening their horizons.

In this book, however, we are concerned only with those delicate, deliciously filled morsels served on napkin-lined silver salvers and elegant china plates at 4 o'clock in the afternoon or thereabouts.

Afternoon-tea sandwiches

Many cookery writers today are bidding us use fresh, crisp, crusty breads of a French nature or, if not French, then made with gutsy wholemeal flour. All of which is a fine idea for making lusty sandwiches for the children's lunch-pack, for an office snack, or for post-football-match sustenance. This kind of sturdy, wholesome bread is designed to contain – and with some good degree of safety – robust fillings, with crisp lettuce leaves cascading out of the sides and mayonnaise brimming appetisingly over the edges. It is not, however, the ideal bread for making the delicate, mouthwatering finger sandwiches served at tea-time, or at an 'At Home' or cocktail party, or at a reception where elegant presentation is called for.

For such morsels was the English sandwich loaf created: square, flat-topped and with a soft, close-textured crumb, which can make it quite difficult to cut into the thin slivers needed to make those delicate sandwiches.

Bread for sandwich-making is best home-made and when it is one day old. It helps to put the loaf into the freezer for an hour or two before cutting: this firms up the crumb. It is also easier to cut if you use a knife with a long, sharp, serrated blade – or you may like to try experimenting with an electric carving knife: after a little practice this can produce excellent results.

It is always easier to work with butters and spreads which are prepared in advance, are at room temperature and are soft. Spread the cut face of the loaf *before* slicing and de-crusting; a flexible small-bladed palette-knife is good for easy spreading.

When making pin-wheels, fluted, shaped or rolled sandwiches, have a dampened tea-towel ready. Take the bread from the freezer, cut off the crust and spread the cut face with butter. Then carefully cut the thinnest possible slices from the full *length* of the loaf. Done this way, the bread will not break up. Lay the slices side by side on the damp towel to prevent the bread drying and curling up at the corners; this will also facilitate the rolling up of a pin-wheel. If the next slice is too frozen, you will have to wait only a couple of minutes for it to become manageable. Fill the first slice and roll it up carefully but tightly. Put each roll into a suitable plastic bag for freezing or storing. Cut them into delicate $\frac{1}{8}$-inch discs which will thaw out in a matter of minutes and be absolutely fresh.

For elegant presentation, sandwiches should be crusted before being cut into squares, fingers, triangles or, when the occasion is special enough, cut into shapes using fancy biscuit- or scone-cutters. (These come in a variety of shapes: round, oval, diamond or heart-shaped.) In order not to be too wasteful, the filling should be contained as near as is feasible within the area of the shape. The off-cuts of the buttered bread can then be toasted in the oven on a baking tray and made into savoury breadcrumbs for use in some other dish.

To keep sandwiches moist, cover them with a piece of greaseproof paper, wetted and lightly wrung out. Then cover the plate or tray with plastic film before refrigerating.

Sandwiches which are made a day in advance, but which you do not wish to freeze, should be packed in plastic bags to avoid contamination with other foodstuffs in your refrigerator.

Freezing sandwiches

Ideally, sandwiches should not be kept in a freezer for more than 3–4 weeks. When packing them for freezing, put a protective wall of foiled card round them to minimise damage to the edges. Fill sandwiches evenly to avoid misshaping and to ensure even defrosting. De-crust the sandwiches before freezing but do not cut them into serving sizes. Freeze in a single layer on open trays. Pin-wheels and rolled sandwiches are better stored uncut in lidded foil boxes to prevent squashing. Wrap sandwiches in cellophane or plastic film before wrapping them again in aluminium foil or freezer bags. Do not put different fillings into the same bag – the flavours may well transfer on defrosting.

Presentation of sandwiches

Crisp, starched cotton-lace doilies or folded linen napkins are the most elegant way of covering plates and dishes. If you do not possess these charming plate covers, use attractively punched paper doilies or dish papers as a more than adequate substitute.

While it is usual to serve piles of tiny sandwiches of one particular filling together on one plate, there is every reason to arrange sandwiches on silver trays, or other attractive platters and baskets, in rows or groups of complementary shapes, colours and fillings. For wedding teas I have frequently used little clusters of mixed sandwiches tied with ribbon bows for each guest to lift on to his or her plate, and of course flower garlands and posies have a place here and can be used *ad lib* to great effect.

The following notion may sound messy but, if freshly made sandwiches are cut small enough, it is a novel and very tasty idea to dip or brush the exposed cut edges with a little home-made mayonnaise, then dip or roll the sandwiches in finely crushed toasted hazelnuts, freshly crushed pistachio nuts, or freshly chopped herbs such as parsley, mint or chives.

Another attractive way of presenting mini-sandwiches for a party or reception is to make a chess-board. Cut the sandwiches into even-sized squares, using both brown and white breads, select a square tray or board, and simply arrange the sandwiches alternately to look like a chessboard, adding a border of freshly picked parsley or watercress sprigs.

Yet another idea is to brush the top of each round of sandwiches with a thin coat of mayonnaise before cutting and crusting, then to make mosaics using the sieved whites and yolks of hardboiled eggs, chopped parsley, a selection of crushed nuts, mock caviare or paprika – all of which will give a variety of textures and colours, and add to the gala effect for a special party.

If cut small or served as open fingers, many of the sandwiches in the book are ideal for a cocktail buffet.

All the sandwich fillings given here can be used on small split bridge rolls or on small split savoury or sweet scones. In that case, do not top the rolls or scones. Serve them as open sandwiches, with a little garnish appropriate to each filling, or just top each open face with a tiny sprig of freshly picked and washed parsley, a watercress leaf, a couple of chive or dill fronds, or a small nut.

Quantity Guide for Sandwiches

An average loaf – 2 lb in weight, 4×4 inches square – will yield 20–24 slices, depending on how deftly you cut the bread. This will make 10–12 sandwiches which, when quartered, will in turn give 40–48 squares or triangles or, when cut into three, 30–36 fingers.

* To spread the bread slices fairly liberally and to the edges you will require 8 oz of softened butter, creamed butter, or any of the other soft savoury and sweet spreads given in the book for 10–12 sandwiches.
* Soft spreadable fillings such as a fine pâté, meat, fish or cheese will require 8–10 oz to fill 10–12 sandwiches.
* Fillings of a coarser nature, such as composite mixtures – crab mayonnaise, chopped chicken, flaked salmon, grated cheese with nuts or fruits, etc. – will require up to 12 oz of filling for 10–12 sandwiches.
* Sliced meats: allow 1 oz per sandwich – i.e. up to 12 oz for 10–12 sandwiches.
* Allow 12 watercress leaves per sandwich.
* Allow 1 small lettuce leaf, de-veined, per sandwich.
* Mayonnaise or other 'flowing' spreads: allow 1 heaped teaspoon per sandwich, or 6 oz for 10–12 sandwiches.

Eventually it is up to the individual host or hostess to establish his or her own generosity. Sandwiches should be well and elegantly filled, but must be manageable for afternoon tea.

Note: At tea-time, you may prefer to omit garlic or spring onions from sandwich fillings.

The Ubiquitous English Non-soggy Tomato Sandwich

There are two traditional English sandwiches that are really difficult to eat and are guaranteed to mess up tie and blouse alike as their filling slithers out: they are the tomato sandwich and the cucumber sandwich. Yet they are the best we have, revealing the essential flavours of the two fillings.

2 lb tomatoes (of a size giving 5 to 1 lb)
salt

freshly ground pepper or old-fashioned white pepper

With a small knife, make a little cross in the base of each tomato. Plunge the tomatoes into a pan of boiling water and count to twenty. Remove the tomatoes to a bowl of cold water, then drain them and peel off their skins.

Now, this is where the mistake often happens. Most people slice them. I don't. I quarter the tomatoes, remove the seeds, press the 'petals' flat and lay them on a slice of buttered bread. If you attempt to use two layers of tomato, you will – or rather, *they* will – come unstuck, so to speak. They will 'slither'. So, one layer only. Then, after seasoning, on goes the top, which is pressed firmly home, and the sandwich is cut into appropriate shapes.

Its Friend, the Victorian Cucumber Sandwich

1 12-inch cucumber
1 tbsp good olive oil
1 tbsp lemon juice
a scant tsp white sugar
salt

ground white pepper (freshly ground black pepper can, of course, be used; it is, however, a small step away from authenticity)

The cucumber must be cut as thin as possible, using a mandoline or a food processor fixed with a metal blade. Very lightly salt the slices and leave them to drain in a colander, lightly weighted with a plate, for two hours or so, pressing from time to time to get rid of excess juices.

Dress the sliced and drained cucumber with a little oil, lemon juice and sugar, and a sprinkling of freshly ground white pepper (no more salt).

Spread thin slices of white or brown bread with creamed butter. Fill in the usual way, but at the last possible moment, as this sandwich quickly becomes 'soggy'.

The Recalcitrant Egg and Cress Sandwich

Along with its two first cousins, the tomato and the cucumber sandwich, this is surely the best known of all English sandwiches, not least because if the eggs are overboiled and crumbly, it too can have a recalcitrant filling!

Try my special version, where I double up on the cress flavour. I think you'll fall for it – and it is certainly safe to present to visitors.

5 eggs, hardboiled (see method)
2 tbsps double cream or 2 oz unsalted butter, softened, or 2 tbsps bland mayonnaise

salt and ground white pepper
1 punnet mustard and cress

Everyone has his or her own way of hardboiling an egg! Whichever method you follow, the egg should still have just a *modicum* of soft yolk in the centre, the white should be softish as opposed to rubbery and, above all, there should be no dark ring round the yolk. This can easily be avoided by ensuring that the shell is cracked after boiling and that the egg is placed under running cold water until it has cooled completely. It's the hot egg that gets the dark rings under its eyes!

Mash the eggs with a fork and bind them with enough double cream, soft butter or mayonnaise to give a spreading consistency.

Snip off the leaves of the cress together with about ¼ inch of the stalk. Mix these into the egg mixture. Season lightly with salt and white pepper – somehow black pepper, tasty though it is, has no place in our traditional sandwich.

Spread brown or white bread with watercress butter (see p. 238) then spread a goodly cushion of the egg filling over it, top with a second slice of bread, press lightly, and crust and cut as desired.

Egg Sandwiches

Proceed as for Egg and Cress Sandwiches, omitting the cress and using plain or lemon butter (see p. 236) to spread the bread.

Potted Meat Sandwiches

Makes 1¼ lb

Potted meat filling

1 lb shin of beef
2 fl. oz medium dry Madeira or
   sherry
1 tsp salt

1 tsp ground mace
1 tsp freshly ground black pepper
a good 4 oz clarified butter (see
   pp. 234–5), cool but not set

Trim the meat of all skin and fat. Cut it into ½-inch cubes and put the cubes into a small casserole or bowl along with the wine and seasonings. Cover with a piece of foil and a lid.

Stand the container in a pan of water and cover the pan too with a lid. Simmer at a very gentle roll for 2½–3 hours, topping up the pan with boiling water if necessary.

In a food processor, make a fine purée of the meat and its juices. Allow to cool. Start the machine again and dribble in three-quarters of the cool clarified butter. Run the machine until you have a smooth paste. Adjust the seasoning.

Transfer the mixture into one large or several individual pots or ramekins. Spoon over a thin film of the remaining clarified butter. Refrigerate. Allow the potted meat to come to room temperature before serving as a sandwich filling or with hot buttered toast.

When used for sandwich fillings, this amount will fill 15–20 sandwiches.

For a different effect, use white bread as the base slice and brown bread as the top slice.

Devilled Salmon Sandwiches

Makes 1 lb

1 lb flaked cooked salmon
1 tbsp Worcestershire sauce
3–4 drops of Tabasco
a squeeze of lemon juice
a little double cream to bind
salt and freshly ground pepper
lettuce leaves, dressed in a little rich
    French dressing

Mix all the filling ingredients except the lettuce to a spreadable paste in a food processor, or mash them well with a fork.

Spread slices of brown bread with tomato butter (see p. 236). Lay a lettuce leaf on each buttered slice, then the filling.

Creamy Tomato and Anchovy Sandwiches

2 lb tomatoes, skinned, seeded and
    chopped
10 anchovy fillets, pounded to a
    paste
enough double cream or cream
    cheese to mix to a spreading
    consistency
$\frac{1}{8}$ **tsp** cayenne pepper

If using cheese, beat it with a fork. Mix the chopped tomato into the cream or cheese. Season with a modicum of cayenne pepper. (Salt will not be necessary as the anchovies will be salty enough.)

Spread brown or white bread first with a little of the anchovy paste, then with watercress butter (see p. 238), then fork over the creamy tomato filling.

Russian Sandwiches

These sandwiches were very popular between the two World Wars.

6 oz red caviare or lumpfish roe
coarse-grained salt

paprika
juice of half a lemon, strained

Spread brown bread slices with watercress butter (see p. 238). Sprinkle with a little coarse-grained salt and a good shake of paprika.

Cover with the red caviare or lumpfish roe. Add a few drops of lemon juice.

Make up at the last minute and keep refrigerated until ready to serve.

Note: Salmon roe may look milky or cloudy when sprinkled with lemon juice. This is all right.

Delhi Sandwiches

This one is straight from the days of the Raj! Shades of *The Jewel in the Crown* or *A Passage to India* – reason enough to have a Raj tea-party.

12 anchovy fillets
12 oz skinless and boneless sardines
2 tsps mild chutney, rubbed through a sieve
1 large hardboiled egg yolk

1½ level tsps mild curry powder
salt, if necessary
4–6 drops of Tabasco or a pinch or two of cayenne pepper

In a blender, make a paste of all the ingredients and cook it in a small pan over a low heat until it has cohered. If it is to be used for spreading, allow it to cool.

Either serve hot, spread on fingers of hot buttered toast or on split toasted muffins, or allow to cool and use with brown bread as a sandwich filling.

Chicken and Almond Sandwiches

8 oz cooked chicken breast, minced
3 oz nibbed almonds, lightly toasted

double cream or bland mayonnaise, to bind
salt and freshly ground pepper

Bind everything together with enough cream or mayonnaise to give a spreading consistency. Spread brown or white bread slices with basil butter (see p. 238). Top with the filling.

Devilled Fish Sandwiches

Perhaps these are more appropriate as post-theatre snacks or cocktail food than for afternoon tea; but no matter, they're unusual and very tasty.

8–10 oz smoked fish (such as haddock, kipper, mackerel)
2 hardboiled eggs, mashed
2 tbsps parsley, chopped
2 tbsps chives, chopped

2 tbsps Worcestershire sauce
3–4 drops of Tabasco
salt and freshly ground pepper
double cream, to bind

Mix all the ingredients together to a textured paste. Spread brown or white bread slices with chive butter (see p. 238), then with the filling.

Lobster Sandwiches

8 oz lobster meat (fresh, canned or frozen), roughly minced or chopped
8 good sprigs of watercress leaves, picked and roughly chopped

salt and freshly ground pepper
a squeeze or two of lemon juice
double cream, to bind

Bind everything together with double cream to a spreading consistency. Spread brown bread slices with watercress butter (see p. 238), then with the filling. Crust and cut into long fingers.

Christmas Turkey Sandwiches

Spread brown or white bread with either lemon and parsley butter (see p. 236) to which has been added a modicum of ground sage, or mustard butter (see p. 239) to which sage has been added. Cover with thinly sliced turkey.

Christmas Cheese Sandwiches

8 oz grated Stilton (not too much of the ripe blue part)
2–3 tbsps port

double cream, to bind
freshly ground pepper

In a liquidiser, make a fine purée of the cheese, port and cream. Season with freshly ground pepper only.

Spread fruit bread or brown bread with walnut butter (see p. 241), then with the cheese mixture.

White Crab Sandwiches

10–12 oz white crab meat (fresh or frozen), finely chopped
4 hardboiled egg yolks, sieved
bland mayonnaise, to bind

2 spring onions, very finely chopped
salt and freshly ground black pepper
lemon juice

Bind everything together with enough mayonnaise to give a spreading consistency. Spread white bread with lemon and parsley butter (see p. 236), then top with the filling.

Note: These sandwiches should not be frozen if frozen fish has been used.

Sardine Sandwiches

2 8-oz tins skinless and boneless sardines in oil, drained and oil reserved
6 hardboiled egg yolks, sieved

lemon juice
2–3 drops of Tabasco
salt and freshly ground pepper

Mash the sardines to a paste with the sieved egg yolks. Season with salt, pepper, lemon juice and Tabasco. Moisten with a little of the reserved oil.

Spread brown or white bread with mustard butter (see p. 239), then top with the filling.

Lettuce Sandwiches I

Known as 'honeymoon' sandwiches, for they have a filling of lettuce ('let us') alone!

10 inner lettuce leaves, finely shredded

Spread brown bread with mint butter (see p. 237), then cover with lettuce leaves.

Lettuce Sandwiches II

10–12 lettuce leaves, finely chopped   bottled tartare sauce

Use the tartare sauce to bind the lettuce to a spreading consistency. Spread the bread with mustard butter (see p. 239), then cover with the filling.

Mock Crab Sandwiches

6 oz Cheshire or Cheddar cheese,
  grated
4 hardboiled eggs, finely chopped
4 tomatoes, skinned, seeded and
  finely diced

soya or olive oil
lemon juice
salt, pepper and Tabasco

Mix the cheese, egg and tomato together and moisten with oil and a drop
or two of lemon juice. Season well. Butter white bread, then spread with
the filling.

Cream Cheese and Walnut Sandwiches

8 oz cream cheese, beaten
4 oz walnut halves, crushed

$\frac{1}{8}$ **tsp** ground nutmeg
salt and freshly ground pepper

Mix all the ingredients together, adding a spoonful of cream if the mixture
is too stiff. Spread the bread with honey butter (see p. 241), then with the
cheese filling.

Cream Cheese and Pineapple Sandwiches

8 oz cream cheese, beaten
4 oz pineapple (fresh or canned),
  finely chopped

2 oz nibbed almonds
salt and freshly ground pepper

Mix all the ingredients to a spreadable paste, using a fork. Spread brown
bread or fruit bread with cinnamon or honey butter (see pp. 240 and 241),
then add the filling.

Cream Cheese and Shrimp Sandwiches

8 oz cream cheese, beaten
8 oz shrimps, finely diced
1 small clove of garlic, crushed

1 heaped tbsp chives or spring
  onions, finely minced
salt and freshly ground pepper

Mix all the ingredients to a spreadable paste using a fork. Spread the bread with lemon and parsley butter (see p. 236), then add the filling.

Cream Cheese, Orange and Hazelnut Sandwiches

8 oz cream cheese, beaten
4 oz orange segments (tinned or fresh), drained
2 oz toasted hazelnuts, roughly crushed

$\frac{1}{2}$ **tsp** cinnamon
salt and freshly ground pepper

Squeeze some of the juice from the orange segments or the mixture will be too wet. Combine all the ingredients, using a fork. Season lightly with salt, pepper and cinnamon, or spread the bread with tomato curry and orange butter or with cinnamon butter (see pp. 236 and 240), then add the filling.

Cream Cheese, Chive and Almond Sandwiches

8 oz cream cheese, beaten
4 oz nibbed almonds, lightly toasted

2 tbsps chives, finely chopped
salt and freshly ground pepper

Combine all the ingredients using a fork. Spread white bread with chive butter (see p. 238), then add the filling.

Caviare Sandwiches

8 oz caviare or lumpfish roe
lemon juice

5 hardboiled egg yolks
1 tbsp double cream

Cut white or brown bread into thick ($\frac{1}{2}$-inch) slices; toast these and split. Scrape away the excess crumb.

Butter the crumb side well with lemon butter (see p. 236), spread with a thin layer of caviare or lumpfish roe, season with lemon juice. Then add a thin cushion of sieved hardboiled egg, seasoned and bound with a spoonful of double cream.
Add the top, cut into bite-sized pieces and serve while the toast is still crisp.

Toasted Oatmeal Sandwiches

6 oz coarse oatmeal, toasted to a
   golden brown in the oven
enough double cream to bind to a
   spreadable paste

1 tbsp honey

Bind the oatmeal with the cream and honey. Spread any fruit bread or tea-bread with honey butter (see p. 241), then with the oatmeal filling.

Celery Sandwiches

8 stalks crisp celery, finely chopped
double cream, to bind

salt and freshly ground pepper

Bind the celery with the cream, then season. Spread any fruit bread with walnut butter (see p. 241), then spread with a layer of the crisp celery filling.

Queen Alexandra's Sandwiches

This sandwich filling was a great favourite of Edward VII's consort.

10 thin slices lamb or ox tongue
8 oz boiled or poached chicken
   breast, minced
enough mayonnaise to bind to a
   spreadable paste

salt and freshly ground pepper
2–3 drops of Tabasco
1 punnet mustard and cress or picked
   watercress leaves

Mix the chicken and mayonnaise using a fork. Season well with salt, pepper and Tabasco. Spread brown bread with mustard butter (see p. 239). Lay slices of tongue on top, spread with the chicken mixture, then add the cress. Trim off the crusts and cut into dainty squares.

Queen Adelaide's Sandwiches

These were said to be a favourite of King George IV.

8 oz boiled or poached chicken
   breast, minced
8 oz lean roast ham (not smoked),
   minced

1 tbsp spring onion, finely chopped
salt and freshly ground pepper
double cream to bind

Combine the chicken, ham and onion in a bowl. Season with salt and pepper and bind with enough double cream to form a thick, spreadable paste. Lightly butter brown or white bread with tomato curry and orange butter (see p. 236) and spread with a layer of the chicken and ham filling.

Fresh Crab Sandwiches

10–12 oz fresh dressed crab or 8 oz frozen crab meat, light and dark, squeezed of excess water
6 spring onions, finely shredded, including an inch or so of the green

4 oz cottage cheese
2–3 tbsps soured or double cream
salt and freshly ground pepper

Bind together all the ingredients. Spread brown bread with lemon or chive butter (see pp. 236 and 238). Spread with a good cushion of the crab filling. Lay a de-veined lettuce leaf on top.

Smoked Salmon, Cheese and Chive Pâté Sandwiches

Makes approximately 1 lb

8 oz smoked salmon or smoked salmon bits
2 oz cream cheese
2 oz unsalted butter
2 heaped tbsps chives, finely chopped

3–4 drops of Tabasco
2 tbsps double cream
sorrel or young spinach leaves
freshly ground pepper

In a liquidiser, make a purée of the smoked salmon, cream cheese, butter, Tabasco and pepper. Scrape into a bowl and stir in the cream and chives.

Pack the mixture into small pots, cover with plastic film and refrigerate until ready for use.

Spread thin slices of rye bread or brown bread with horseradish butter (see p. 239) or with plain unsalted butter, then add a good layer of the pâté. Cover with sorrel or young washed spinach leaves.

This pâté can also be served as a starter at dinner.

Cream Cheese, Date and Pecan Nut Sandwiches

8 oz cream cheese
2 oz pecans or walnuts, roughly
  chopped

6–8 dates, stoned and roughly
  chopped
¼ tsp finely grated orange zest

Beat the cheese with the zest. Mix with the rest of the ingredients. Spread currant or brown bread with cinnamon butter (see p. 240), then cover with the filling.

Salmon and Cucumber Sandwiches

This sandwich combines three of our favourite summer flavours.

12 oz cold poached salmon, flaked
  and mashed
¼ cucumber, peeled, seeded and
  finely diced

stiff bland mayonnaise, to bind
salt and freshly ground pepper
lemon juice

Mix the ingredients to a spreadable paste, using a fork. Spread brown bread slices with mint butter (see p. 237), then add the filling.

Egg and Curry Sandwiches

1 tsp curry paste or curry sauce
double cream to bind

6 hardboiled eggs, sieved
salt and freshly ground pepper

Mix the curry paste or sauce with a little cream, then with the eggs. Season with salt and pepper. Spread brown or white bread with watercress butter (see p. 238), then top with the filling.

Crab and Artichoke Sandwiches

8 oz white crab meat (fresh or frozen)
1 8-oz tin of artichoke bottoms or
  hearts
1 oz fresh Parmesan cheese, finely
  grated

bland mayonnaise to bind
salt and freshly ground black pepper
a good squeeze of lemon juice
2–3 drops of Tabasco

Roughly chop the crab meat. Finely dice the artichoke bottoms, or shred and chop the hearts if these are used. Mix everything together and season to taste with salt, pepper, lemon juice and Tabasco. Spread brown bread with lemon butter (see p. 236), then with the filling.

Sardine and Chestnut Sandwiches

2 4-oz tins of sardines in tomato
6–8 chestnuts, cooked and shelled or
  use drained chestnuts in brine

2–3 **tsps** lemon juice
a little salt

Fillet and bone the sardines (if you like, though I never do, as the bones are soft). Chop the chestnuts. Mash everything to a rough-textured paste. Season sparingly. Spread brown bread with chive or watercress butter (see p. 238), then with the filling.

Mangetout and Shrimp Sandwiches

20 small to medium mangetouts
8 oz shrimps (fresh, frozen or tinned)
4 oz cream cheese
2–3 **tsps** lemon juice

1 **tbsp** chives and/or parsley, finely
  chopped
ground white pepper
a little salt

Squeeze excess moisture out of the shrimps if frozen ones are used. Chop the shrimps finely, mix with the cheese, lemon juice and herbs, and season to taste (be sparing with the salt).

In fast-boiling salted water, blanch the mangetouts for 15–20 seconds. Cool under running cold water. Drain well and pat dry with kitchen towels.

Using kitchen scissors, snip off the top and tail of each mangetout and cut the thinnest sliver off the side to remove the 'string'. Open the mangetout out flat, discarding any 'seeds' if you wish. Pat dry again.

Spread white or brown bread with tomato curry and orange or chive butter (see pp. 236 and 238), then lay a couple of mangetouts spread with a cushion of the shrimp filling on top.

Bacon and Avocado Sandwiches

2 ripe Hass avocados, peeled and
  stoned
4 rashers of lean back bacon, rinded
  and finely diced
1 **scant tbsp** olive oil (or use the
  bacon fat)

2–3 **tsps** lemon juice
salt and freshly ground black pepper
  or ground mace

Fry the bacon until crisp. Drain and cool. Mash the avocado with the lemon juice and oil, season well (but be sparing with the salt) and mix in the bacon. Spread brown bread with mustard butter (see p. 239), then add a good cushion of the filling.

Smoked Salmon, Cream Cheese and Pistachio Sandwiches

½ **lb** smoked Scotch salmon, sliced
6 oz cream cheese
2 oz pistachio or cashew nuts, coarsely crushed

salt and freshly ground pepper, to taste
2–3 drops of Tabasco

Beat the cheese with the seasoning until soft. Mix in the crushed pistachio nuts. Spread brown bread with horseradish butter or chive butter (see pp. 238 and 239), then lay slices of smoked salmon on top, followed by a cushion of the cheese mixture.

Cream Cheese, Olive and Walnut Sandwiches

6 oz cream cheese
2 oz walnuts, crushed
2 oz pimento-stuffed olives, finely chopped

salt and freshly ground pepper

Beat the cheese until soft. Mix in the other ingredients. Spread white or brown bread with walnut butter (see p. 241). Spread the filling over.

Smoked Haddock Sandwiches

8 oz smoked haddock, cooked, skinned and boned (10–12 oz uncooked weight)

enough mayonnaise to bind

Make a purée of the fish and mayonnaise in a liquidiser. Spread brown bread with watercress butter (see p. 238). Spread a good cushion of the filling on top.

Stir-fried Salmon and Ginger Sandwiches

1 12-oz piece of salmon, fresh or frozen
1 small clove of garlic, crushed
a 1-inch piece of green ginger,
  peeled and finely chopped

2 tbsps soya oil
¼ **tsp** ground ginger
salt

Skin, bone and cut the salmon into ½-inch cubes.

In a large frying pan heat the oil until smoking well. Add the green ginger and garlic and fry for 10 seconds, stirring with a straight-edged wooden spatula to prevent burning.

Add the salmon all at once. Spread it around and stir-fry it for 3–4 minutes, sprinkling with the ground ginger and salt. Remove the pan from the heat and let the fish cool completely. Reserve the pan juices.

In a liquidiser, make a purée of the fish, incorporating the pan juices. Give a little texture to the purée by using the stop/start method.

Spread brown bread with lemon butter (see p. 236). Spread a good cushion of the fish purée on it, and a few slivers of cucumber if liked.

Smoked Chicken and Belgian Endive Sandwiches

12 oz smoked chicken fillet, skinned
2–3 tbsps double cream, to bind
salt and a little freshly ground pepper

1–2 heads Belgian endive, split into
leaves

In an old-fashioned mincer, mince the chicken and bind it to a spreadable paste with 2–3 tablespoons of double cream. Season to taste (be sparing with the salt). Spread white bread with tomato butter (see p. 236) or plain butter. Spread a cushion of the smoked chicken paste on top, then add two or three crisp endive leaves.

Pâté, Pickled Walnut and Peanut Sandwiches

8 oz fine textured pâté
2 oz salted peanuts, roughly crushed

2 pickled walnuts, drained and finely diced

Beat the pâté until soft. Mix in the peanuts, then the astringent pickled walnuts. Spread white or brown bread with walnut butter (see p. 241), then cover with the filling.

Beetroot and Sour Cream Sandwiches

8 oz beetroot, cooked and peeled
1 tsp caster sugar
salt and freshly ground pepper

½ **tsp** orange zest, finely grated
2 tsps lemon juice
2–3 tbsps sour cream, to bind

Make a purée of the first five ingredients, adding enough sour cream to give a spreading consistency. Try this on the currant or rye bread (see pp. 111 and 61) with cinnamon butter (see p. 240)! Or just use brown bread spread with lemon or horseradish butter (see pp. 236 and 239).

Note: This filling will inevitably stain the bread.

Rolled or Pin-wheel Sandwiches

Asparagus Rolls with Hollandaise Sauce

Makes 20–24 pin-wheels

12 asparagus tips, lightly cooked   ½ **pint** *hollandaise* sauce

Spread slices of crusted brown bread with the *hollandaise* sauce. Place one fat or two or three slim asparagus tips on the front edge of each slice and roll up the slices tightly.

Cut the roll into two pieces with a diagonal stroke of the knife to give an interesting pointed shape.

Smoked Salmon Pin-wheels

Makes approximately 40 pin-wheels

¾ **lb** smoked Scotch salmon, thinly
   sliced

lemon juice
freshly ground black pepper

Using an uncut brown or white loaf, slice the bread along its length. Cut off the crusts at this stage. Spread the slices evenly with chive or basil butter (see p. 238).

Cover the slices with slivers of smoked salmon, leaving a ½-inch border uncovered on the back edge. Season with lemon juice and pepper.

Roll up the slices tightly from the front edge. Wrap the rolls in greaseproof paper and refrigerate until ready for use.

To serve, unwrap the rolls and cut into ¼-inch thick pin-wheels or discs.

Cut each roll into discs.

Roll the moistened edges in crushed nuts or parsley.

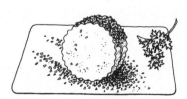

Rolled Muscatel Raisin and Rum Pin-wheels

8 oz seedless Muscatel raisins   **4 oz** cream cheese, beaten
2 tbsps dark rum

Soak the raisins in the rum for 2 hours. In a liquidiser make a coarse purée of the cheese, raisins and their liquid.

Cut any of the fruit breads or brown bread lengthways. Take off the crusts at this stage. Spread with Cumberland rum butter (see p. 240) then with the filling. Roll as for Smoked Salmon Pin-wheels.

The 'New' English Sandwich

So far I have dealt with the more delicate type of sandwiches served for afternoon tea. But what if you find yourself saddled with a dozen strapping fifth-formers who are celebrating winning some match or other, a fellow pupil's elevation to the rank of school prefect, or just a birthday? In such a case, the sandwich has to take on a different form in order to satisfy lusty teenage appetites.

Here are some *new* English sandwiches for you to try out on them when next the door bursts open, mid-afternoon, a teenage rabble arrives and afternoon tea is required.

Each recipe or amount is for one full round.

Breakfast Buttie

Toast 1 white teacake on the inside only, then spread it with 1 oz bacon dripping or tomato butter (see p. 236).

Fill it with 4 rashers of streaky bacon, crisply fried, and 1 egg made into a thin 'wet' omelette and then folded to fit the teacake surface.

Make-a-Date

Take 2 slices of ¼-inch-thick date and walnut bread (see p. 241) and spread them with 1 oz cinnamon butter (see p. 240). Fill with a quarter of a sliced banana and a quarter of a green apple, grated and tossed in lemon juice.

Creamy Chicken Lickin'

Toast 2 slices of white bread on the outside only, then spread them with ½ oz mustard butter (see p. 239). Fill with 1 oz chopped chicken, bound with a little thick mayonnaise or cream and seasoned well. Add ½ oz tiny white mushrooms, thinly sliced and fried in a knob of butter until crisp.

Banger Special

Take 2 slices of wholemeal bread and spread them with 1 oz mustard butter (see p. 239). Fill with 2 cooked pork sausages, sliced lengthways, and a cushion of apple sauce.

Salami Special

Take 2 slices of rye bread (see p. 61), and spread them with 1 oz mustard butter (see p. 239). Fill with 8 slices of salami, and a quarter of a green pepper, shredded and tossed in a teaspoon of oil and vinegar dressing, then add 4 thin raw onion rings.

Fillet o' Fish

Take 2 slices of brown bread and spread them with $\frac{1}{2}$ oz lemon butter (see p. 236). Fill with 3 sardines, filleted and boned (not mashed). Add a cushion of watercress leaves and a squeeze of lemon.

Christmas Special

Take 2 slices of herb bread (see p. 64) and spread them with 1 oz mustard butter (see p. 239) and 1 oz cranberry jelly. Fill with 2 oz thinly sliced turkey breast and top with stuffing.

Kipper Tie-break

Take 2 slices of brown bread, toast them on the outside and spread them with $\frac{1}{2}$ oz of lemon and parsley butter (see p. 236). Fill with a $\frac{1}{2}$-inch layer of kipper pâté.

Orange Nut

Take 2 slices of brown bread and spread them with $\frac{1}{2}$ oz orange butter (see p. 240). Fill with 1 oz cream cheese, mixed with $\frac{1}{2}$ oz crushed walnuts and 2 chopped orange or mandarin segments.

Cheese 'n' Apple

Take 2 crispbreads and spread them with 1 oz tomato curry and orange butter (see p. 236). Fill with 4 thin slices of Dutch cheese. Top with half a grated apple mixed with a little mayonnaise.

Crowd o' Shrimps

Take 2 slices of brown bread and spread them with 1 oz watercress butter (see p. 238). Fill with 2 oz chopped shrimps mixed with a little thick mayonnaise. Top with a cushion of picked watercress leaves.

Hawaiian Bite

Take 2 slices of banana bread (see p. 113) and spread with 1 oz honey butter (see p. 241). Fill with 1 oz cream cheese mixed with 1 oz chopped pineapple and a pinch of cinnamon.

Salmon Season

Take 2 slices of herb bread (see p. 64) and spread with $\frac{1}{2}$ oz lemon butter (see p. 236). Fill with 2 oz cooked salmon, loosely mashed with 1 heaped teaspoon of lemon mayonnaise. Top with thin wafers of cucumber soaked in a modicum of oil and lemon juice, seasoned with salt and pepper.

Ham 'n' Nut

Take 2 slices of rye bread (see p. 61) and spread them with 1 oz bacon drippings or unsalted butter. Fill with 1 oz diced ham, cooked until crisp, then cooled. Add 1 oz roughly crushed toasted hazelnuts bound with 1 teaspoon of very thick cream or mayonnaise.

Egg 'n' Cress

Take 1 bap and split it. Spread it with $\frac{1}{4}$ oz mustard butter (see p. 239). Fill with 1 nearly hardboiled egg mashed with 1 teaspoon of thick cream. Top with a cushion of well-chopped box cress.

Corny Cake

Take 1 brown teacake and split it. Spread it with 1 oz mustard butter (see p. 239). Fill with 2 oz corned beef, 6 thin onion rings, and 1 dessertspoonful of apple chutney.

Choc Full o' Nuts

Take 2 slices harvo bread (see p. 116) and spread them with 1 oz honey butter (see p. 241). Fill with 2 oz grated chocolate, and 1 oz crushed toasted hazelnuts bound with 1 teaspoon of thick cream.

Nursery Tea Sandwiches

Nursery sandwiches, to be tempting, should be crusted and cut into mini bite-size shapes.

Egg Sandwiches

4 hardboiled eggs, sieved   double cream, to bind
salt and freshly ground pepper

Season the egg and mix together with the cream. Spread the bread with chive butter (see p. 238) if serving adults, and add the egg mixture.

Banana and Jam Sandwiches

2 bananas, mashed   a little brown sugar
a little jam, sieved

Spread buttered bread with the sieved jam, sprinkle with sugar, then spread on the mashed banana.

Honey Sandwiches

Use one or other of the fruit breads (see pp. 111 and 113) spread with unsalted butter or cream cheese and thick honey (not the clear type).

Cream Cheese Sandwiches

Spread any of the fruit breads with cream cheese.

Brown Sugar and Chocolate Sandwiches

Spread brown bread with a little cream cheese or creamy butter. Sprinkle with brown sugar and grated chocolate. Top with a second slice of bread and press together well with a weight. Cut into pointed 'soldiers'.

95

The Magic Picnic Tree

The very thought of giving a party for children between the ages of four and eight fills the average mum or dad with horror, not only at the thought of all the food preparation but also at the thought of how to entertain such a mini-mob. If only mothers would realise that even if children of this age-group are quite savage, they do have simple needs where food is concerned and a good gimmick will solve the problem.

Leave yourself free to devote your energies to quelling the more dangerous events of the afternoon. This means that all food must be at the ready before kick-off, and the party picnic tree is the ideal answer. It will start them *wondering* what's in store when they arrive, and when the time comes for them to have their food it should create at least half an hour's diversion as they search for named parcels and discover the contents. You will need a soft drinks 'bar' for the thirsty children.

If your party is to be a large one and you need a big tree, then chipboard panels will be the best medium to use. Don't use hardboard as there is too much 'whip' in it and you may find it very difficult to cope with.' Chipboard comes in panels measuring 8×4 feet; so, for an 8-foot tree, you will need two panels. A fret-saw, or better still a jig-saw, will quickly see to the shaping of the branches, which you will first have sketched out on the board. For a smaller tree, stiff cardboard will suffice; buy thick *mounting* card, which can be obtained in different colours at any good art shop, and use a scoring knife for the cutting and shaping.

Drill holes an inch from the tip of each branch. Thread and loop cord, ribbon or tinsel through. Paint the whole tree in polyurethane varnish, which has a clear finish; this will bring out the grain in the wood. A little clear adhesive and some sequins or coloured glitter at the tips of the branches will add to the party effect, as will tiny Christmas baubles and lights if the party is around Christmas time. Bows of silsheen ribbon, paper flowers or plastic shapes are another way of decorating the tree.

Now hang the surprise food on the tree, each item in its own name-tagged container. Use colourful paper to make such things as 'sausage' crackers (the sausage itself wrapped in plastic film and slipped into a paper tube saved from 'you know where'!), crêpe-paper reticules or dolly bags holding crisps and biscuits, or sandwich or biscuit parcels tied with bright ribbons. Paint funny faces on hardboiled eggs if the party is around Eastertime, and hang toffee apples from drawstrings. For the more adventurous and adept, mini-carrier bags can be made to hold popcorn or Twiglets. Those are just a few ideas to start you off: use your imagination and add anything that is bright and fun to eat.

A Magic Picnic Tree is a charming novelty and easy to make.

Scones
and
Tea-breads

Scones

The word 'scone', thought by many to be Scottish Celtic, is derived from the Dutch word *schoonbroot* or 'beautiful bread'. A scone is at its best when eaten almost straight from the oven, or certainly within an hour or so of baking. However, they do freeze well; after thawing they should be served gently warmed through in a low oven or in a microwave. Leftover scones are excellent when split and toasted.

Traditionally scones are served in the afternoon at tea. Freshly baked, split and buttered, then topped with home-made preserves and, to gild the lily, with whipped double cream or rich clotted cream, as in Devon and Cornwall.

Here are some guidelines for making successful scones:

* Pre-heat the oven and the baking tray.
* Measure the flour before sieving, then sieve it twice with any other dry ingredients that may be called for in the recipe.
* The dough should be handled very gently and deftly, especially when kneading.
* Rub the fats into the flour thoroughly until the mixture looks like soft breadcrumbs or damp sand.
* Bake the scones as soon as you can after mixing the dry and liquid ingredients. To prepare ahead, rub in the fat and add other dry ingredients such as nuts or fruit, but leave adding the liquids until just before rolling, shaping and baking.
* Avoid twisting the scone-cutter when stamping out the shapes. This can cause them to bake lopsided.

Basic Rich Scone Recipe

Makes approximately 10 scones

8 oz plain flour	**2 oz** unsalted butter
3 tsps baking powder	**1 oz** lard
½ **tsp** salt	**1 egg**, beaten with ¼ pint milk
2 oz caster sugar	

Place a well-buttered baking tray in the oven and pre-heat to Gas 8/ 450°F/230°C.

Sieve the flour twice with the baking powder, salt and sugar (and other fine ingredients, such as powdered mustard, depending on the recipe).

Dice the fat into the dry ingredients, then lightly rub it in with cool fingertips, or use a wire pastry blender, until completely blended in.

Make a well in the centre and stir in the beaten egg and milk. Lightly gather the mixture together with a fork until the ingredients form a soft dough.

Turn this dough on to a lightly floured board or work surface and knead *very lightly* to a soft mass.

Roll out the dough with a rolling pin, or pat it with your hand, until it is approximately ¾ inch thick. Scones do not rise as much as you might expect.

With a 2-inch cutter, stamp out the scones, or cut the dough into triangles with a sharp knife. Lightly knead together any trimmings, re-roll and stamp out.

With a palette-knife, lift the scones on to the *hot* baking tray, placing them 1 inch apart. Brush only the tops with lightly beaten egg or milk; avoid getting egg on the sides as this will impede rising.

Bake towards the top of the oven for approximately 10 minutes until the scones are risen and golden brown.

Lift them with the palette-knife on to a cooling rack.

Variations

Savoury
Omit the sugar. Serve savoury scones with cream cheese, potted cheeses, fish or meats.

Cheese
To the above recipe add 8 oz very finely grated *mature* cheddar cheese and a good pinch of dry English mustard. Omit sugar.

Sage and Walnut
To the basic recipe add 8 oz finely chopped walnuts, plus 3 tablespoons of chopped fresh sage or 1 tablespoon of dried rubbed sage. Omit sugar.

Wholemeal
Use 6 oz wholemeal flour and 2 oz self-raising flour. After sieving, tip any bran remaining in the sieve back into the flour you are using. Omit sugar.

Fruit Scones
Sift ¼ teaspoon of mixed spice with the flour, and before adding the liquids stir in 3 oz sultanas or sultanas and currants mixed.

Treacle Scones
In a measuring jug dissolve 2 tablespoons of black treacle in 2 tablespoons of hot water. Make up to ½ pint with milk. Use also as the liquid for Wholemeal Scones.

Batch Scone

Made in minutes, this very short, light round scone needs no rolling or cutting out. Serve it straight from the oven, cut into wedges, split and buttered.

Makes 10–12 wedges

8 oz self-raising flour
3 tsps baking powder
3 oz unsalted butter
1 oz lard
3 oz caster sugar
4 oz sultanas or sultanas and
   currants mixed

1 oz mixed cut candied peel
1 egg, beaten
¼ pint milk
extra sugar for top

Pre-heat the oven to Gas 6/400°F/200°C and place a large, well-buttered baking tray in it.

Sieve the flour and baking powder twice, then rub in the butter and lard with your fingertips, or use a wire pastry blender, until the mixture looks like breadcrumbs. Stir in the sugar, sultanas and candied peel. Beat together the egg and milk, and gently mix into the dry ingredients until a soft dough is formed.

Tip the dough on to a floured board or work surface and knead it lightly to shape it into a ball. Place it on the hot baking tray, flatten it slightly until it is 1–1½ inches thick, and sprinkle with additional sugar. Mark into 'V' wedges without cutting through.

Bake for approximately 25 minutes or until golden brown.

Cool slightly, then cut into ten or twelve wedges, split them across and serve them warm with butter.

Old English Buttermilk Scones

Makes 30–40 small scones

1 lb sieved white unbleached flour
2 oz caster sugar
1 tsp salt
4 oz lard

4 oz unsalted butter
½ pint buttermilk or yoghurt
double cream, to glaze

Put a well-buttered baking tray inside the oven and pre-heat to Gas 6/400°F/200°C.

Rub the two fats into the flour until a moist sand-like texture is reached. Mix in the sugar and salt.

Make a well in the centre and pour in the buttermilk or yoghurt. Gather the mixture together with a fork. Turn it on to a lightly floured work surface and knead it *lightly*. Form the dough into a rectangle.

Roll the dough into an oblong ¾ inch thick. Cut through into 1½-inch squares, but do not separate them entirely; just ease them a little apart. Glaze with a little double cream and place on the baking tray.

Bake for 12–15 minutes. Do not over-cook.

Split the scones and serve them with clotted cream or butter and jam or fruit cheese.

Wholemeal Fruit Scones

Makes 16–18 scones

8 **oz** wholemeal flour
3 **tsps** baking powder
½ **tsp** ground mace
½ **tsp** cinnamon
4 **oz** unsalted butter, cubed

1 **oz** Muscovado sugar
4 **oz** sultanas or chopped seedless
    Muscatel raisins
1 large egg, beaten with ¼ pint milk

Place a lightly buttered baking sheet in the oven and pre-heat to Gas 7/ 425°F/220°C.

Sieve the flour, baking powder and spices together into a bowl. Rub in the butter with your fingertips until you have a sand-like texture. Mix in the sugar and fruit. Mix to a soft dough with the egg and milk, using a large fork.

Roll or press out the dough on a lightly floured work surface to approximately ¾–1 inch thick. Cut it into 2-inch rounds. Place these cheek by jowl on the baking tray.

Bake for 12–15 minutes.

Serve the scones warm, split and buttered.

Girdle Scones

These are popular for tea in Scotland and Wales, where the girdle or griddle – a round, flat iron sheet with a hooped handle – is used. At one time this would have been suspended from a ratchet over the hot, dying embers of an open fire. Today a heavy-bottomed frying pan is often used to make these delicious pancakes.

Makes 6–8 scones

10 oz self-raising flour
½ tsp bicarbonate of soda
1 tsp cream of tartar
a pinch of salt

2 tsps caster sugar
8 fl. oz buttermilk, milk or natural
  yoghurt

Sieve all the dry ingredients into a bowl. Add enough of the liquid to mix to an elastic dough.

Turn the dough on to a floured work surface and knead lightly until smooth. Form the dough into a square, rolling it out to ½ inch thick. Cut it into six or eight squares.

Put the squares on to a heated griddle or into a heavy-bottomed frying pan, brushed with a little butter or lard, and cook over an even, low to medium heat until the scones are risen and starting to brown. Turn them over and continue cooking on the other side. Cooking takes about 8–10 minutes in all.

Cool the scones on a wire rack. Serve them warm, split and buttered, with jam or honey.

Drop Scones or Scotch Pancakes I

These quick and easy tea-time treats are also traditionally cooked on a girdle or griddle, but will be just as successful made in a heavy-based frying pan.

Makes approximately 18 scones

6 oz self-raising flour
a pinch of salt
2 oz unsalted butter

2 tsps caster sugar
1 egg, beaten
4 fl. oz milk, to mix

Pre-heat a griddle or a heavy-based frying pan.

Sieve the flour and salt into a large bowl. Rub in the butter with your fingertips, or use a pastry blender, and stir in the sugar.

Make a well in the centre of the dry ingredients, add the egg and enough milk to make a thick, smooth batter.

Using about ½ tablespoon for each scone, 'drop' the batter – hence the name – on to the very hot griddle, spacing the scones well apart. As a check for consistency, when you drop a spoonful on the griddle it should spread to a circle approximately 3 inches in diameter, then stop. Cook for 2–3 minutes until the scones are slightly puffy and the surface bubbles. Turn the scones over and cook for a further 2–3 minutes until both sides are golden brown.

Place the scones between two teatowels on a wire cooling rack while you cook the remaining batter.

Serve the scones freshly cooked and hot, buttered, and with preserves if wished.

Variation. Add a few sultanas, chopped dates or raisins to the uncooked batter.

Drop Scones II

Makes 18–20 scones

10 oz plain flour
¼ tsp bicarbonate of soda
1 tsp cream of tartar
4 tbsps caster sugar
1 tbsp golden syrup

1 tsp grated lemon zest
4 oz sultanas, soaked in 1 tbsp
   whisky (optional)
1 large egg, beaten
milk, to mix

Sieve all the dry ingredients together into a bowl.

Make a well in the centre and put in the egg, syrup and enough milk to make a thick, heavy dropping batter. Mix in the sultanas if used.

Heat a griddle or heavy-based frying pan; brush it with a little butter or lard. Using ½ tablespoon for each scone, 'drop' the mixture from the point of a spoon to form several scones and cook until set and brown on one side, with bubbles coming to the surface of the batter.

Turn the scones over and cook until the edges are no longer sticky. The scones should be about ⅓ inch thick, so test one before thinning down the batter too far. Keep the scones warm between two teatowels on a wire cooling rack.

Serve, buttered.

Mini Orange 'Muffins' with Sultanas

Makes 20–24 muffins

2 heaped tbsps self-raising flour,
   sieved
½ tsp salt
1 good tbsp caster sugar
2 oz sultanas

2 large eggs plus 1 egg yolk, beaten
   together
grated zest of half an orange
juice of half an orange
milk, to mix

In a bowl mix the flour, salt and sugar together.

Make a well in the centre and pour in the egg mixture, grated orange zest and orange juice. Using a fork, gather and mix to a smooth batter, adding enough milk to give a soft dropping consistency. Mix in the sultanas.

Heat a griddle or heavy-bottomed frying pan, brush it with a little soya oil or melted butter, and drop a teaspoonful of the batter on to it.

As soon as bubbles rise and the batter is just set, flip the muffins over and cook for just a few seconds on the other side.

Keep the muffins warm in a clean teatowel on a wire rack.

Serve buttered.

Bracks and Briths, Muffins, Crumpets and Pikelets – the Confusion!

It is in the field of baking that most old names are still in use today.

In Northern Ireland, and in the Irish Republic, *brack* is the Celtic word for salt and is used to mean bread. 'Barm brack' is leavened bread, the word *barm* meaning yeast. 'Barm cakes' are still baked, sold and eaten in the northern counties of England, and are a flat bread cake, usually served split and filled with meat, cheese or fish as a workman's midday meal. It is the richer types of these breads that have found their way on to the afternoon-tea table.

In Wales, spiced fruit breads were baked on a girdle or griddle, and were known as 'pitchy bread' – *pice'r pregethwr* which name has survived and is with us as the 'pikelet' in the Midlands, the north of England and Wales. Today pikelets are made from a batter of milk, flour and egg, and are baked in metal rings on a griddle, then cooled. They are served toasted and spread with butter. In the south of England a close relation of the pikelet is the 'crumpet', the name coming from the Middle English word *crompid*, meaning to bend or curl up – which is what home-made crumpets do at the edges.

A 'muffin' (hardly ever seen in England today, although English muffins abound in the United States) is a more bread-like affair than its aforementioned first cousins. The derivation of its name is more readily recognisable, as it stems from the Old French dialect word *moufflet*, meaning soft bread. A 'muffineer', by the way, is not the dome-lidded dish with its hot-water liner used to keep toast or crumpets warm; it is a small silver dredger with a pierced domed lid used in olden days for sprinkling buttered muffins with salt or spices, which have given way to jam and honey today.

Pikelets

The name is the anglicised version of the Welsh *pice'r pregethwr*. A griddle or heavy-based frying pan is the traditional place for cooking these pancakes.

Makes 12–16 pikelets

10 oz self-raising flour
4 oz caster sugar
1 egg, beaten
milk

3 oz unsalted butter
$\frac{1}{4}$ teaspoon bicarbonate of soda
1 tsp vinegar

Sieve the flour with the sugar. Add the egg and enough milk to make a thick batter. Melt the butter and add the bicarbonate of soda and vinegar, mixing well into the batter.

Using 2 teaspoonsful for each pikelet, drop the batter on to a hot greased griddle or heavy-based frying pan or use pikelet rings. Cook until bubbles appear on the surface and the bottoms of the pikelets are brown, then turn them over and cook the other side.

Serve hot and well buttered. If made in advance, pikelets are always toasted and served crisp and hot, their holes oozing with butter!

Crumpets

Eaten more often with a savoury topping or just with butter rather than with jam or honey, crumpets may be served fresh and hot or, if made the day before, toasted with a slice of cheese on top.

Makes approximately 16 crumpets

12 oz strong white flour	⅓ **pint** milk
1 tbsp dried or ½ oz fresh yeast	½ **tsp** bicarbonate of soda
½ **tsp** caster sugar	**1 tsp** salt
½ **pint** warm water	

Sieve half the flour into a large bowl. Add the yeast, sugar and water, and mix until smooth. Leave in a warm place for about 20 minutes until frothy.

Add two-thirds of the milk to the remaining ingredients. Beat the two batters together well, adding more milk if needed, to make a thick pouring batter.

Lightly grease a griddle or heavy-based frying pan and 6–8 metal crumpet rings approximately 3 inches in diameter. Arrange the rings on the griddle and heat thoroughly. Pour about 2 tablespoons of the batter into each ring and cook for 10 minutes or until the crumpets are set and the characteristic holes appear. Remove the rings and turn the crumpets over. Cook for a further 5–6 minutes.

Repeat the process with the remaining batter.

Cool the crumpets on a wire rack and eat them fresh, toasted and buttered, with any of the potted foods on pp. 217–22 as a topping.

Muffins

Traditional English muffins, with their distinctive 'holey' texture, are best eaten fresh, split and buttered. If they are a day or so old, split them with a fork to give a rough texture, then toast and butter them.

Makes 12–16 muffins

1 tbsp dried or ½ oz fresh yeast
1 tsp caster sugar
½ pint warm water

1 lb strong white flour
1 tsp salt
flour or fine semolina

Dust a baking tray with flour or semolina.

Mix the yeast, sugar and water in a small bowl and leave it in a warm place for 10 minutes or until frothy. Sieve the flour and salt into a large bowl. Add the yeast liquid and mix with a fork to form a soft dough. Turn out on to a lightly floured work surface and knead for about 10 minutes until the dough is smooth.

Place the dough in a large, lightly oiled plastic bag and leave to rise in a warm place for 1–1½ hours until it has doubled in volume. Punch back and knead again for about 5 minutes until the dough is smooth and firm.

Roll out the dough ½ inch thick, cover it with a teatowel and leave it to relax for a further 10 minutes. Cut it into 10–12 rounds with a 3-inch plain cutter.

Place the muffins on the prepared baking tray and dust them with the same flour or semolina used for the tray. Put the tray inside the oiled plastic bag and leave in a warm place for 30–40 minutes until the muffins have risen and doubled in volume.

Pre-heat the oven to Gas 8/450°F/230°C.

Bake for about 10 minutes, turning over carefully after 5 minutes. Cool on a wire rack.

Bara Brith

Makes three 1lb loaves

1 tbsp dried or ½ oz fresh yeast
16 fl. oz warm milk
1 tsp caster sugar
3 lb strong white flour
1 tsp salt
1 lb 2 oz unsalted butter

12 oz soft brown sugar
8 oz currants
4 oz chopped candied peel
2 tsp mixed spice
3 eggs, beaten

Mix the yeast with the warm milk. Rub the butter into the flour, then add all the remaining ingredients except the eggs and the yeast mixture.

Make a well in the centre and add the eggs and the yeast mixture.

Mix to a soft dough, then cover and leave in a warm place for 1½ hours until it has risen to twice its original volume. Turn the dough on to a floured board, divide it between three greased 1lb loaf tins and stand them in a warm place for approximately 20 minutes to let the dough rise.

Pre-heat the oven to Gas 6/400°F/200°C.

Bake for 1½–2 hours. When cold, cut the bread into thin slices and serve spread with plenty of butter.

Irish Tea Brack

This is an easy-to-make version of the Barm Brack, using no yeast.

Makes one 2lb loaf

12 **oz** mixed dried fruit   4 **tsps** marmalade
8 **fl. oz** boiling black tea   8 **oz** caster sugar
1 egg, beaten   14 **oz** self-raising flour
1 **tsp** mixed spice

Place the mixed fruit in a bowl, cover it with hot tea and leave it to soak overnight. Next day, add the remaining ingredients to the tea and fruit and mix well.

Pre-heat the oven to Gas 5/375°F/190°C.

Bake in a greased 7-inch square tin on the middle shelf for 1½ hours. Allow the loaf to cool in the tin.

Slice and serve buttered. Store in an air-tight tin.

Tea-breads

Tea-breads are halfway between bread and cake, with those made without yeast more towards the cake end. They are best kept for a day or two after making, well wrapped in plastic film, to allow the flavour to mellow. Serve them sliced and buttered.

Treacle Bread

Serves 4

1 lb plain flour	**1 oz** caster sugar
1 tsp salt	**2 tbsps** treacle
1 tsp bicarbonate of soda	**8 fl. oz** buttermilk
1 tsp ground ginger	

Pre-heat the oven to Gas 8/450°F/230°C.

Sieve the dry ingredients together. Mix the treacle with 4 tablespoons of buttermilk and add to the dry ingredients.

Add more buttermilk, sufficient to form a soft dough. Turn it on to a floured board and shape it into a round cake. Mark the cake into quarters.

Bake for 30–35 minutes.

Serve, split and buttered, with or without jam or honey.

Currant Bread

Delicious served thinly sliced and buttered, with the added luxury of home-made jam or with honey. If any stays around long enough to lose its freshness – which is doubtful – it is equally good toasted.

Makes two 1lb loaves

1 tbsp dried or ½ oz fresh yeast	**1 oz** lard
1 tsp caster sugar	**8 oz** currants
¾ **pint** warm milk	**1 oz** peel
1¼ lb strong white flour	**1 tbsp** each caster sugar and milk, to
2 tsps salt	glaze

Grease two 1lb loaf tins.

Mix the yeast and sugar with two-thirds of the milk and leave it in a warm place for about 10 minutes or until frothy.

Sieve the flour and salt into a large bowl and with your fingertips rub in the lard. Stir in the currants and peel. Stir in the yeast mixture and enough of the remaining milk to make a soft dough.

Turn out the dough on to a lightly floured surface and knead it for about 5 minutes or until it feels firm and elastic. Place it in an oiled plastic bag and leave it in a warm place for about 1–1½ hours or until the dough has doubled in volume.

Punch back and knead the dough again for 5 minutes, then divide it into two pieces. Shape each to fit a loaf tin and place inside. Slip the tins into the oiled plastic bag and leave for about 20–30 minutes or until the dough has risen to the top of the tins.

Pre-heat the oven to Gas 7/425°F/220°C.

Bake for about 50 minutes.

Stir together the milk and sugar for the glaze and brush it on the tops of the loaves.

Reduce the oven temperature to Gas 5/375°F/190°C and bake for a further 15 minutes. Turn out on to a wire rack to cool.

Sultana and Lemon Tea-Bread

Makes two 1lb loaves

1 tbsp dried or ½ oz fresh yeast	**6 oz** sultanas
1 tsp honey	finely grated zest of a lemon
¼ **pint** warm water	¼ **tsp** mixed spice
1 lb plain flour	**1** egg
1 tsp salt	**4 oz** icing sugar, sieved
2 tbsps caster sugar	**2 tbsps** lemon juice, strained

Grease two 1lb loaf tins.

In a small bowl, mix together the yeast, honey and half of the water, and leave in a warm place for 10 minutes until frothy.

Sieve the flour and salt into a large bowl and mix in the sugar, sultanas, lemon zest and spice.

Add the egg and the yeast liquid, then enough of the remaining water to make a soft dough.

Turn the dough on to a lightly floured surface and knead it for 5 minutes. Place it in an oiled plastic bag and leave in a warm place to rise for about 1 hour or until doubled in size.

Knead the dough again for 2–3 minutes, divide it into two and place it in the prepared tins. Place the tins in the oiled plastic bag and leave to rise again for 40–60 minutes.

Pre-heat the oven to Gas 6/400°F/200°C.

Bake for about 30–35 minutes.

Turn the bread out on to a wire cooling rack. When cold, mix the icing sugar with enough lemon juice to make a coating consistency. Spread over the top of the loaves.

Serve fresh, sliced and buttered, with or without honey or lemon cheese.

Banana Bread

Makes 1 large loaf

4 oz unsalted butter, softened	2 large ripe bananas, mashed
6 oz caster sugar	**1 tsp** vanilla essence
2 large eggs, beaten	**2½ fl. oz** single cream
8 oz plain flour	**2 oz** hazelnuts or walnuts, crushed
1 tsp bicarbonate of soda	and toasted
1 tsp salt	**½ tsp** ground nutmeg

Pre-heat the oven to Gas 4/350°F/180°C.

Cream the butter, sugar and eggs until light and fluffy. Mix in the mashed banana. Sieve together the flour, bicarbonate of soda, salt and nutmeg and fold them into the creamed mixture.

Mix in the cream and vanilla essence. Finally, stir in the nuts.

Pour the mixture into a buttered and lined baking tin (approx. 9×5 inches).

Bake for an hour, by which time the bread should spring back when lightly pressed with your forefinger.

Turn out on to a wire rack. Serve thinly sliced and lightly buttered.

Banana Nut Loaf

Makes one 2lb loaf

2 oz unsalted butter	**9 oz** plain or wholemeal flour
2 oz caster sugar	**3 level tsps** baking powder
6 fl. oz honey	**2 oz** chopped nuts (almonds, walnuts
2 large eggs, beaten	or hazelnuts)
3 ripe bananas	

Pre-heat the oven to Gas 5/375°F/190°C.

This recipe can be made by putting everything in a food processor or as follows.

Cream the butter and sugar. Beat in the honey. Add the eggs and beat well. Mash the bananas well and mix them in. Sieve together the flour and baking powder, and fold into the mixture. Finally, fold in the nuts and turn the mixture into a buttered 2lb loaf tin.

Bake for 45 minutes and then reduce the heat to Gas 4/350°F/180°C and bake for a further 30 minutes or until the loaf has risen and is firm to the touch.

If almonds or hazelnuts are used, toast these lightly for an unusual flavour.

Banana Pecan Bread

This is a deliciously moist tea-bread, even more delicious when three or four days old and served toasted and liberally spread with honey butter (see p. 241)!

Makes two 1lb loaves

3 **oz** unsalted butter
4 **oz** soft brown sugar
1 large egg, beaten
4 **oz** plain flour
4 **oz** wholewheat or wholemeal flour
   sieved together

1 **level tsp** ground mace
2 **tsps** baking powder
4 ripe bananas, well mashed
5 **oz** pecan nuts, roughly crushed

Pre-heat the oven to Gas 4/350°F/180°C.

Cream together the butter and sugar until light and fluffy. Dribble in the egg and beat well in.

Sieve the two flours, the ground mace and the baking powder together and mix in, adding any bran which has remained in the sieve.

Mix in the mashed bananas, which should be soft enough to give a dropping consistency; if they are not ripe enough, mix in a little sherry or milk. Fold in the crushed pecan nuts.

Spoon the mixture into two buttered and lined 1lb loaf tins. Bake for 45–55 minutes or until a skewer comes out clean when inserted into the centre of the bread and the bread is leaving the sides of the tin.

Leave to cool for half an hour before turning on to a wire cooling rack.

In recipes calling for pecans, walnuts can be substituted.

Date and Nut Loaf

This is based on a very old recipe, dating from *c*.1730.

Makes one 1½ lb loaf

6 oz dates, chopped
8 fl. oz boiling water
1 tsp bicarbonate of soda
2 oz unsalted butter, softened
1 oz lard

4 oz caster sugar
1 egg, beaten
4 oz mixed almonds and walnuts,
   chopped
8 oz plain flour

Pre-heat the oven to Gas 6/400°F/200°C.

Cover the dates with the boiling water and leave them to cool. Drain them and reserve the water. Add the bicarbonate of soda to the water. Cream the butter, lard and sugar together, and add the egg, nuts and dates.

Stir in the flour together with the liquid from the dates.

Mix well and put into a well-greased loaf tin. Bake for 1 hour.

Serve sliced and buttered.

Date and Walnut Loaf

Makes one 2lb loaf

9 oz dates, roughly chopped
6 fl. oz boiling water
1 tsp bicarbonate of soda
12 oz self-raising flour

3 oz unsalted butter
½ tsp salt
7 oz caster sugar
4 oz walnuts, chopped

Mix the bicarbonate of soda into the boiling water, pour over the dates and leave to soak for 2 hours.

Pre-heat the oven to Gas 2/300°F/150°C.

Sieve the flour and rub in the butter. Add the salt, sugar and walnuts. Mash the dates well into the water and soda mixture, and add with the beaten egg to the dry ingredients. Mix well.

Put the mixture into a buttered 2lb loaf tin and bake for 1½ hours. Cool on a wire rack.

Freda Mary Lord's Date and Walnut Loaf

This is my younger sister's favourite offering at tea-time. The ingredients in this recipe are measured in a 5 fl. oz teacup.

Makes one 2lb loaf

1½ **teacups** dates, coarsely chopped
¾ **teacup** water
1 **tsp** bicarbonate of soda
2½ **teacups** self-raising flour
3 **tsps** baking powder

½ **tsp** salt
⅓ **teacup** unsalted butter
1 **teacup** caster sugar
1 **teacup** walnuts, coarsely chopped
1 large egg, beaten

Over a medium heat, slowly bring the dates and water just to the boil. Remove from the heat and beat in the bicarbonate of soda. Leave to cool.

Pre-heat the oven to Gas 2/300°F/150°C.

Sieve the flour, baking powder and salt into a large bowl. Rub in the butter with your fingertips, or use a pastry blender. Stir in the sugar and nuts.

Add the date mixture and the egg to the dry ingredients, and mix thoroughly together. Spoon into a greased and floured 2lb loaf tin and smooth the top.

Bake for 1½ hours. Allow the loaf to cool in the tin before turning it out on to a wire rack. When completely cooled, wrap and keep for at least two days before eating.

Cut into thick slices, and butter.

Harvo Loaf

Simply mix together all the ingredients and bake – this is one of the simplest of tea-breads to make. Again, it is best kept for a day or two to allow the flavours to mellow before slicing. Serve buttered. It is also good made into sandwiches with a sweet filling such as cream cheese and chopped dates or bananas.

Makes one 2lb loaf

8 **fl. oz** milk
1 **tbsp** golden syrup
5 **oz** plain flour
5 **oz** wholemeal flour

1 **tbsp** baking powder
7 **oz** soft brown sugar
4 **oz** mixed dried fruit
golden syrup, to glaze

Pre-heat the oven to Gas 4/350°F/180°C.

Gently heat the milk and syrup just long enough to melt the syrup.

Sieve the two flours and the baking powder into a large bowl, tipping in any bran left in the sieve. Stir in the sugar and fruit. Beat in the milk and syrup mixture.

Spoon the mixture into a greased and floured 2lb loaf tin and bake for 45–60 minutes.

Allow to cool in the tin, then turn out on to a wire rack. Brush the top of the hot loaf with a little golden syrup for a shiny, sticky finish. Cool completely, then wrap and mature.

Nellie Smith's Harvo Bread

This is the recipe used by my mother all her life. It uses a 5 fl. oz teacup.

Makes two 1lb loaves

2 **teacups** wholemeal flour
2 **teacups** plain flour
1 **teacup** sultanas, chopped dates or
    raisins
½ **teacup** caster sugar

1 **teacup** golden syrup
½ **teacup** milk, approx.
1 **tsp** bicarbonate of soda
2 **oz** lard

Pre-heat the oven to Gas 4/350°F/180°C.

Melt the syrup and lard together and stir in the bicarbonate of soda. Add to the dry ingredients and mix well. Add enough milk to make a dropping consistency.

Bake in two well-buttered 1lb loaf tins for about an hour or until a knife inserted into the middle comes out clean.

Saffron Cake

It is said that saffron was introduced to Cornwall by the Phoenicians when they came to trade for tin. It is well worth paying the high price asked today for these delicate yellow strands for the bonus of colour and aroma they give to Cornwall's greatest cake.

Though called a cake, this to me is a rich fruity tea-bread.

117

Whole quantity: makes two 2lb cakes

$\frac{1}{2}$ **oz** dried yeast (usually 1 packet)
1 heaped tsp caster sugar
7 fl. oz warm water
$\frac{1}{4}$ **tsp** saffron strands, crumbled
3 tbsps boiling water
1 lb 9 oz strong white flour
2 tbsps milk powder

1 tsp salt
2 oz caster sugar
7 oz fat ($\frac{1}{2}$ unsalted butter, $\frac{1}{2}$ lard)
yellow colouring (optional)
10 oz currants
4 oz sultanas
2 oz mixed peel

Half quantity: makes one 2lb cake

2 tsps dried yeast
1 tsp caster sugar
7 fl. oz warm water
$\frac{1}{4}$ **tsp** saffron strands, crumbled
3 tbsps boiling water
12 oz strong white flour
1 tbsp milk powder
$\frac{1}{2}$ **tsp** salt

1 oz caster sugar
2 oz unsalted butter
2 oz lard
yellow colouring (optional)
5 oz currants
2 oz sultanas
1 oz mixed peel

Put the dried yeast into a small bowl with the teaspoon of sugar. Pour in the water, whisk with a fork and leave aside to froth for about 10–15 minutes.

Put the saffron into a separate bowl. Add 3 tablespoons of boiling water and leave to infuse.

Sieve 7 oz of the flour (4 oz if you are making the half quantity) into a bowl. Stir in the milk powder. Pour in the frothed yeast and mix to a batter; it will probably be rather lumpy but, worry not, this will right itself at a later stage. Cover the bowl with plastic film or a cloth and leave it in a warm, draught-free place for 30 minutes to froth.

While that is busy doing its stuff, put the balance of the flour into a large mixing bowl. Add the salt and sugar and rub in the fats until the mixture resembles fresh breadcrumbs. Pour in the frothed mixture, followed by the saffron and its soaking water. (Some people strain off the saffron and discard it, using only the soaking water. My philosophy is that the stuff is so damned expensive I am not prepared to throw any of it away!)

Now the hard part: you can either beat the mixture with a spoon or your hand or, best of all, with an electric beater fitted with an S-hook. It really is hard work, but the mixture needs to be beaten for 10 minutes by spoon or hand, or for 5 minutes with the beater. When ready, the dough is silky and very elastic and, though soft, it should leave your hands and utensils clean and should not stick tackily to anything. Cover it again with plastic film and leave it in a warm place to rise. The mixture should double in bulk, which usually takes about 1 hour.

Knock back the dough and bash it around for about another 5 minutes by hand, or for a couple of minutes with the beater. Yellow colouring can be added at this point if necessary. Work in the dried fruit and peel, and transfer the dough to two well-greased 2lb loaf tins. Slip the tins inside a plastic bag, trapping a little air inside so that the bag balloons up, and tie it with a tie-tag. Leave it in a warm, draught-free place for about 40 minutes or until the mixture has risen to the tops of the tins.

Pre-heat the oven to Gas 6/400°F/200°C.

Bake for 50 minutes. Turn off the heat, remove the saffron cakes from the tins, and return the cakes to the oven, lying them on one side. Close the door and leave for 5 minutes, then remove them and leave to cool on a wire rack.

Serve sliced thinly and liberally buttered. The bread is ideal for some sandwiches.

Sally Lunn Cakes

Legend has it that Sally Lunn touted her special Bath buns in the streets of that city. There is reference in 1727 to 'Lun's Cakes', and these were in fact probably made at a baker's shop at that time.

We do know that an enriched bread with caraway seeds and sprinkled with crushed sugar loaf *was* popular for breakfast in eighteenth-century Bath homes, and was called *sol-et-lune* – which was Norman French for sun and moon, and referred to the golden sun colour of the egg-glazed top of this cake or bread (the moon being the whiter, paler under part).

However, it is also said – and not without good reason – that Sally Lunn, when crying her wares in the streets, called out 'Soleilune'. Which story came first, we don't really know; the truth probably lies somewhere between the two.

What is perhaps even more interesting is that at one time it was traditional to eat Sally Lunn cakes with a fork – sliced horizontally and bathed with scalded cream! Today, we eat them fresh, sliced thinly and well buttered, or, when a day or two old cut somewhat thicker and toasted in front of a roaring fire.

Makes 2 cakes

2 oz unsalted butter	1 lb strong white flour
6 fl. oz milk	1 tsp salt
1 tbsp dried or ½ oz fresh yeast	6 tsps each caster sugar and water,
1 tsp caster sugar	mixed, to glaze
2 eggs, beaten	

Grease two 5-inch cake tins or 1-pint ovenproof soufflé dishes.

Over a low heat, slowly melt the butter in the milk with the sugar. Sprinkle over the yeast and leave in a warm place for 10 minutes until frothy. Beat in the eggs.

Sieve the flour and salt into a bowl, add the yeast liquid and mix well.

Turn the dough out on to a lightly floured surface and knead it for 10 minutes. Shape it into two balls and place them in the prepared tins or dishes. Place in oiled plastic bags and leave in a warm place for about 1 hour until the dough fills the tins.

Pre-heat the oven to Gas 8/450°F/230°C.

Bake for about 20 minutes or until golden brown. Turn the cakes on to a wire rack and glaze while still hot. Serve sliced horizontally and buttered.

A variation of the plain Sally Lunn is achieved by adding a mixture of dried fruits along with the flour. Add 12 oz of mixed sultanas, raisins, currants, finely chopped mixed peel and candied cherries.

Chelsea Buns

Made of enriched dough stuffed with dried fruit and peel and with a sticky glaze, these buns get their name from the Chelsea Bun House where they were a speciality in the eighteenth century when Chelsea was a village.

Makes approximately 8–10 buns

1 tbsp dried or ½ oz fresh yeast	**Filling**
¼ **tsp** caster sugar	
4 fl. oz warm milk	**1 oz** butter, melted
8 oz strong white flour	**3 oz** mixed dried fruit
½ **tsp** salt	**1 oz** candied peel
1 oz unsalted butter	**2 oz** soft brown sugar
1 egg, beaten	clear honey, to glaze

Grease a 7-inch square cake tin.

Mix the yeast and sugar with the milk in a small bowl and sprinkle 1 oz of the flour on it. Leave in a warm place for about 15 minutes or until frothy.

Sieve the remaining flour and the salt into a large bowl. Rub in the fat with the fingertips. Add the yeast mixture with the beaten egg and mix to a soft dough. Turn out on to a lightly floured work surface and knead for about 5 minutes until smooth.

Place the dough in an oiled plastic bag and leave to rise in a warm place for about 1–1½ hours or until double in size. Punch the dough back, knead it, and roll it out to a rectangle 14×10 inches. Brush with the melted butter and sprinkle the fruit, peel and sugar over it to within ½ inch of the edges.

Roll up the dough from the longest side and pinch the edges. Cut the roll into nine equal slices and place them, cut-side down, in the greased tin, three in a row.

Pre-heat the oven to Gas 5/375°F/190°C. Slip the tin into the oiled plastic bag and leave to rise in a warm place for about 30 minutes or until doubled in size.

Bake for about 25–30 minutes or until the buns are a rich golden brown. Turn them out on to a wire rack and, while still warm, brush them with melted honey for a shiny, sticky glaze.

Note: Don't expect Chelsea Buns to be as rich and delicate as Danish pastries, which they closely resemble in appearance. Chelsea Buns are more bread-like in texture and are more for the high-tea table, served with butter and jam.

Bath Buns

These sweet buns, with their crunchy sugar topping, were popular with the wealthy visitors to the spa town of Bath in the eighteenth century.

Makes 18 buns

2 tbsps dried or ½ oz fresh yeast
¼ **pint** warm milk
4 tbsps warm water
1 lb strong white flour
1 tsp salt
2 oz caster sugar
2 oz unsalted butter, melted

2 eggs, beaten
6 oz sultanas
2 oz chopped mixed peel
beaten egg, crushed sugar lumps or
    preserving sugar crystals for the
    topping

Mix the yeast, liquids and 4 oz of the flour in a small bowl and leave in a warm place for 20 minutes until frothy.

Sieve the remaining flour and salt into a large bowl. Add the sugar, butter, eggs, yeast liquid, sultanas and peel, and mix all together to a soft dough. Turn out on to a lightly floured surface and knead the dough for 10 minutes until smooth. Place it in a large oiled plastic bag and leave the dough in a warm place to rise for 1 hour. Knock back and knead the dough again for 5 minutes.

Divide the dough into eighteen pieces. Roll each one with the palm of your hand into a round bun shape and put on a greased baking tray. Put the tray into the oiled plastic bag and leave in a warm place for 30 minutes until the buns have doubled in size.

Pre-heat the oven to Gas 5/375°F/190°C.

Brush the buns with beaten egg and sprinkle them with some of the crushed sugar or sugar crystals.

Bake for 15–20 minutes until the buns are risen and golden brown. Cool on a wire rack.

Serve plain or split and buttered.

Devonshire Splits

Soft, sweet buns filled with cream and jam – traditionally Devonshire clotted cream and home-made strawberry jam, but whipped cream is almost as good.

Makes 12–14 buns

1 tbsp dried or ½ oz fresh yeast
½ **pint** warm milk
1 lb strong white flour
1 tsp salt
2 oz unsalted butter

2 tbsps caster sugar
raspberry or strawberry jam,
    whipped cream and icing sugar
    for the filling

Mix the yeast and 1 tablespoon of the sugar with half the milk in a small bowl and leave in a warm place for 10 minutes or until frothy.

Sieve the flour and salt into a large bowl. Melt the butter and the rest of the sugar in the remaining milk until lukewarm. Stir this and the yeast liquid into the flour and beat to an elastic dough.

Turn out the dough on to a lightly floured surface and knead for 10 minutes until smooth.

Slip the dough into a large oiled plastic bag and leave in a warm place for 1–1½ hours until doubled in size.

Knead the dough again for another 5 minutes. Divide it into twelve or fourteen pieces and shape these into round buns. Place them on a greased baking tray, flattening them slightly with the palm of your hand.

Put the tray into the oiled plastic bag and leave to rise in a warm place for about 20 minutes.

Pre-heat the oven to Gas 7/425°F/220°C.

Bake for 20 minutes. Cool on a wire rack. Dust with icing sugar.

To serve, make a diagonal slit in each bun, cutting almost through, and fill with jam and cream.

Brighton Rocks

Makes 16–18 buns

6 oz unsalted butter	**10 oz** plain flour
6 oz caster sugar	**2** eggs, beaten
6 oz ground almonds	**1 tsp** rose water
8 oz currants	beaten egg, to glaze

Pre-heat the oven to Gas 7/425°F/220°C.

Cream the butter and sugar. Work in the ground almonds and currants. Add the flour with the beaten eggs and rose water. Mix to a stiff dough. Fork into small mounds and place on greased baking trays.

Glaze the buns with a little beaten egg and bake for about 12–15 minutes. Cool on a wire rack.

Lardy Cake: see p. 190.

Cheshire Souling Cake: see p. 202.

CAKES

Victoria Sponge

This very traditional English cake was named after Queen Victoria, though history omits to tell us whether it was actually her favourite cake. It is a very light, melt-in-the-mouth sponge simply filled with jam and dredged with icing sugar. For a more elaborate filling, whisk lemon cheese into whipped double cream and spoon it between the layers.

The traditional recipe involved creaming the fat and sugar together until very fluffy, beating in the eggs one at a time, and then very carefully folding in the flour with a metal spoon. With the development of soft fats and quick-beating electric mixers and processors, the following far simpler, foolproof method has become very popular. The flavour and texture are just as good, if not better, than in the traditional method.

Serves 8–10

8 oz self-raising flour
2 tsps baking powder
8 oz caster sugar
4 eggs, beaten with 2 tbsps cold
 water

8 oz unsalted butter or soft
 margarine
raspberry jam
icing sugar

Pre-heat the oven to Gas 3/325°F/170°C.

Sieve the flour and baking powder together twice.

With an electric mixer or a food processor beat together the eggs, water, sugar and margarine until very light and creamy. Add the flour and baking powder, and continue to beat until the batter is a pale creamy colour and looks glossy. Divide between two 8-inch sandwich tins, the sides and bottom of each lightly buttered and the base lined with a circle of buttered paper.

Bake for 20 minutes or until the top springs back when pressed with your fingertip. (If space doesn't allow both tins to be put on the middle shelf together, place one lower and reverse positions halfway through the cooking time.)

Stand the cake tins on wire cooling racks for 5 minutes, then turn the cakes out, removing the base papers. Cool completely before filling.

Spread the top of one cake with raspberry jam. Sit the second cake on top and dredge with icing sugar.

The same quantity will make 30 individual sponge cakes – delicious topped with a spoonful of lemon glacé icing and half a candied cherry.

Plain Sponge Cake

This is a fatless sponge.

Serves 8

4 large eggs
half their total weight in caster sugar
  and half in self-raising flour

raspberry or strawberry jam
icing sugar

Pre-heat the oven to Gas 5/375°F/190°C.

Butter two non-stick 7-inch sandwich tins. Dust well with flour, shaking away any surplus.

Arrange a warmed bowl over a pan of faintly simmering water. Put in the eggs and sugar, and whisk the mixture until light and creamy. The whisk should leave a distinct trail when drawn through the mixture. Remove from the heat.

Sieve the flour into the egg mixture, incorporating it by cutting and folding it in with a flexible balloon whisk. Divide the mixture equally between the two tins.

Bake for 20 minutes. Turn out on to a wire cooling rack.

Spread the top of one cake with plenty of the good red jam. Sit the second cake on top. Dredge with icing sugar. Eat the same day.

Eighteenth-century Sponge Cake

As far as I can tell from my many years of research, Mrs Elizabeth Raffald gives the first recipe 'To make a Cake without Butter' in the first (1769) edition of her excellent book of eighteenth-century receipts, *The Experienced English Housekeeper*, and it is interesting to read her exact directions:

'Beat eight Eggs half an Hour, have ready pounded and sifted a Pound of Loaf sugar, shake it in, and beat it half an Hour more, put to it a quarter of a Pound of Sweat Almonds beat fine, with Orange Flower Water, grate the Rind of a Lemon into the Almonds and squeeze in the Juice of the Lemon, mix them all together, and keep beating them 'till the Oven is ready, and just before you set it in, put to it three quarters of a Pound of warm dry fine Flour; rub your Hoop with Butter, an hour and a half will bake it.'

Many people make this type of cake without butter, although I find that the odd ounce of unsalted butter makes it just that little bit more moist.

Serves 8

4 eggs	4 oz self-raising flour, sieved with
4 oz caster sugar	1 oz ground almonds
1 tsp finely grated lemon zest	1 oz unsalted butter, melted but cold

Pre-heat the oven to Gas 5/375°F/190°C.

Beat the eggs and sugar together with the lemon zest until quite stiff and thick. Fold and cut in the sieved flour and almonds, mixing lightly but thoroughly. Dribble in the butter, again mixing well.

Butter well and dredge with caster sugar a lightweight 8-inch diameter metal cake tin. Spoon in the mixture and bake for 20–25 minutes. Serve in slices, spread as you would a scone with jam, cream cheese, whipped or clotted cream.

2–4–6–8 Cake

So called in Britain as 2 eggs, 4 oz butter, 6 oz sugar and 8 oz flour are used.

Serves 8

4 oz unsalted butter, softened	2 tsps baking powder
6 oz caster sugar	$\frac{1}{4}$ tsp salt
8 oz self-raising flour, sieved	2$\frac{1}{2}$ fl. oz rich milk, to which add
2 eggs, separated	1 tsp vanilla essence

Pre-heat the oven to Gas 4/350°F/190°C.

Sieve the flour, baking powder and salt together. Cream the butter and sugar until light and fluffy. Beat in the egg yolks with 1 teaspoon of the flour mixture. Beat well. Mix in the remaining flour mixture and the milk.

Beat the egg whites until they stand in peaks. Cut and fold these into the cake mixture.

Divide between two 7-inch non-stick sandwich tins. Bake for 25–30 minutes. Cool a little before turning out on to a wire cooling rack.

Split each cake and layer it with your favourite butter cream, then dredge the top with icing sugar.

Sand Cake

Eat as a plain cake or serve with zabaglione in place of the more usual sponge fingers.

Makes 8 good slices

2 **oz** self-raising flour
1 **level tsp** baking powder
2 **oz** ground rice
6 **oz** unsalted butter

4 **oz** caster sugar
1 **tsp** vanilla essence
3 eggs, beaten
1 **tbsp** milk (optional)

Pre-heat the oven to Gas 4/350°F/180°C.

Liberally butter and sugar a fluted mould or deep loose-bottomed cake tin 7 inches in diameter.

Sieve the flour and baking powder together. Mix with the ground rice. Put on one side.

Cream the butter, sugar and vanilla essence until light and fluffy. Beat in the eggs slowly. Gradually beat in the flour mixture, adding a little milk or water until you have a soft dropping consistency. Turn into the mould or tin and bake for 1–1¼ hours.

Pound Cake

This is one of the earliest cakes – in the way we think of cake today – and is unchanged from its original form in the rather extended appendix of the fifth edition of Hannah Glasse's book *The Art of Cookery Made Plain and Easy*, which appeared in 1763.

8 **oz** caster sugar
1 **lb** self-raising flour
8 **oz** unsalted butter, softened

5 eggs
1 **tsp** finely grated lemon zest
brandy or sherry, to mix

Mix all the ingredients together and beat well. (This cake can also be made in a food processor using the all-in-one method. Allow it to be beaten well for 10 minutes or so.)

Pre-heat the oven to Gas 3/325°F/170°C.

Bake for an hour or until it is firm to the touch and is leaving the sides of the tin.

Madeira Cake

6 **oz** unsalted butter
6 **oz** caster sugar
3 eggs, beaten
4 **oz** self-raising flour
2 **oz** plain flour

2 **oz** ground almonds
zest and juice of a lemon
a little milk (if necessary)
1–2 slices of candied citron peel

Pre-heat the oven to Gas 3/325°F/170°C.

Grease and line with greaseproof paper a round, 7-inch cake tin.

Cream the butter and sugar until light and fluffy. Add the eggs slowly, beating well all the time.

Sieve the flours and ground almonds together and fold half into the mixture, then add the lemon zest and juice. Fold in the remaining flour. Add a little milk, if necessary, to give a dropping consistency.

Put the mixture into the prepared cake tin. Arrange the citron peel on top. Bake for 1–1¼ hours. Turn on to a wire rack to cool.

Madeira Cake can be used to make Mini Iced Cakes (see pp. 171–2).

Lemon Rice Cake

8 oz ground rice
8 oz self-raising flour
8 oz unsalted butter, softened
6 oz caster sugar

4 eggs, beaten
2 tsps finely grated lemon zest
milk, to mix

Pre-heat the oven to Gas 3/325°F/170°C.

Sieve the ground rice and flour together twice on to a paper.

Cream the butter, sugar and lemon zest until light and fluffy. Dribble and beat in the eggs gradually. Mix in the flour and ground rice mixture, adding a little milk to arrive at a soft, spoonable mixture.

Butter the sides of an 8-inch round cake tin and line the base with a circle of buttered paper. Spoon in the cake mixture and level the top. Bake for 1¼–1½ hours or until done.

FRUIT CAKES

Dundee Cake

2 oz almonds
11 oz flour (3 oz self-raising and 8 oz
   plain)
a pinch of salt
a pinch of mixed spice
8 oz unsalted butter
8 oz soft brown sugar

grated zest of an orange and a lemon
4 large eggs
8 oz currants
8 oz sultanas
6 oz raisins
4 oz chopped mixed peel
4 oz chopped cherries

Pre-heat the oven to Gas 3/325°F/160°C.

Grease and line an 8-inch round cake tin.

Blanch the almonds and chop half of them; reserve the other half. Sieve the flour, salt and spice together. Cream the butter and sugar, add the grated orange and lemon zest, then add the eggs one at a time, alternating with the flour.

Mix in the remaining ingredients, including the chopped almonds. Place in the prepared tin, smooth the top and arrange the remaining split almonds neatly on top. Bake for approximately 3 hours.

Plain Christmas Cake

Makes 2 cakes

8 oz sultanas
12 oz seedless raisins
4 oz cut mixed peel
4 oz glacé cherries, roughly chopped
4 oz unsalted butter
4 oz lard

8 oz caster sugar
4 large eggs, beaten
8 oz plain flour, sieved
2 oz split or whole almonds,
   blanched

Pre-heat the oven to Gas 4/350°F/180°C.

Wash and dry the sultanas and raisins if necessary. Roughly chop the raisins after washing. Beat the fats and sugar until light and fluffy. Beat in the eggs a little at a time, adding a spoonful of flour if they start to 'split'. Beat the mixture well until fluffy. Fold in the flour, without beating. Fold in the fruits.

Line two 2-lb tins with buttered paper and two-thirds fill them with the mixture. Top with the almonds. Bake for 1 hour, then lower the temperature to Gas 3/325°F/170°C for a further 1–1½ hours.

Rich Dark Plum Cake or Christmas Cake

This cake is heavy with fruit, sticky and all the things a good Christmas cake should be. Dare I suggest you try eating fingers of it, as we do in my home county of Yorkshire, together with a sliver of Wensleydale, Cheshire or any other crumbly English cheese?

Serves 30–40

8 oz currants
8 oz sultanas
8 oz seedless Muscatel raisins, chopped
6 oz blanched almonds, roughly crushed
6 oz glacé cherries, halved
4 oz glacé apricots, roughly chopped
4 oz prunes *fourrés* or stoned prunes, soaked overnight in 1 cup of rum and chopped
4 oz mixed candied peel

12 oz self-raising flour
1 dsp mixed spice (mace, cinnamon and a ground clove)
¼ tsp salt
10 oz unsalted butter, softened
10 oz Muscovado or Barbados or moist brown sugar
5 large eggs, beaten
4 tbsps black treacle or syrup
juice and grated zest of a large lemon
light rum or brandy

Pre-heat the oven to Gas 3/325°F/170°C.

Sieve together the flour, salt and spice. In a large bowl mix together the fruits, peel and spiced flour, coating all the fruits with the flour.

In a second bowl cream the butter and sugar until quite light in colour. Beat in the eggs, then the treacle, lemon juice and zest.

Combine the two mixtures in one bowl. Mix well, adding enough rum or brandy to arrive at a soft dropping consistency.

Butter and line the bottom and sides of a 7–8lb square or round cake tin with double buttered paper. Fill with the mixture and level the top. Bake for 1 hour, then reduce the temperature to Gas 1½/275°F/140°C for a further 2–2½ hours. Test with a needle for doneness.

Cool. Store for 1 month. Cover with marzipan and royal icing if liked (see pp. 136 and 134).

Rosie's Wedding Cake

I have written reams in other books and in magazine articles about the delightful problems posed by arranging a wedding. So here, in my afternoon tea book, I want to talk only about the cake and to tell you briefly how I came to terms with that for my own daughter Rosie's wedding.

You see, I am a cake fanatic – an absolute addict. I will kill for cake, particularly chocolate cake and rich moist fruit cake of a kind that can only be made at home.

Wedding (or Christmas or Christening) cakes can be the best thing in the world – or they can be abysmal failures. Towering edifices, with iced cherubs and garlands piped everywhere and attendant panels of brittle lacey icing to be guarded against shattering for weeks before the nuptials, are all very fitting for the cake-cutting photograph – but to eat? Absolutely not. They're out of my scheme of things. The strength and dryness of the icing necessary to support each towering tier as it is built up by professional confectioners is of a hardness to break one's teeth, not to mention making an unholy mess on the carpet as the groom's sword rasps into it.

Wedding cake has to be moist, packed to the point of indecency with liquor-soaked fruits and topped with a thick cushion of crunchy almond paste – which in itself poses a problem, as the oil from such a rich paste stains the virgin white of the bridal coating. But, it *is* delicious to eat and it doesn't stain *my* icing, which is a soft, lemony, pristine white confection spread evenly, or forked, over the almond layer of a large round *single*-tier cake: no other tiers to support and therefore no pillars to sink!

'Won't that look odd?' you might rightly ask. Maybe, but it will 'eat well', as the old saying goes. And it won't look nearly so 'odd' if you follow my instructions for its setting and decorating. Having achieved the layers of almond and white icing, the next job is to arrange a garland of fresh or silk flowers around the *base* of the cake and then arrange a cushion of roses or whatever flowers take your fancy on a board of a size to cover the *top* of the cake completely. Next, yards of tulle or muslin should be swagged around the cake table. The cake is then placed on an ornate silver stand, readily hired from your local silversmith, and further lush garlands and posies of flowers are attached to this table skirt . . . and hey presto – it will look more bridal than the bride!

Serves 80–100

2 lb good unsalted butter (the flavour of the butter is all-important)	2 lb Muscatel raisins, stoned and chopped
2 lb soft brown sugar	2 lb sultanas
1 lb black treacle or syrup	1 lb currants
24 eggs, separated	1 lb glacé cherries, roughly chopped
finely grated zest of 2 lemons and 2 oranges	4 oz stem ginger, finely chopped
1 heaped tsp each of mace and cinnamon	4 oz mixed candied peel, finely chopped
2 tsps bicarbonate of soda	½ bottle of brandy, rum, or pale sherry (use the same liquor as in the almond paste if making this)
2 lb plain flour	fresh orange juice
1 lb ground almonds or semolina	

Cream the butter and sugar until the granules are totally dissolved. Beat in the treacle. Beat in the eggs *yolks* only. Add the orange and lemon zests, spices and bicarbonate of soda. Beat in the flour and ground almonds, using enough orange juice as necessary to arrive at a softish, spoonable mix. Add the fruits, candied peel, ginger, etc., and the chosen liquor. Stiffly beat the egg whites. Cut and fold these into the mixture well.

Pre-heat the oven to Gas 4/350°F/180°C.

Line the bottom and sides of a large, 14-inch diameter cake tin – or one 9-inch and one 6-inch tin (making two tiers) – with double-thickness paper. Butter the tin and paper well with unsalted butter. Spoon the mixture into the tin and level the top.

Bake for 1 hour, then lower the temperature to Gas 2/300°F/150°C for a further 2½–3 hours. Test for doneness by the needle method.

Crunchy Marzipan

2 lb ground almonds, made by mincing freshly blanched almonds
1½ lb caster sugar

2 eggs
2 tbsp rum, dry sherry or brandy

Make as for ordinary marzipan (see p. 136).

Royal Icing

Sufficient for a thick cushion of semi-soft icing for a 14-inch diameter cake.

2 lb icing sugar, sieved
4 large egg whites

juice of a large lemon (or more)

Put the icing sugar into a bowl and make a well in the centre. Beat the egg whites until well broken up. Incorporate them into the icing sugar, adding the lemon juice as you go along. The icing should be just spreadable.

Cover the sides and top of the cake with marzipan, allow it to dry, then spread and fork the icing over and leave to set. Leave overnight to set (it will not set *hard* overnight, but will get firmer in due course).

Simnel Cake with Yeast

During Lent, Sundays are traditionally exempt from the general fast. The first real festival Sunday in the church's calendar is the fourth Sunday in Lent – Mothering Sunday. Years ago children, and in particular maid-servants who lived away from home, made a visit to their parents on this day, taking with them presents in the form of a bouquet of flowers or a Simnel Cake.

Simnel Cake is rich in fruits, with a marzipan 'seam' baked inside and a topping of eleven balls of marzipan toasted under a hot grill. (These balls represent the apostles. Judas is rightly missed off!)

This recipe comes from the Women's Institute's *A Cook's Tour of Britain*.

Serves 16–20

8 oz strong plain flour	4 oz sultanas
$\frac{1}{2}$ tsp mixed spice	4 oz currants
4 oz unsalted butter	1 lb marzipan, bought or home-
4 oz caster sugar	made (see below)
$\frac{1}{4}$ oz dried or $\frac{1}{2}$ oz fresh yeast	2 tbsps apricot jam
$\frac{1}{4}$ pint warm milk	a little beaten egg white to glaze
3 egg yolks	

Sieve the flour and spice into a warm bowl and rub in the butter until the mixture resembles fine breadcrumbs. Reserve 1 teaspoon of sugar and stir the rest into the flour. Mix the fresh yeast with the reserved sugar and add to the milk (or sprinkle dried yeast on the milk with the sugar) and leave until frothy. Add to the flour with the egg yolks and knead until smooth. Cover and prove for about 1 hour until the dough has doubled in size.

Pre-heat the oven to Gas 5/375°F/190°C.

Knead the dough again, working in the fruit. Put half the dough into a greased and floured cake tin, 7 inches in diameter.

Take one-third of the marzipan and roll it into a circle to fit the tin exactly. Place this on the dough and cover with the remaining half of the dough. Prove for 30 minutes, then bake for $1\frac{1}{2}$ hours.

Leave the cake in the tin for 30 minutes so that the marzipan firms up, then turn out on to a wire rack to cool.

Roll out half the remaining marzipan to fit the top of the cake. Brush the top of the cake with apricot jam and use the marzipan to cover the cake. Make the remaining marzipan into eleven balls and press them round the top of the cake. Brush with a little beaten egg white and put under a hot grill until the almond paste is lightly coloured (this happens very quickly, so keep an eye on the cake all the time).

If liked, put a frill or ribbon around the cake and a decoration of tiny 'eggs' or 'flowers' round the top of the cake.

Marzipan

4 oz ground almonds   **2** egg whites
12 oz icing sugar   water to mix

Mix the ground almonds, icing sugar and egg whites to a smooth paste, adding a little water if necessary.

Bible or Scripture Cake

Oh ye of little faith,
Believe it or not (sic) this actually works;
even if you never bake it, it's fun to look up
the passages from the Bible!

1	**8 oz** unsalted butter	8 oz Judges 5, xxv, last clause
2	**8 oz** caster sugar	8 oz Jeremiah 6, xx
3	**1 tbsp** honey	1 tbsp I Samuel 14, xxv
4	**3** eggs	Jeremiah 17, xi
5	**8 oz** raisins	8 oz I Samuel 30, xii
6	**8 oz** figs, chopped	8 oz Nahum 3, xii, chopped
7	**2 oz** almonds, blanched and chopped	2 oz Numbers 17, viii, blanched and chopped
8	**1 lb** plain flour	1 lb I Kings 4, xxii
9	season to taste with spices	season to taste with II Chronicles 9, ix
10	a pinch of salt	a pinch of Leviticus 2, xiii
11	**1 tsp** baking powder	1 tsp Amos 4, v
12	**3 tbsps** milk	3 tbsps Judges 4, xix

Pre-heat the oven to Gas 3/325°F/170°C.

Beat Nos. 1, 2 and 3 to a cream. Add 4, one at a time, still beating, then 5, 6 and 7, and beat again. Add 8, 9, 10 and 11, having previously mixed them, and lastly add 12.

Bake for 1½ hours.

Note: References are to passages in the Authorized Version.

George Washington Cake

This recipe was taken over to the United States from England in the eighteenth century.

This version is adapted from the American recipe taken from The American Museum at Claverton Manor, near Bath, Avon.

12 oz unsalted butter	**1 tsp** cinnamon
12 oz caster sugar	**1 tsp** salt
4 eggs, separated	**½ pint** milk
1 lb plain flour, sieved	**4 oz** seedless raisins
2 dsps baking powder	**2 oz** currants
1 tsp mace	**1 oz** finely chopped lemon zest

Pre-heat the oven to Gas 3/325°F/170°C.

Cream the butter and sugar until smooth. Add the egg yolks.

Sieve the flour, baking powder, salt and spices and add them, alternately with milk, to the mixture. Beat well. Stir in the fruits and zest. Beat the egg whites stiff, but not dry. Fold them into mixture.

Bake in a deep, 8-inch square tin, buttered and lined with greaseproof paper, for 1½ hours. When cool, split and sandwich with butter icing, and top with glacé icing.

Saffron Cake: see pp. 117–19.

CUT-AND-COME-AGAIN CAKES AND PARKINS

The strange name 'Cut-and-Come-Again Cake' refers to a cake or loaf, sometimes buttered, sometimes not, with a high sugar content, which on baking in old-fashioned fire or faggot-heated ovens tended to dry out, the sugar caramelising to a certain extent because of over-baking.

These enriched breads – for that is what they really are – were kept in an air-tight tin (in country districts they were often wrapped in a blanket and buried in the garden) until the crumb matured and the caramel softened or 'came again'.

The same rich tea-breads are also known as 'Cut and Butter Breads' – which name is perhaps more self-explanatory.

Dales Cut-and-Come-Again Cake

This type of cake can often be found on WI market stalls. It is not to be missed; the deep chocolate tones married with raisins make it very different from other cut-and-come-again cakes, in which dates and walnuts are usually the partners.

Serves 12–16

12 oz unsalted butter, softened
9 oz caster sugar
3 large eggs
3 tbsps lemon juice
grated zest of a small lemon
6 oz chopped mixed peel, dredged
   in 1 tbsp flour

3 tbsps golden syrup or honey
12 oz seedless raisins
14 oz self-raising flour
2½ rounded tbsps cocoa

Pre-heat the oven to Gas 4/350°F/180°C. Butter and line with buttered paper a deep 10-inch cake tin.

Cream the butter and sugar until light and fluffy. Beat in the eggs, syrup or honey, lemon juice and zest. Stir in the fruit and peel.

Sieve together the flour and cocoa, then cut and fold into the mixture. Pour into the tin. Bake for 30 minutes. Lower the temperature to Gas 3/325°F/170°C for a further 3 – yes, 3 – hours until the cake is firm to the touch in the middle and is 'quiet' – that is, not bubbling when you listen to it.

Cool for 30 minutes before turning out. Eat cut into slices, with or without butter but certainly with cheese!

Note: The cake may sink a little, but this is no detriment to its 'eating quality; in fact, it is an improvement if anything.

Grasmere Gingerbread

Serves 16–18

1 lb plain flour
2 tsps ground ginger
1 tsp bicarbonate of soda

1 tsp cream of tartar
8 oz unsalted butter or margarine
8 oz soft brown sugar

Pre-heat the oven to Gas 2/300°F/150°C.

Sieve together the flour, ginger, bicarbonate of soda and cream of tartar. Rub in the fat, then add the sugar and mix well.

Grease a 10×12-inch flat tin, 1 inch deep, and press the mixture into it. Bake for about 35–40 minutes. Allow to cool slightly before cutting into pieces.

Orange and Ginger Parkin

Serves 16–20

4 oz unsalted butter
1 lb golden syrup or old-fashioned
  brown (not black) treacle
12 oz caster sugar
4 oz self-raising flour
a good pinch of salt
1 lb medium oatmeal
1 level tsp ground ginger

2 eggs
1 tbsp stem ginger, cut into thin
  shreds or finely chopped
2 tbsps candied orange peel,
  chopped
3 pieces stem ginger, cut into
  thinnest slivers, to decorate
milk or rum

Pre-heat the oven to Gas 4/350°F/180°C.

Melt the butter and syrup in a non-stick pan over a low heat (it should be fully melted but not hot). Mix all the dry ingredients together. Mix in the syrup and butter and then the eggs. Mix to a soft dropping consistency with milk or rum.

Pour the mixture into a 9-inch square, well-buttered, paper-lined loaf tin. Bake for 1–1¼ hours or until cooked. Scatter the pieces of ginger on the top.

The parkin should be left for 2 weeks or more to mature properly, stored in an air-tight tin.

Wholemeal, Fruit and Bran Cake

This cake is good when sliced, well buttered and served with a mild, crumbly cheese such as Wensleydale or Cheshire. Alternatively, it is delicious toasted for breakfast.

Serves 8–12

8 oz All Bran
8 oz sultanas and currants, mixed
8 oz Muscovado sugar
4 oz hazelnuts, lightly toasted and roughly chopped
2 tsps vanilla essence

1 tsp ground ginger
1 tsp ground mace
¾ pint milk
8 oz wholemeal flour
3 tsps baking powder

Pre-heat the oven to Gas 4/350°F/180°C.

Put the All Bran, fruits, sugar, hazelnuts and vanilla essence into a bowl. Cover with the milk and mix well. Leave to soak for 2 hours.

Sieve the flour, baking powder and spices together and gradually fold into the mixture.

Bake in an 8-inch square tin lined with buttered paper for 1¼–1½ hours. Leave to cool before turning on to a wire cooling rack.

Sponge Rolls

Swiss Roll

I wonder who would have invented half the world's recreations had not the Victorians taken it upon themselves to educate 'the foreigner'? Wasn't it our own Arnold Lunn who persuaded the Swiss that ski-ing should become a sport and not just a means of getting about in the snow-covered mountains? St Moritz was where the *crème de la crème* of British society went to 'take the air' and it soon began to grow into the international resort we know today. It is said that there was an excellent pâtisserie there to which our ladyfolk resorted to partake of tea in the afternoons, and here a delicate jam-filled sponge cake could be enjoyed. The recipe was dragged out of some poor unsuspecting pastrycook, brought back to England and made into a cake today more associated with us than with the Swiss!

I love it; the plainer the better. That said, the technical idea of rolling things up in a sponge blanket has been the inspiration for richer versions, some of which I give you here.

My version, again from home, differs from present-day ideas in that it is rolled up with its jam while still hot. This allows the jam to permeate the sponge cake a little.

Serves 8

3 eggs	**1 tbsp** boiling water
4 oz caster sugar, sieved	caster sugar for dredging
4 oz plain flour, sieved	raspberry jam

Pre-heat the oven to Gas 7/425°F/220°C. Butter and line with buttered paper a 12×9-inch Swiss roll tin.

Whisk the eggs and sugar in a bowl over a pan of simmering water until thick and the whisk leaves a distinct trail when drawn across the surface of the mixture.

Sieve the flour over the mixture and, using a wire balloon whisk or a slotted spoon, cut and fold it in lightly but thoroughly. Stir in the boiling water.

Pour the mixture into the lined tin and spread to the corners. Bake near the top of the oven for 7–9 minutes or until the sponge springs back when pressed lightly with your forefinger.

Have ready a damp teatowel spread out on a work surface. Over this lay a sheet of greaseproof paper. Dredge this evenly and thoroughly with caster sugar. Turn the sponge on to this, carefully remove the base paper and trim the edges if necessary.

Spread the warm surface of the sponge with plenty of good raspberry jam and roll it up quickly and carefully. Leave to cool on a wire rack. Dredge with caster sugar before serving.

Apple, Lime and Lemon Roll with Apple Cream Sauce

The notion of eating a cake with a sauce for tea may at first sound bizarre: but I assure you it's not as odd as you may think.

Serves 6–8

Roulade

2 large eggs
2½ oz caster sugar
2 tsps lemon zest, grated or
  shredded
2 oz plain flour, sieved
caster or icing sugar for dredging
⅔ lb lime marmalade

Sauce

6 oz Cox's Orange Pippins
2 oz caster sugar
2 fl. oz brandy
3 fl. oz single cream

To decorate

1 Cox's Orange Pippin
juice of half a lemon
½ oz sugar

To make the roulade. Pre-heat the oven to Gas 5/375°F/190°C. Grease and line with buttered paper a Swiss roll tin, 14×9 inches.

Whisk the eggs and sugar until they form a heavy trail when the whisk is drawn through. Mix in the zest. Cut and fold in the flour.

Pour into the tin and spread into the corners. Bake for 10–12 minutes, by which time the cake will be firm to the touch in the centre.

Meanwhile, wring out a teatowel in cold water and spread it on a work surface. Lay on top of it a sheet of greaseproof paper dredged evenly with caster sugar. Invert the cooked roulade on to this and carefully remove the lining paper.

Roll up the roulade fairly tightly lengthways (i.e. making a long slim roll) using the paper and the cloth to help you. The paper stays inside as you roll; the damp cloth does not. Leave to cool.

Unroll. Spread with plenty of lime marmalade. Re-roll and dredge with more caster or icing sugar. Cut into six V-shaped wedges (and eat the offcuts from each end!).

To make the sauce. Peel and core the apples, slice them thinly and toss them in the sugar. Add the brandy (or 2 fl. oz water) and cook, covered, over a minimum heat until soft. Blend to a fine purée and cool. Stir in the cream. Chill.

To decorate. Peel and core the single apple and cut it into twelve slim wedges. Toss these in lemon juice and sugar. Cook in a shallow pan in one layer over a minimum heat, covered, until the wedges are transparent but still hold their shape. Cool.

Serve the wedges of roulade decorated with a couple of slivers of cooked apple and a tiny blob of lime jelly or marmalade, with a spoonful of the sauce served alongside. Best eaten the same day, although it can be frozen.

Chestnut Cream Cheese and Vanilla Roll

Serves 8

Sponge

3 eggs
3 oz vanilla sugar or 1 tsp vanilla essence
3 oz self-raising flour, sieved on to paper
1 scant oz unsalted butter, melted but cool

Filling

1 19-oz tin Faugier Marrons au Syrop (chestnuts in syrup, *not* marrons glacés; the latter could be used – but at what cost!)
8 oz Philadelphia cream cheese
1 tsp icing sugar
1 tsp vanilla essence
6 fl. oz double cream

To decorate

icing sugar
whipped cream
1–2 drops vanilla essence

To make the sponge. Pre-heat the oven to Gas 5/375°F/190°C. Butter a 14× 9-inch Swiss roll tin with unsalted butter and line the base with grease-proof paper, also lightly brushed with melted butter.

Whisk the eggs and sugar (and the vanilla essence if used) until thick and the whisk leaves a very distinct trail. Briskly whisk in the flour and incorporate the cool melted butter at the same time.

Pour into the lined tin. Spread the mixture, paying particular attention to the corners. Bake for 12 minutes.

Have ready a clean teatowel, well wrung out in cold water. Turn out the sponge on to this and remove the base paper. Leave to cool (but not to go cold, or it won't roll successfully).

To make the filling. Drain the chestnuts and roughly chop them (reserve 4 or 5 for decoration if you like). Beat the cheese with the icing sugar and vanilla essence. Whip the cream until it stands in soft peaks and carefully fold it into the cream cheese (don't try to do this in a machine or you will end up with a curdled mess).

Spread the sponge liberally with the filling and roll it up gently but firmly, using the towel to hold everything together as you roll.

Leave to cool completely. Dredge liberally with icing sugar and decorate at will with spirals or blobs of cream whipped with ½ teaspoon of icing sugar and a drop or two of vanilla essence. If you have reserved chestnuts, these too can be added as luxury decoration.

Hazelnut, Raspberry and Redcurrant Swiss Roll

I sometimes serve this hot as a light pudding with a real English custard sauce.

Serves 8

Sponge	Filling
2 large eggs	8 oz redcurrant jelly or raspberry jam
2 oz caster sugar	
3 oz hazelnuts, finely crushed and well-toasted	3 oz hazelnuts, roughly crushed and toasted
1 oz self-raising flour, sieved and mixed with the nuts	4 oz fresh or frozen raspberries, mashed to a rough pulp

Pre-heat the oven to Gas 7/425°F/220°C.

Butter and line with buttered paper a 14×8-inch Swiss roll tin.

Using an electric mixer, beat the eggs and sugar until they are light and fluffy and the whisk leaves a distinct trail. Cut and fold in the flour and nut mixture, using a balloon whisk.

Pour the mixture into the tin and spread to the corners. Bake for 10–12 minutes or until the sponge is firm to the touch.

Turn out the baked sponge on to a paper well dredged with caster sugar.

Warm the redcurrant jelly in a bowl over simmering water. Mix in the nuts. Allow to cool but not to set again.

Spread the sponge with the jam and nut filling and spread a broad band of the fresh raspberry pulp over this (it needs to go edge to edge, but not down the full length.)

144

Roll up the sponge tightly using the paper as an aid. Transfer the cake to a wire cooling rack. Dredge well with icing sugar. Serve, cut on the diagonal into 1-inch slices.

Coconut Kirsch Roll

Light as air with its yummy cream filling laced with Kirsch. Nothing that a health-fiend should even think about, but everything a gourmet should.

Serves 8

Sponge

4 large eggs
4 oz caster sugar
1 oz desiccated coconut, toasted (see method)
3 oz self-raising flour, sieved

Filling

6 large egg yolks
1½ oz sugar
½ pint single cream

1 heaped tsp gelatine crystals
3 fl. oz Kirsch
3 oz unsalted butter, softened

Topping

1 oz extra toasted coconut
⅓ pint double cream for whipping
2 tbsps Kirsch
1 tbsp icing sugar
8 pieces of glacé or fresh pineapple to decorate

To make the sponge. Pre-heat the oven to Gas 5/375°F/190°C. Butter and line a 14×9-inch Swiss roll tin with buttered greaseproof paper.

Using a rotary or electric hand whisk, cream the eggs and sugar until the whisk leaves a very distinct trail when drawn through the mixture.

Mix the coconut and flour together, then cut and fold this into the egg mixture. Pour into the lined tin and bake for 12 minutes.

Put a clean teatowel, wrung out in cold water, on to a flat surface. Cover with a piece of greaseproof paper at least 18×12 inches, and dredge this evenly with caster sugar. When the sponge is ready, turn it out on to the prepared paper. Carefully remove the base paper and leave the sponge for 30 seconds to allow the steam to escape. Trim the edges.

Ease and gradually roll up the sponge very loosely, using the teatowel to help. Unroll, and re-roll it loosely in the paper only. Leave to cool.

To make the filling. In a round-bottomed bowl arranged over a pan of *boiling* water, whisk the egg yolks, sugar, cream and gelatine until thick and ribboning. Remove from the heat and pour in the Kirsch immediately. This will remove any residual heat as well as giving flavour.

Put the bowl in a sink of cold water to cool the mixture. At the same time, whisk in the softened butter bit by bit. Cool and chill, and whisk from time to time to ensure a thick, even-textured mixture – it should be just spreadable. If necessary, add a little more Kirsch or single cream to thin it down.

Unroll the sponge and spread to the edges with the cream filling. Dredge with extra toasted coconut, then roll up again.

To make the topping. Whip the double cream, Kirsch and icing sugar to a piping consistency. Pipe a garland down the centre of the roll. Dredge with a little more toasted coconut and spike with pieces of glacé or fresh pineapple. The roll should be eaten the day it is made, although it will freeze.

To toast the coconut. Pre-heat the oven to Gas 6/400°F/200°C. Spread 6 oz desiccated coconut on an oven tray. Using the blade edge of a palette-knife, gather up and re-spread the coconut at regular intervals (every 2 minutes once the edges start to turn light gold). When evenly browned and *dry*, turn on to a tray or paper to cool.

Chocolate and Raisin Roll

This deliciously rich dessert is more of a mousse than a cake, as it has no flour. Make it the day before you need it.

Serves 6–8

6 oz plain chocolate	¼ **pint** double cream
5 eggs, separated	1 **tbsp** brandy or sherry
6 oz caster sugar	icing sugar
3 oz raisins	

Pre-heat the oven to Gas 4/350°F/180°C. Grease and line a 13×9-inch Swiss roll tin.

Break up the chocolate and place it in a bowl over hot water until it has melted.

Place the egg yolks and sugar in a bowl over hot water and whisk until the mixture is pale and fluffy; this will take about 5 minutes. Whisk in the chocolate gradually, then stir in half the raisins.

Whisk the egg whites until stiff, then fold carefully into the chocolate mixture, taking care not to knock out the air. Pour into the prepared tin and shake the tin to level the mixture. Bake for 25 minutes, until firm. Remove from the oven and cover with a sheet of aluminium foil. Leave for at least 3 hours, until completely cold.

Whisk the cream until it holds its shape, then stir in the remaining raisins and the brandy or sherry. Turn out the roll on to a sheet of sugared paper and spread the roll with cream. Roll up carefully from a short end and place on a serving plate. (The mixture will crack slightly as you roll it.) Sprinkle with icing sugar and chill until ready to serve.

Plain Chocolate Sherry Sponge Cake

Serves 8

6 oz unsalted butter or margarine
6 oz caster sugar
3 eggs, beaten

6 oz self-raising flour, sieved
1 oz cocoa powder
2 tbsps sweet sherry or milk

Pre-heat the oven to Gas 5/375°F/190°C. Butter and line with buttered paper an 8-inch cake tin.

Sieve the flour and cocoa together on to a paper. Cream the butter and eggs until light and fluffy. Cut and fold in the flour mixture, adding the sherry or milk to give a dropping consistency.

Bake for 15–20 minutes or until firm when pressed lightly with your forefinger.

Chocolate and Gooseberry Cake

My favourite chocolate cake – which I eat for breakfast – is not a pretentious gâteau like those made in other countries, but a good, wholesome, light-textured though rich cake made with honest ingredients tasting as they are meant to.

If you don't have gooseberry jam, then any sharp-edged jam will do, such as raspberry, redcurrant (Krakus do a very tangy redcurrant jam which I can recommend for this recipe).

Serves 12–14

Sponge

8 oz unsalted butter, at room
  temperature
4 oz caster sugar
4 large eggs
6 oz self-raising flour
1 tsp vanilla essence
1 tsp baking powder
2 oz cocoa powder
2 oz ground almonds or an extra
  2 oz self-raising flour
2–3 tbsps milk or water
gooseberry jam

Butter cream

4 oz unsalted butter
4 oz icing sugar
2 oz cocoa powder
1 tsp vanilla essence

Icing

4 oz plain chocolate
1 oz unsalted butter
1 tbsp brandy

Chocolate leaves

bay, rose or camellia leaves
8 oz plain chocolate

148

To make the sponge. Pre-heat the oven to Gas 5/375°F/190°C.

Cream the butter and sugar thoroughly. Beat the eggs and fold them into the creamed mixture gradually, adding a little of the flour if the mixture shows signs of curdling. Add the vanilla essence.

Sieve together the flour, baking powder and cocoa powder. Fold thoroughly into the mixture, adding the ground almonds as you go along. Add milk or water to arrive at a loose dropping consistency.

Line the bases of two well-buttered 8-inch sandwich tins with greaseproof paper. Divide the mixture between the tins and bake for 35–40 minutes. Leave for 5 minutes before turning on to a wire cooling rack. Remove the paper.

To make the butter cream. Blend together all the ingredients for the butter cream.

To make the icing. Break the chocolate into bits. Soften together with the butter and brandy in a bowl over a pan of simmering water. Leave the mixture to cool. This is a softish icing.

To make up the cake. Spread a good cushion of gooseberry jam over one of the cakes. Spread the butter cream over it. Lay the second cake on top so that it is flat-side up. Spread the icing over the top.

To make the chocolate leaves. Melt the chocolate in a bowl over simmering water. Take a selection of even-sized bay, rose or small camellia leaves and brush melted chocolate over the fronts of the leaves. Allow them to set in the refrigerator until they are hard. Peel off the leaves carefully and decorate the cake with them.

Three-nut Chocolate Layer Cake

Serves 12–14

Sponge

2 **oz** walnuts
6 large eggs
6 **oz** caster sugar
4 **oz** self-raising flour
1 **tsp** baking powder
1½ **oz** cocoa powder

Apricot purée

¾ **lb** apricot jam
1 **tbsp** Kirsch, gin or whisky

Hazelnut chocolate butter

8 **oz** hazelnuts
8 **oz** icing sugar
3 **tbsps** cocoa powder
8 **oz** unsalted butter, softened
1 **tbsp** Kirsch, gin or whisky

Ganache

10 **oz** plain chocolate
½ **pint** single cream

Topping

12 marrons glacés
4 **oz** chocolate-coated almonds or
    other chocolate sweets

To make the sponge. Pre-heat the oven to Gas 6/400°F/200°C. Roughly crush the walnuts, spread them on a baking tray and toast in the oven for 4–6 minutes. Watch carefully and shake the tray gently several times to prevent them burning or scorching at the edges, but make sure they are toasted thoroughly.

Using a rotary or electric whisk, whisk the eggs and sugar until light and fluffy and the whisk leaves a distinct trail. Sieve the flour, baking powder and cocoa powder together twice. Mix the toasted walnuts with the flour mixture, then fold into the egg mixture.

Pour into a lined, 10×4-inch deep, round non-stick cake tin. Bake on the middle shelf of the oven at Gas 6/400°F/200°C for 50 minutes–1 hour or until the cake begins to leave the sides of the tin and is firm to the touch.

Allow to cool for a few minutes, then turn on to a wire cooling rack and remove the lining paper.

To make the apricot purée. Warm the apricot jam, then press it through a fine-meshed wire sieve. Cool slightly, then cover with plastic film to prevent a skin forming. Just before using, whisk in the Kirsch, gin or whisky.

To make the hazelnut chocolate butter. Toast and finely crush the hazelnuts as you did the walnuts in the sponge mixture, making sure to rub away the skins first. Sieve the icing sugar together with the cocoa powder, and beat into the butter. Add the toasted hazelnuts and mix in well. Just before spreading, whisk in the Kirsch, gin or whisky.

To make the ganache. Break up the chocolate and melt it gently with the cream in a bowl over a pan of boiling water. Cool. Just as the mixture is about to set, whisk it until it is light in colour and of a piping consistency.

To make up cake. When the sponge is completely cool, cut it into three equal layers. If the top layer is not even, carefully shave off a little until it is level. Turn it on to a board and spread it with half the apricot purée. Then spread half the hazelnut chocolate butter on top of this and repeat the process with the second layer of sponge, using the rest of the apricot purée and hazelnut chocolate butter. Using two palette-knives, carefully lift the second layer of sponge and place it on top of the first layer. Put the third layer on top. Spread two-thirds of the ganache over the top and sides, using the last third to pipe a collar around the edge of the cake. Decorate with marrons glacés and split chocolate-coated almonds.

Serve at room temperature so that the butter cream is soft and the sponge moist.

Chocolate Caramel Cake

Serves 6–8

Sponge	Butter cream
3 large eggs	8 oz plain chocolate
4 oz caster sugar	8 oz unsalted butter
4 oz plain flour	1 lb icing sugar
a pinch of salt	
	2 tbsps apricot jam, sieved

Caramel

6 oz caster sugar
cold water

To make the sponge layers (the day before). Pre-heat the oven to Gas 6/400°F/ 200°C. Prepare *five* flat trays lined with aluminium foil or buttered greaseproof paper (cake tins and roasting tins upside down can be used to improvise). Draw a 7-inch circle on each piece of lining paper.

Break the eggs into a large bowl, add the sugar and whisk over simmering water until the mixture is thick and the whisk forms a definite trail when drawn through.

Sieve the flour with a pinch of salt on to a piece of paper, then carefully fold and cut this into the eggs and sugar with a slotted spoon. Divide between the five papers and spread evenly with a palette-knife to the edges of the drawn circles.

Bake in batches for 7–8 minutes or until cooked and golden brown, and perhaps slightly crisp at the edges. Turn on to a wire rack, remove the paper carefully, and leave the cakes to cool.

Using a paper template, trim the edges of the sponge circles to size.

To make the caramel. Put the sugar into a heavy-bottomed pan, just cover it with cold water, place the pan over a low heat and bring to the boil. Do not stir. Boil rapidly until a golden-brown caramel develops.

While this is happening, stand two of the sponge bases on a wire cooling rack, nice side uppermost. When the caramel is ready, hold the pan with a cloth and pour half of the caramel over each base, starting in the centre and working round and out in a circular movement. *Do not touch the caramel with your fingers as it sticks and burns.* Before it sets hard on one of the cakes, mark serving portions with a knife blade by pressing it into the half-set caramel (about 6–8 segments is right). Leave on one side: do not refrigerate or the caramel will soften.

To make the butter cream. Break the chocolate into pieces and put it into a bowl over a pan of simmering water. Cream the butter, then beat in the icing sugar. Beat until smooth and fluffy. Gradually add the melted chocolate, scraping it out of the bowl with a plastic or rubber spatula.

151

To assemble the cake. Stand the plain caramel-covered base on a board or icing turntable. Spread some of the butter cream over the caramel. Place a plain sponge cake on top of this and spread it with a good cushion of apricot jam or purée, then a cushion of the butter cream. The third piece of sponge is spread with butter cream only, as is the fourth. The fifth sponge, the top of the cake, is the segmented caramel-covered layer.

Spread the remaining butter cream round the sides of the cake and fork a pattern round it, or pipe columns of the butter cream up the sides. Pipe lines of butter cream across the top of the cake to mark the portions.

Rainbow or Marble Cake

A marble cake with a difference, as mine has a seam of moist redcurrant jelly running through the marbling. This adds an interesting dimension to its overall appearance.

Serves 12–14

12 oz unsalted butter	2 **tsps** essence de framboise
12 oz caster sugar	(optional)
6 eggs	1 **tbsp** cocoa powder
12 oz self-raising flour	grated zest of a lemon
2 **tsps** baking powder	1–2 drops of yellow colouring
1 oz ground almonds	1 **tsp** essence de pistache
2–3 **tbsps** milk or water	1–2 drops of green colouring
2–3 drops of cochineal	2 **tsps** redcurrant jelly

Pre-heat the oven to Gas 4/350°F/180°C. Butter and line a 12×4×4-inch cake tin.

Cream the butter and sugar thoroughly. Beat the eggs and fold them into the creamed mixture gradually, adding a little of the flour if the mixture shows signs of curdling.

Sieve together the flour, baking powder and ground almonds. Fold thoroughly into the mixture. Add milk or water to arrive at a loose dropping consistency. Divide the mixture into three or four equal parts, depending on whether you want three or four colours.

To the first part, add the cochineal and the essence de framboise. To the second, beat in the cocoa powder. To the third, add the grated lemon rind and yellow colouring. To the fourth, add the essence de pistache and green colouring.

Spoon small amounts of the different coloured mixtures along the bottom of the prepared tin. Give the tin a sharp bang on the work surface to settle things in. Add tiny bits of the redcurrant jelly right down the centre. Continue adding the mixture at random in blobs until it is used up, but do not put jelly on the top.

Bake for 30 minutes, then lower the heat to Gas 4/350°F/180°C for a further 35–40 minutes or until cooked. Test with a clean knitting needle or skewer, which should come out clean when inserted in the centre of the cake. The cake will also sound 'quiet' if you listen with your ear to it. Finish by dredging the surface of the cake with icing sugar when cold.

Battenburg Cake

Called after Prince Henry of Battenburg, this cake is sometimes known in my family as 'Tennis Cake' because it resembles the four sections of a tennis court.

Serves 8

6 oz self-raising flour	**6 oz** soft margarine
1½ tsps baking powder	4 drops of red colouring
3 large eggs, beaten	apricot jam
3 tbsps tepid water	marzipan (see method)
6 oz caster sugar	

Use a cake tin approximately 10×8 inches and 2 inches deep. Cut a triple thickness of greaseproof paper the width of the tin and the length plus 4 inches. Pleat the paper so that when placed in the tin the fold divides the tin in half across the width; this enables you to bake two colours of cake in the same tin.

Pre-heat the oven to Gas 5/375°F/190°C.

Sieve the flour and baking powder together twice. With an electric mixer or a food processor beat together the eggs, water, sugar and margarine until creamy. Add the flour and continue to beat until the mixture is a pale creamy colour and looks glossy.

Divide equally into two and place one half into one side of the prepared tin. Beat the red colouring into the second half of the mixture and spoon it into the other part of the tin. Level the tops and bake for approximately 40 minutes.

Leave to cool for 5 minutes, then turn out on to a wire cooling rack, peeling off the paper and separating the two sponges. When quite cold, trim the sponges to make two equal-sized cakes. Cut each one in half lengthways.

Spread each piece with jam and sandwich together in pairs, giving two layers with alternating colours. Coat the whole of the outside except for the ends with jam.

On a lightly sugared board roll out the marzipan to an oblong the length of the cake and wide enough to wrap all the way round it – about 16×8 inches. Wrap the marzipan completely around the cake, pressing the joins together and trimming the edges.

Using your thumb and forefinger, pinch the outer edges decoratively – rather as you would the edge of a pastry case. Score the top with a knife in a criss-cross pattern.

To cover the cake with marzipan, use half the quantity made from the recipe on p. 136 or 1lb bought marzipan.

Tangy Lemon Sponge Cake

For the family, this recipe can be made as two separate sticky-topped cakes, in which case you will need 10 extra lemon slices. Or make it as one deep, rich layered cake which lifts it into a special category for party use. It can be made by the all-in-one method in a food processor.

Serves 10–12

1 12-oz jar of lemon curd	4 large eggs, beaten
1 lemon, cut into 10 slices	7 oz self-raising flour
4 oz unsalted butter, softened	3 oz cornflour
4 oz caster sugar	1 tsp baking powder
finely grated zest of a small lemon	lemon juice

Pre-heat the oven to Gas 5/375°F/190°C.

Butter, and line with buttered papers on the bases, two 7-inch sandwich tins. Spread the base of one with one-third of the jar of lemon curd. Arrange the lemon slices, slightly overlapping, in a circle on this.

Cream the butter, lemon rind and sugar thoroughly. Gradually beat in the eggs. Sieve the flour, cornflour and baking powder together twice and mix into the creamed mixture. Add a little lemon juice and beat until you have a softish dropping consistency.

Divide the mixture between the two tins, levelling the tops. Bake for 35–40 minutes or until the cakes are firm to the touch. Turn on to wire cooling racks and leave to cool completely.

Divide each cake in half; or, if you have a good eye and stable hand, three layers makes for a gooier finish. Spread all the layers apart from the one decorated with lemon slices liberally with the remaining lemon curd. Arrange in layers with, obviously, the one decorated with the lemon slices uppermost.

Light Coffee Cake

Serves 8

1 heaped tsp instant coffee, Continental-blend	**3** large eggs, beaten
1 tbsp boiling water	**3 oz** caster sugar
	3 oz plain flour

Pre-heat the oven to Gas 5/375°F/190°C.

Butter and line with buttered paper an 8-inch deep cake tin.

Dissolve the coffee in the water.

Using an electric mixer, whisk the eggs and sugar in a heatproof bowl arranged over a pan of simmering water until the whisk leaves a distinct trail when drawn across the mixture. Remove the bowl from the heat and whisk in the coffee essence. Whisk from time to time until cool.

Using a hand whisk, gradually cut and fold in the flour. Pour into the tin and bake for 30–35 minutes or until the cake is firm to the touch. Turn out on to a wire rack to cool.

Serve either plain, the top of the cake simply dredged with icing sugar, or split and spread with ⅓ pint double cream whipped to a spreadable consistency with a scant tablespoon of caster sugar and a tablespoon of sweet sherry.

Dark Coffee Cake

This is a cheap cutting cake.

Serves 8

4 oz unsalted butter, cubed	**1 tsp** mixed spice
4 oz Muscovado sugar	**2 fl. oz** strong coffee, cold
2 oz golden syrup (approx. 2 tbsps), warmed in a teacup	**6 oz** sultanas or raisins
10 oz self-raising flour	**1** large egg, beaten

Pre-heat the oven to Gas 3/325°F/170°C.

Sieve the flour and spice into a bowl. Rub in the butter until you have a moist sand-like texture. Mix in the sugar. Make a well in the centre.

Beat together the eggs, syrup and coffee, and pour into the mixture. Gather the flour into the liquids using a fork. Beat well until you have a soft dropping consistency; add a little water if necessary. Stir in the dried fruit.

Line the base of a 7-inch square, deep cake tin or an 8-inch round one with buttered paper. Butter the sides of the tin. Spoon in the mixture, and level the top.

Bake for 1¼–1½ hours or until the cake is firm to the touch and leaves the sides of the tin. Cool completely before turning out.

Walnut Cake

Serves 12–14

Sponge

8 oz self-raising flour, sieved
4 oz walnuts, finely crushed
6 oz unsalted butter
6 oz caster sugar
3 large eggs, beaten
2 tbsps milk
1 tsp finely grated orange zest

Icing

8 oz icing sugar, sieved
1 tsp instant coffee granules,
  Continental-blend
1–2 tbsps boiling water

Butter Cream (optional)

8 oz unsalted butter, softened
6–8 oz icing sugar, sieved
3–4 tbsps brandy, whisky or sherry,
  warmed
4 oz walnuts, finely crushed

To decorate

12–18 half walnuts

Pre-heat the oven to Gas 4/350°F/180°C.

Cream the butter, sugar and zest until light and fluffy. Dribble and beat in the eggs.

Stir and beat in the flour and walnuts alternately, adding enough milk to arrive at a soft, dropping consistency.

Line the bases of two 7-inch non-stick cake tins with circles of buttered paper. Spoon in the mixture. Level the top and bake for 45 minutes–1 hour or until cooked.

To make the icing. Mix the coffee granules with the water, then dribble enough of the coffee essence into the icing sugar to arrive at a just-flowing consistency.

To make the butter cream. In a liquidiser make a smooth paste of the sugar, butter and brandy. Just mix in the walnuts.

Split each cake in two. Spread butter cream on three layers. Place the fourth layer on top, ice with the coffee icing (which should be spooned over the walnuts) and let it dribble down the sides if it wants to.

Coffee Walnut Cake

A light and quite delicious cake with a butterscotch and coffee icing – ideal for morning or afternoon breaks or even as a rich special pudding.

Serves 8

Sponge

4 egg yolks
3 oz caster sugar
2 tbsps coffee essence
grated zest of an orange
1 oz fresh white breadcrumbs
3 oz walnuts, finely crushed
3 egg whites
a pinch of salt

Icing

2 oz unsalted butter
6 oz icing sugar
3 tbsps single cream
2 tbsps coffee essence
1 oz walnut pieces, to decorate

Prepare and line an 8-inch round, deep cake tin (*not* a loose-bottomed tin).

Whisk the egg yolks and sugar in a bowl over a pan of gently simmering water until thick and creamy and the whisk leaves a trail. Cool, whisking occasionally, then whisk in the coffee essence and zest. Fold in the breadcrumbs and nuts.

Whisk the egg whites until stiff and carefully fold them in. Spoon the mixture into the tin.

Bake for 1 hour until the cake no longer 'sings' when you listen to it. Cool it upside down and leave it to get completely cold before you remove the tin and paper. Split the cake in half.

To make the icing, sieve the icing sugar into a large bowl. In a small saucepan, melt the butter and allow it to bubble until it starts to turn brown round the edges. Watch it like a hawk so that it does not burn. Remove it immediately and pour it on to the icing sugar. Beat vigorously, adding the cream and coffee essence. You should have a soft icing that drops from the spoon.

Use half the icing to sandwich the cake halves together and swirl the rest attractively on top. Sprinkle the walnuts over the top and allow the icing to 'set' before cutting the cake.

Coconut Cake

Serves 8

Sponge

3 **oz** desiccated coconut
¼ **pint** milk
1 **tbsp** Kirsch or 1 tsp vanilla essence
6 **oz** self-raising flour
1 **tsp** baking powder
a pinch of salt
4 **oz** unsalted butter, softened
4 **oz** caster sugar

2 eggs, beaten
raspberry jam

Icing

8 **oz** icing sugar, sieved
juice of a lemon
1 **tsp** grated lemon zest
1 **oz** desiccated coconut
boiling water to mix

Grease and line an 8-inch round, deep cake tin, or a 7-inch square one.

Soak the coconut in the milk with the Kirsch or essence for 15 minutes.

Pre-heat the oven to Gas 4/350°F/180°C.

Sieve the flour, baking powder and salt together. Cream the butter and sugar together until light and fluffy, then gradually beat in the eggs. Fold in the flour and the coconut milk mixture.

Spoon into the cake tin and bake for about 1 hour until risen and cooked. Cool upside down, then, when quite cold, split in half and sandwich together with jam.

For the icing, mix the lemon juice with the icing sugar and zest, adding boiling water if too thick. Stir in the coconut, then spread on top of the cake, allowing it to run down the sides.

Orange and Almond Liqueur Cake

Serves 10–12

Sponge

8 **oz** self-raising flour
1 **tsp** baking powder
4 **oz** ground almonds
8 **oz** unsalted butter
8 **oz** caster sugar
2 **heaped tsps** finely grated orange
  zest
4 eggs, beaten
2 **tbsps** cold water
orange 'jelly' marmalade
flaked almonds and candied orange
  slices for decoration

Special butter cream

4 egg whites
8 **oz** icing sugar
2 drops red colouring
2 drops yellow colouring
8 **oz** unsalted butter, very soft
1 **tsp** grated orange zest
2 **tbsps** orange liqueur (Cointreau,
  Grand Marnier or Curaçao)

Icing

6 **oz** icing sugar
2 **tbsps** orange liqueur (as above)

To make the sponge. Pre-heat the oven to Gas 5/375°F/190°C.

Butter and line the bases of two 8-inch sandwich tins. Sieve the flour, baking powder and ground almonds together on to a paper, twice. Cream the butter, sugar and zest until light and fluffy. Beat in the eggs, then the flour mixture, using a little cold water to arrive at a soft dropping consistency.

Divide the mixture equally between the two tins. Level the tops and bake for 35–40 minutes or until firm when pressed lightly with the finger.

Turn the cakes on to a wire cooling rack and cool completely. Halve each cake.

To make the special butter cream. Stiffly beat the egg whites, then beat in half the icing sugar, adding the colouring at this stage. Fold in the remaining sugar. Cream the butter and zest very well. Gradually beat in the meringue mixture and liqueur.

To make the icing. Sieve the icing sugar into a bowl. Heat the liqueur over a low heat in a metal soup-ladle (do not allow it to ignite). Stir then beat into the sugar.

Spread this over the baked base-side of one of the cakes, using a palette-knife dipped in boiling water to ease the process and to give a smooth finish. Set aside.

Spread one-third of the butter cream on the crumb face of one of the cakes. Arrange a second cake on this and splash it with a little liqueur, then spread it with some of the remaining butter cream. Spread the next cake with the jelly, fit it on top of the second layer and spread it with some butter cream. Finally, top with the iced layer.

Spread butter cream round the sides of the cake. Press the flaked almonds into this. Decorate at will with any remaining butter cream piped in blobs and stuck with candied orange. Cut with a hot, wetted knife.

Fresh Raspberry Cake

Serves 10

Sponge

6 large eggs
6 oz caster sugar
finely grated zest of a lemon
2 oz unsalted butter, melted but cool
6 oz self-raising flour, sieved

Butter cream

8 oz unsalted butter, softened
8 oz icing sugar, sieved
8 oz raspberries, fresh or frozen
2 tbsps eau de vie de framboise or
   gin

Icing

6 oz icing sugar
juice of half a lemon
a few drops of pink colouring

Piping cream

$\frac{1}{2}$ **pint** double cream
1$\frac{1}{2}$ **oz** icing sugar
a drop of carmine colouring
1 **tbsp** of your selected liqueur
1 **tsp** lemon juice
8 **oz** extra raspberries (optional)

To make the sponge. Pre-heat the oven to Gas 5/375°F/190°C.

Butter and line with buttered paper two Swiss roll tins about 14×9×$\frac{1}{2}$ inch deep.

Whisk the eggs, sugar and zest until light and fluffy and the whisk leaves a distinct trail. Whisk in the cool melted butter, then cut and fold in the flour.

Divide the mixture equally – it pours readily – between the two tins and spread it evenly into the corners. Bake for 12–14 minutes or until it is springy to the touch. Turn out on to a wire cooling rack, remove the paper and leave to cool completely.

To make the butter cream. Cream the butter and sugar. Beat in the raspberries and liqueur. Rub the mixture through a fine-meshed wire sieve, using the back of a wooden spoon to do this.

Cut each cake in half lengthways, spread the layers with the raspberry butter cream and assemble the layers.

To make the icing. Put the icing sugar in a bowl and add enough lemon juice (or cold water) to achieve a spreading consistency. Add a tiny touch of colouring to make a very pale pink colour. Arrange the extra raspberries over this.

Whip together the ingredients for the piping cream decorate the base edges of the cake.

Raspberry Cream Layer Cake

Lagkage, or Layer Cake, is Denmark's national cake, served not only at tea-time, freshly made, but as a dessert after dinner and with morning coffee.

Fiddling, but not difficult to make – and worth any effort!

Serves 10–12

Sponge

6 eggs
8 oz vanilla sugar or 8 oz caster
    sugar plus 2 tsps vanilla essence
6 oz self-raising flour
1 tsp baking powder

Cream filling

1 oz caster sugar
½ **tsp** cornflour
3 large egg yolks
9 fl. oz double cream
2 tbsps eau de vie de framboise or a
    few drops of raspberry essence

Jam filling

4–6 oz good-quality raspberry jam

Icing

4 oz icing sugar, sieved
2 drops of red colouring
1–2 tbsps eau de vie de framboise,
    gin or vodka, to mix

To decorate

½ **pint** unsweetened whipped cream
6 oz fresh raspberries

Line *two* baking trays with buttered greaseproof paper or aluminium foil. With a pencil, draw two circles on each paper, using a 7–8-inch flan ring as your guide.

Pre-heat the oven to Gas 6/400°F/200°C.

Beat the eggs, vanilla sugar (or sugar and vanilla essence) together until white and thick. If you can see the trail left by the beater when it is drawn slowly through the mixture, then it is thick enough. Sieve together the flour and the baking powder and fold in gradually, using a slotted spoon.

Divide the mixture equally into four portions, and with a palette-knife spread two on each paper, spreading to the edges of the drawn circles. Bake for 10–12 minutes. Turn on to a wire cooling rack and remove the papers. Allow to cool and, using the same flan ring as a template, trim the layers neatly.

To make the cream filling. Cream together the sugar, cornflour, egg yolks and, for added luxury, the liqueur or essence. Heat the cream to boiling point and add it to the mixture, then put the mixture in a double boiler or arrange the bowl over a pan of boiling water. Stirring continuously, let the sauce cook for a minute or so. Allow it to cool, sprinkling the surface with a little caster sugar to prevent a skin forming. If the finished cream or custard appears oily, beat in a spoonful or two of hot water.

To make the jam filling. Put the raspberry jam into a bowl over hot water until it becomes soft. Press it through a wire sieve and allow to cool. Sprinkle the surface of the purée with caster sugar to prevent a skin forming.

To make up the cake. Spread the jam on to the first base, covering this with the second base, on to which spread the cream filling, covering it with the third base. Spread this with jam and any remaining cream filling and top with the fourth base.

To make the raspberry icing. Mix the ingredients to a spreading consistency and, using a hot, wetted palette-knife, spread the icing to the edges of the top (fourth) sponge. Garnish the cake with a collar of fresh raspberries.

Cranberry Cheesecake

A deliciously light and fluffy cheesecake, best eaten chilled.

Serves 8

6 **oz** digestive biscuits, crushed
3 **oz** butter, melted but cool
6 **oz** Ocean Spray fresh cranberries
¼ **pint** red wine
1 packet of raspberry jelly, cubed

4 **oz** caster sugar
4 **oz** cream cheese
finely grated zest of half a lemon
1 **tbsp** lemon juice
1 egg white, beaten until stiff

Mix the crushed biscuits with the butter and use to line the base and sides of an 8½-inch pie plate. Chill.

Simmer the cranberries in the wine until tender, then sieve. Return them to a gentle heat and add the jelly cubes and sugar, stirring until dissolved. Cool to the point of setting.

Beat the cheese with the lemon zest and juice until smooth. Stir in 4 tablespoons of the setting jelly. Fold in the stiffly whisked egg white. Spoon half the rest of the jelly into the crust. Chill quickly.

Pile the cheese mixture on top. Refrigerate to set. When the rest of the jelly is set, chop it with a damp knife on wet greaseproof paper, and use it for decoration.

Toffee Cake

Ideal for a children's birthday treat.

Serves 8

8 oz unsalted butter, softened
8 oz caster sugar
2 tsps vanilla essence
4 eggs, beaten

4 oz plain chocolate
6 oz plain flour
4 oz walnut halves, crushed

Pre-heat the oven to Gas 3/325°F/170°C.

Put the chocolate to melt in a bowl over a pan of simmering water.

Cream the butter, sugar and essence until light and fluffy. Gradually beat in the eggs. Mix in the melted chocolate, then the flour and crushed nuts.

Spoon into a well-buttered cake tin, approximately 9×12 inches, and bake for 40–45 minutes. Allow to cool a little. Turn on to a wire cooling rack and cut into 3-inch fingers before cooling completely.

MERINGUES

Meringues first appear under a different guise in 'To Make Cream Cakes', a 'receipt' in Elizabeth Raffald's *The Experienced English Housekeeper* (1769 edition). This gives a sure indication that meringues were popular in Britain well over two hundred years ago. In the original recipe, the reader is bidden to 'beat the whites of nine eggs to a stiff froth' before 'shaking in softly' double-refined sugar. The meringues were then sandwiched together with a purée of fresh raspberries – and whipped cream, no less!

Today the meringue is still the most popular of the fancy cakes presented at tea-time, and although we no longer fill them with raspberries, we do sandwich them with rich cream. I now return the favour, so to speak, by garnishing each cream meringue with three or four fresh raspberries.

Light as air, crisp outside and aerated inside, meringue can form the basis of many delicious cakes and desserts. Pipe it into cones or baskets, or simply spoon it on to lined baking trays and literally dry it out at a very low temperature. After cooling, meringues will keep for about a week in an air-tight container. Serve them filled with whipped cream and, if liked, fruit.

Here are some guidelines for successful meringues.

* The whisk or beaters and the bowl used must be absolutely clean, free from any grease and dry.
* Ideally, use egg whites from 2–3-day-old eggs that are at room temperature. When separating, be very careful to avoid even the slightest trace of yolk in the whites.
* Use caster sugar or equal quantities of caster and icing sugar.
* Line the baking tray with greaseproof paper which may be used more than once.

Basic Meringues

Makes approximately 12–16 shells or 6–8 whole pairs

2 large egg whites
their exact weight (which can be approximately 2½–4 oz) in caster sugar

Line a baking tray with aluminium foil.

In a large bowl, whisk the egg whites until stiff. Sprinkle half the sugar over them and continue to whisk until the texture is smooth and close, and stands in stiff peaks when the whisk is removed. Lightly fold in the remaining sugar with a metal balloon whisk.

Pre-heat the oven to Gas ½/250°F/130°C.

Using a metal spoon and a spatula, spoon the mixture into ovals on the baking tray. Alternatively, spoon the meringue into a fabric piping bag fitted with a large star nozzle and pipe it into cone or finger shapes.

Bake for 3–4 hours or until dry. Cool on a wire rack. Sandwich together with whipped cream shortly before serving.

Hazelnut Cake

This recipe was adapted by Elisabeth Smith, my wife, for use in the kitchens of my restaurant, Foxhill, in Yorkshire way back in 1955. The original meringue 'bases' are from one of Maria Floris's books. At Foxhill, two full cakes were sandwiched together with 8 oz fresh (or whole frozen) raspberries, topped with ½ pint whipped heavy cream, before the second cake was placed in position and dredged heavily with icing sugar.

Malcolm Reid and Colin Long from The Box Tree Restaurant in Ilkley enjoyed this so much that they introduced it into the menu at their beautiful restaurant and have, over the years, refined and developed it into a multi-layered gâteau. However, much as I enjoy theirs, I still hanker after my own rough-hewn and crunchy textured version.

It adds a further note of luxury if you pour a double measure of Kirsch or Maraschino into the cream before whipping it.

Serves 8–10

5 largish egg whites
10 oz caster sugar
6 oz toasted hazelnuts, finely crushed

8 oz whole raspberries (fresh or frozen)
½ pint whipped cream, lightly sweetened

Pre-heat the oven to Gas 5/375°F/190°C.

Stiffly beat the egg whites as for a meringue, incorporating half the sugar as you beat and the second half towards the end of the beating time as the meringue 'peaks'. Fold in the crushed hazelnuts with a slotted spoon.

Divide the mixture evenly between two 8-inch sandwich tins which have been lined with aluminium foil. Bake for 35–40 minutes.

The cake bases can be made days in advance and stored in an air-tight tin. However, do not assemble the cakes for serving too far in advance as the raspberries will make the base-cake too soggy.

An hour or so before you want to serve, place the first cake on a piece of greaseproof paper. Cover it with the raspberries and, using a 1-inch star nozzle, pipe a wall of the whipped cream around. Fill in with the remaining cream. Top with the second cake, crusty side up, and dredge the top heavily with sieved icing sugar. Use a large fish slice to assist in lifting the cake – which is fragile – on to a serving plate.

Walnut and Pineapple Meringue Cake

Ideal for a special Sunday tea in the garden, or as a rich pudding after a dinner. Try sipping a glass of crème de cacao with it as you munch away.

Serves 8–10

7 large egg whites
15 oz caster sugar, sieved
9 oz walnuts, crushed
1 small pineapple
1 pint double cream

2 tbsps Kirsch (optional)
1 level tbsp icing sugar
2 pieces glacé pineapple, cut into
   small pieces, to decorate (optional)

Pre-heat the oven to Gas 5/375°F/190°C.

Butter the sides and bases and paper-line the bases only, of three 8-inch sandwich tins (or make the cakes in batches to suit your supply of such tins: the mixture holds well enough for them to be cooked in batches).

Beat the egg whites until they stand in peaks. Beat in half the sugar, bringing the mixture back to stiff peak consistency. Using a balloon whisk, quickly whisk in the remaining sugar and cut and fold in the crushed nuts.

Divide the mixture into three parts, pour equal amounts into the prepared tins and bake for 20 minutes. If, after 20 minutes, there is evidence of scorching, reduce the oven temperature to Gas 4/350°F/180°C, and add a further 10 minutes to the baking time. These cake bases are quite fragile, so turn them carefully on to a wire cooling tray. Remove the papers and leave the cakes to cool.

Peel, core and chop the pineapple. Whip the cream with the Kirsch and icing sugar until it stands in peaks.

Place one of the cakes upside down on a serving dish. Pipe round a collar of cream, then fill the centre with the chopped pineapple. Arrange the second cake on top, the right way up. Spread with the remaining cream. Arrange the third cake on top of that. Dredge with icing sugar, a few blobs of cream and the glacé pineapple if used.

Cut into pieces with a serrated knife. Serve the same day, as the cake will soften – though some people think it the better for it!

Praline Vacherin Cake

Meringues and praline are the *bêtes noires* of many otherwise confident cooks. However, take them step by step and make this delicious vacherin.

Serves 8–10

Almond meringue

6 egg whites
12 oz caster sugar, sieved
4 oz nibbed almonds, toasted

Praline

8 oz flaked almonds
8 oz caster sugar

Filling

1½ **pints** double cream
2 **fl. oz** Amaretto di Saronno
1 **oz** caster sugar
12 glacé apricots, diced using a hot, wetted knife

To decorate

12 glacé apricots, roughly chopped

To make the meringue. Pre-heat the oven to Gas 1/275°F/140°C. Whisk the egg whites until stiff. Gradually whisk in half the sugar, stopping when the mixture begins to subside. Fold in the remaining sugar and the nibbed almonds.

Line two baking trays with buttered greaseproof paper. Draw a 10–11-inch circle on each piece of paper. Spread the meringue mixture in the circles and bake for 1–1¼ hours until beige and crisp.

Turn out on to cooling racks and carefully remove the paper. Leave to cool.

Crucial. *To make the praline.* Mix the almonds and sugar in a heavy-based pan over a low heat. Stir all the time and cook until caramelised. When the mixture is a deep golden colour, tip it on to an oiled tray and leave it to cool completely.

Using a food processor or a rolling pin, crush 3 oz of the praline roughly and the remaining 5 oz finely.

To make the filling. Whip the cream, Amaretto di Saronno and sugar until thick. Divide the cream mixture in two and mix the diced apricots and roughly crushed praline into half of it.

Place one of the meringues on a serving plate. Spread it with the praline and cream mixture and put the second meringue on top of it. Carefully spread the remaining cream over the top and sides. Sprinkle the finely crushed praline on top and press any that remains on to the sides. Decorate with glacé apricots.

Almond and Apricot Vacherin

Serves 8–10

Cake bases

5 egg whites
10 oz caster sugar
6 oz toasted almonds, crushed

Almond custard ice-cream

8 egg yolks
3 oz caster sugar
1 pint single cream or half cream
  and half milk
1 tsp almond essence or 2 tbsps
  Kirsch

Filling

12 fresh apricots, stoned, soaked in
  2 tbsps Amaretto di Saronno,
  crème de banane, Kirsch, brandy
  or other liqueur
½ pint double cream, whipped to
  piping consistency
icing sugar

To make the cake bases. Pre-heat the oven to Gas 5/375°F/190°C. Stiffly beat the egg whites, as for meringues, incorporating half the sugar as you beat and the second half towards the end of the beating when the mixture must stand in peaks. Using a slotted spoon, fold in the crushed almonds.

Divide the mixture evenly between two 8-inch sandwich tins lined with aluminium foil. Bake for 35–40 minutes. Leave to cool a little before turning on to a wire cooling rack and removing the papers.

These bases can be made days in advance and stored in an air-tight tin or frozen.

To make the almond custard ice-cream. Beat the egg yolks and sugar until fluffy and all the granules of sugar are dissolved. Bring the cream and almond essence to the boil and pour it over the egg mixture, whisking briskly all the time.

Arrange the bowl over a pan of boiling water and, stirring gently all the time, thicken the custard until it is the consistency of double cream and coats the back of a wooden spoon well; if you draw your finger across the back it should leave a definite trail.

Leave the custard to cool completely, then chill it, either following the instructions for your ice-cream maker or in a suitable container which will fit into the ice-making compartment of your refrigerator or freezer. If the latter method is used, stir the mixture every 30 minutes or so to prevent ice crystals from forming.

To form the ice-cream-layer. Line an 8-inch sandwich tin with plastic film. Press the ice-cream into this to make a thick round cake. Freeze.

To assemble the vacherin. Turn out one of the meringue bases on to a serving plate. Remove the ice-cream from its mould and take off the plastic film. Place the ice-cream on top of the meringue base. Pipe a collar of whipped cream round the edge of the ice-cream. Fill with apricot halves and splash with a suitable liqueur.

Rest the second meringue on top of this and dredge liberally with icing sugar.

Small Cakes

Madeleines

Makes 20–24 cakes

4 oz caster sugar, sieved
4 eggs
3½ oz self-raising flour, sieved twice
3½ oz unsalted butter, melted but cool

1 tsp finely grated orange or lemon zest or 1 tbsp rose or orange flower water

Pre-heat the oven to Gas 5/375°F/190°C.

In a bowl, using a rotary or hand whisk, whisk the eggs, sugar, zest and flower water until *thick* and pale and the whisk leaves a distinct trail when drawn across the mixture. Whisk in the cool melted butter, then lightly but thoroughly cut and fold in the flour.

Lightly butter and dredge with caster sugar two trays of bun tins or madeleine tins (these can be bought in specialist cook shops). Two-thirds fill them with the mixture. Bake for 10 minutes or until risen, golden brown and resistant to light pressure from your forefinger. Remove to a wire cooling rack.

Depending on the size of your tins and on how hard you whisk (upon which will depend the volume of the mixture), you may need to make a third tray of the buns.

Florentines

Home-made Florentines are quite delicious, if a little involved to make. As timing is important, make them in batches. Although the chocolate base is traditional, they are also very good without it.

Makes 8 cakes

2 oz unsalted butter
6 oz caster sugar
1 oz self-raising flour
½ pint double cream
8 oz blanched almonds, roughly chopped

4 oz chopped mixed peel
3 oz angelica, washed and chopped
3 oz glacé cherries, washed and chopped
8 oz plain chocolate

Pre-heat the oven to Gas 5/375°F/190°C.

Melt the butter with the sugar then stir in the flour. Cook for 1 minute, then stir in the cream and cook again until thickened.

Stir in the nuts, peel, angelica and cherries.

Line two baking trays with non-stick paper and put 4 dessertspoons of mixture on to each, spacing well. Pat down to a round shape with the back of a spoon.

Bake each tray for about 15 minutes or until a mid-brown. Pat the edges back to a neat round shape with a knife while the biscuits firm up on the trays, then after about 5 minutes lift the biscuits with a palette-knife on to a wire cooling rack.

When the biscuits are cold and firm, melt the chocolate in a bowl over a pan of gently simmering water. Turn the Florentines upside down, and coat each with a generous teaspoon of chocolate, spreading with a knife and marking in wavy lines with a fork. Cool upside down until set.

Store in an air-tight tin. Florentines are best eaten within 24 hours, otherwise they go a little chewy – but are still quite delicious.

Mini Iced Cakes

Makes 20–30 cakes

1 2lb oblong Madeira Cake (see pp. 129–30)
½ lb apricot or raspberry jam, sieved

Icing

2 egg whites
1 lb icing sugar, sieved
1 tsp glycerine
boiling water, liqueur or lemon juice

To make the icing. Beat the egg whites to slacken them. Beat in the icing sugar and glycerine. Adjust to a strong coating consistency with your chosen liquid.

Test the icing on the back of an egg cup: it should take quite a few seconds to fall over the edge and down.

Trim the cake to an oblong. Carefully cut it across into four even layers, approximately ½ inch thick. Sandwich two layers together with the jam. Cut these into approximately 1-inch lengths, then 1-inch cubes. Arrange the cubes on a wire rack.

Gently bang the rack to shake away surplus cake crumbs, then place the cubes on a spotlessly clean work surface.

Coat the cubes with icing (give them two coats if the icing is too thin). Scrape up any icing overflow and re-use it or refrigerate it for future use.

Optional additives for the icing:

1–2 drops of instant coffee, Continental-blend, dissolved in 1 tbsp boiling water
lemon juice, and 1–2 drops of yellow colouring or 1 drop of green-coloured pistachio essence

4 oz toasted almond nibs added to coffee icing
12 oz plain chocolate plus 2 oz unsalted butter, dissolved over hot water (do not use icing mixture with this coating)

Lady's Fingers

Makes approximately 36 fingers

3 large eggs, separated
6 oz caster sugar
1 tsp vanilla essence
1 tbsp caster sugar

a pinch of salt
6 oz self-raising flour, sieved
icing sugar

Pre-heat the oven to Gas 2/300°F/160°C.

Beat the egg yolks, vanilla essence and sugar with a balloon or electric hand whisk until the mixture 'ribbons', or leaves a distinct trail when the whisk is drawn through it.

In a separate bowl, beat the egg whites with the salt and 1 tablespoon of caster sugar until they peak.

Sieve and mix the flour into the yolk mixture. Cut and fold in the beaten egg whites. The mixture should be 'airy'.

Fit a piping bag with a ½-inch plain nozzle. Pipe 4-inch lengths of the mixture on to lightly but evenly buttered and floured baking trays.

Dredge lightly with icing sugar, brushing away any surplus from the sheet with a dry pastry brush.

Bake for 15–20 minutes. Remove to a wire cooling rack, using a spatula. Dredge with extra icing sugar.

These delicate sponge fingers can also be used for dinner, served with ice-creams or fruit salad.

Cream Sponge Fingers

Take two Lady's Fingers from the above recipe. Smear the first well with sieved home-made raspberry or apricot jam. Pipe a column of sweetened whipped cream on to this, then lay the second finger on top.

Orange and Ginger Gobbet Cakes

So called by me as these little cakes illustrate perfectly that eighteenth-century word for a mouthful. Flavoured with orange and ginger, they can be served not only at tea-time but also with coffee after dinner, where they would make a tasty and lightweight conclusion to the meal instead of a pudding.

Makes about 4 dozen baby buns

4 oz unsalted butter
4 oz caster sugar
juice and finely grated zest of a small
    orange

3 oz self-raising flour
2 level tsps baking powder
2 eggs
slices of stem ginger (about 4 pieces)

Pre-heat the oven to Gas 5/375°F/190°C.

Cream the butter and sugar with the orange zest. Sieve the flour and baking powder together. Beat the eggs and gradually fold them into the creamed mixture. Add the sieved flour, using a little orange juice to arrive at a dropping consistency.

Use mini tartlet tins if you have them (the best kind are manufactured by Tala) and butter them well. Put teaspoons of the mixture into the tins, with a slice of stem ginger on top. Bake for 12–15 minutes or until done.

Orange Blossom Cakes

Makes 16–20 cakes

Sponge

12 oz unsalted butter, softened
12 oz caster sugar
6 large eggs, beaten
10 oz self-raising flour
2 tsps baking powder
6 oz ground rice
4 tsps finely grated orange zest
¼ **pint** fresh orange juice, strained

Butter cream

4 oz unsalted butter, softened
4 oz icing sugar, sieved
2 tbsps any orange-flavoured
    liqueur (Cointreau, Grand
    Marnier, etc.)

Marzipan

1 lb marzipan (bought variety or
    make up half the quantity on
    p. 136)
icing sugar
jam or jelly, sieved

Icing

3 oz icing sugar, sieved into a bowl
1 drop of orange colouring
1 tsp glycerine
2 tsps triple-strength orange flower
    water or orange liqueur

Pre-heat the oven to Gas 3/325°F/170°C.

Butter and line with buttered paper the base of a tray measuring approximately 10×8×3 inches.

Cream the butter and sugar together until light and fluffy. Beat in the eggs gradually, adding a sprinkling of flour to prevent curdling.

Beat in the orange zest and a little of the juice. Sieve the flour, baking powder and ground rice together, and cut and fold it into the butter and egg mixture. Mix to a soft dropping consistency, using more juice (or cold water) if necessary.

Spoon into the baking tray. Level the top. Bake for $1\frac{1}{4}$–$1\frac{1}{2}$ hours or until the cake is springy to the touch and is leaving the sides of the tin. Leave for 10 minutes to cool.

Turn out on to a wire cooling rack. Remove the paper carefully. When cool, trim the top level, trim off the browned sides, and cut the cake in half across the middle.

Beat all the ingredients for the butter cream to a smooth paste. Spread it on the cut surface of the split cake and cover with the second layer of cake.

Cut the cake into $1\frac{1}{2}$–2-inch squares or, using a plastic aerosol top as a template, cut it into rounds with a long pointed knife. (Use all the debris for a trifle or Queen's Pudding).

To cover with marzipan, stand the sieved jam in a bowl in a pan of simmering water to warm and melt somewhat. Make a template of paper $\frac{1}{8}$ inch deeper than the cut cakes and $\frac{1}{8}$ inch longer than their circumference.

Knead the marzipan until completely pliable, working on a surface well dredged with icing sugar. Use the heel of the hand to do this: it takes quite a bit of strength initially. Form into a rectangular block, then press and roll this into a sheet $\frac{1}{8}$ inch thick.

Using the template and a ruler as a guide, cut out the required number of strips and trim lengths to size. Using the same aerosol top, cut out the required number of circles. Brush one side of the marzipan strips with jam or jelly, then wrap it round each cake. Brush one side of circle and fit it inside the top, jam down. Prise or crimp the edges together. Dredge with icing sugar, or coat with icing made by mixing together the icing ingredients with boiling water so that the icing *just* flows.

Brownies

There are many different recipes for Brownies, some more 'cakey' than others. I prefer mine to be chewy, and this is what these are. They are also quite sweet – and all the better for that, too!

Makes 16–20 squares

4 oz plain chocolate	**2 eggs**, lightly beaten
4 oz unsalted butter	**4 oz** self-raising flour
12 oz caster sugar	$\frac{1}{2}$ **tsp** salt
1 tsp vanilla essence	**4–6 oz** walnuts, roughly crushed

Pre-heat the oven to Gas 4/350°F/180°C.

Butter and line an 8-inch square tin.

Soften the chocolate in a bowl over hot water. Beat in the butter away from the heat. Beat in the sugar and vanilla essence. Beat in the eggs a little at a time. Sieve together the flour and salt, and quickly stir them in. Fold in the nuts.

Spoon and spread the mixture evenly into the cake tin. Bake for 35–40 minutes. Allow to cool slightly, then cut into squares. Store in an air-tight tin, or freeze.

Chocolate Coconut Squares

Makes approximately 24 squares

For the base

- **4 oz** unsalted butter, softened
- **2 tbsps** cocoa powder
- **2 oz** caster sugar
- **1 egg**, beaten
- **2 tsps** vanilla essence
- **8 oz** digestive biscuit crumbs
- **5 oz** desiccated coconut

Icing

- **4 oz** unsalted butter, softened
- **2 tbsps** single cream or top of the milk
- **10 oz** icing sugar, sieved

To decorate

- **4 oz** plain chocolate

To make the base. Melt the butter, cocoa powder and sugar in a pan over a low heat. When melted and mixed together, remove from the heat. Add the beaten egg, vanilla essence, biscuit crumbs and coconut.

Pour the mixture into a $\frac{1}{2}\times9\times12$-inch Swiss roll tin. Level the top and put to chill for 30 minutes.

To make the icing. Cream the butter, stir in the cream or top of milk, add the sieved icing sugar and beat until smooth. Spread the icing over the chilled base mixture and return to the fridge to set.

Meanwhile, melt the chocolate in a bowl over hot water. Put it into a piping bag fitted with a $\frac{1}{16}$-inch plain nozzle.

Mark the set mixture into 1-inch squares (or any other shape you wish). Dribble the melted chocolate over the tops. Refrigerate again until set, then cut into the squares or other appropriate shapes.

Coconut Macaroons

The name derives from the French *macaron*, which is distantly related to the Italian *maccaroni*, which in turn (dubiously) means paste.

Almond Macaroons (see pp. 209–10) have been popular sweetmeats in England since mediaeval times. Coconut Macaroons are a Victorian version of the original recipe using desiccated coconut in place of ground almonds. Made this way, children love them!

Makes 12

2 egg whites	rice paper
6 oz caster sugar	glacé cherries
8 oz desiccated coconut	

Pre-heat the oven to Gas 3/325°F/160°C. Lay the rice paper on ungreased baking trays with the smooth side of the paper uppermost.

Whisk the egg whites until stiff. Whisk in the sugar and then fold in the coconut.

Pile the mixture in twelve pyramid shapes on the rice paper. Top with a small slice of cherry.

Bake for 20–30 minutes or until a pale golden brown.

Leave on the baking tray until cold. Cut around the rice paper to separate.

Cherry Whirls

Makes 16–18 whirls

6 oz unsalted butter	**6 oz** plain flour, sieved
2 oz icing sugar, sieved	**16–18** halves of glacé cherries
1 tsp vanilla essence	

Pre-heat the oven to Gas 3/325°F/160°C.

Cream the butter until it is light and soft. Add the icing sugar and vanilla essence and beat until light and smooth, then stir in the flour.

Transfer the mixture to a large piping bag fitted with a 1-inch nozzle. Pipe 16–18 fairly small whirls on to two buttered baking trays and top each whirl with half a cherry. Bake in the centre of the oven for 20 minutes or until a pale golden colour.

Leave on the baking tray to set for 5 minutes before transferring carefully to a wire rack. Store in an air-tight container when cold.

Mini Mocha Éclairs

Makes about 20 éclairs

choux pastry (see pp. 187–8)

Mocha pastry cream

4 egg yolks
1 tsp cornflour
1½ oz caster sugar
½ pint single cream
2 oz unsalted butter
2 tsps instant coffee, Continental-blend, dissolved in 2 tbsps boiling water

Mocha icing

8 oz icing sugar, sieved
1 dsp almond oil or glycerine
coffee essence (as before)

Alternative liqueur cream filling

1 pint double cream
2 oz icing sugar
finely grated zest of an orange
2 tbsps Cointreau or Grand Marnier
a drop each of yellow and red colouring, mixed to a very pale orange colour

Alternative liqueur icing

8 oz icing sugar, sieved
2 tbsps Cointreau or Grand Marnier
2 tbsps glycerine (not essential, but helps keep icing glossy)
1 tsp finely grated orange zest

To make the choux pastry cases. Follow the instructions on pp. 187–8, piping the dough into 2–2½-inch fingers.

To make the mocha pastry cream. Whisk the egg yolks with the cornflour and sugar. Bring the cream to the boil and pour it over the egg mixture, whisking all the time. Return the mixture to the pan and, over a low heat, stir until thick. Remove from the heat and whisk in the butter, bit by bit. Beat in coffee essence to taste and leave to cool.

Put the mixture into a piping bag fitted with a plain ½-inch nozzle. Make an incision in the side of each éclair, insert the nozzle and fill with the mocha cream.

To make the mocha icing. Put the icing sugar into a bowl. Add the oil and enough coffee essence to make into a spreadable icing. Spread a little on each éclair.

These mini éclairs are also delicious when filled with a liqueur cream filling and finished with a liqueur icing. To make the filling, whip the cream, then add the icing sugar, orange zest, liqueur and colouring. Fill as before. For liqueur icing, put the icing sugar into a bowl, then add the liqueur, glycerine (if used) and the orange zest. Spread a little on to each éclair.

Chocolate Fudge

It is quite useful to have a plate of fudge at tea-time for those who kid themselves that they don't want to eat cake, yet want a little something sweet!

Makes ½ lb

4 oz plain chocolate, broken up
2 oz unsalted butter
1 tsp vanilla essence

2 tbsps milk
1 lb icing sugar, sieved

Line a Swiss roll tin with plastic film.

Melt the chocolate and butter in a bowl over a pan of boiling water. Stir to ensure even melting. Remove the bowl from the heat. Stir in the essence and milk. Beat in the icing sugar a little at a time.

Turn the mixture into the tin. Spread and level with a palette-knife to ½-inch thick. Cool and chill in the fridge. Turn out and remove the plastic film.

Cut into squares or oblongs. Wrap each piece in coloured tissue paper for added interest.

Brandy Snaps

Makes 20–24

4 oz unsalted butter
4 oz caster sugar
4 oz golden syrup
4 oz plain flour

½ tsp mixed spice (optional)
½ tsp ground ginger
strained juice of half a lemon

Pre-heat the oven to Gas 5/375°F/190°C.

Line two baking trays with greaseproof paper.

Put the butter, sugar and syrup into a pan and heat gently until melted. Remove from the heat. Sieve the flour, spice and ginger together, then add to the melted mixture. Mix in the juice. Mix well and drop teaspoonfuls of the mixture on to the lined trays allowing plenty of room for the mixture to spread.

Bake for 5–6 minutes or until bubbly and golden brown. Bake them in batches, as they harden quickly. Remove from the oven and, as the mixture begins to firm up, roll each quickly around a greased wooden-spoon handle. Leave until set, then twist slightly and remove to a wire rack to cool.

Repeat with the remaining mixture. If liked, fill with whipped brandy cream, made from $\frac{1}{2}$ pint double cream beaten to stiff peaks with 1 fl. oz brandy and 1 oz icing sugar.

Do not fill more than 30 minutes in advance of serving as they quickly soften.

Note: This same mixture is used for making crisp cups to hold ice-creams or sorbets. These are moulded over the rounded butt of a rolling pin or over a suitably shaped round-bowled cup or tin mould.

Petits Fours

Petits fours, small iced cakes and stuffed fruits have a place on the afternoon-tea table in the 1980s, not just because they are attractive and add an extra dimension to your menu but also because they appeal to the diet-conscious who, in spite of themselves, have a sweet tooth.

Stuffed Fruits

Makes 15–18 fruits

30–36 pieces of fruit – dates, glacé cherries, glacé apricots, soaked prunes, halves of walnuts or pecans, etc.

1 lb marzipan (bought variety or see p. 136)

Roll out ½-inch pieces of marzipan and sandwich them between two pieces of your chosen fruit or fruits. Press the two halves together, dredge with caster or icing sugar and place each fruit into a paper *petit four* case.

Variations

Into each 1 lb of marzipan, knead well any of the following:

4 oz toasted hazelnuts, crushed
1 tbsp finely grated orange zest, soaked in 1 tbsp rum, brandy or Cointreau
4 oz pistachio nuts, roughly crushed

4 oz chocolate chips or grated chocolate
4 oz walnuts, crushed and soaked in 2 tbsps rum or brandy

Marzipan Strawberries

Makes approximately 30–36 pieces

8 oz caster sugar
4 fl. oz water
tip of a tsp cream of tartar, dissolved in a little water

8 oz ground almonds, sieved
a small tsp rose water (triple strength) or lemon juice
red and green colouring

Bring the sugar and water to the boil. Add the cream of tartar. Continue boiling to a heat of 240°F/116°C (measured on an all-purpose food thermometer). Remove from the heat.

Stir in the ground almonds and flower water and enough *drops* of colour to give a pretty strawberry pink. If you want to make different colours, then add the colouring at the kneading stage, having divided the paste into appropriate batches.

When cool, turn the paste on to a work surface dusted with icing sugar, and knead until smooth. Leave for a day or two to mature, wrapped in greaseproof paper and in an air-tight container in the refrigerator.

Form into cylinders 1 inch in diameter. Cut these into pieces and form into strawberry shapes. Leave to 'set'.

Make marzipan leaves using green colour in a little of the original marzipan, or clip plastic leaves off some suitable cheap plastic flowers. Artificial leaves can be purchased for this purpose. To arrive at a more realistic strawberry, meticulously mottle the surface of the formed 'fruits' using a small paint brush and red colouring.

PASTRIES

Pastry

English cookery embraces many different types of pastries, from the simplest shortcrust through rich, melt-in-the-mouth, sweetened flan pastry to the more complicated puff or flaky varieties.

Ordinary shortcrust pastry is the most widely used as a base for both sweet and savoury recipes. Rich shortcrust pastry has a higher proportion of fat to flour, with sugar included, and eggs are used as the liquid ingredient. It should be rolled slightly thinner than basic shortcrust pastry and always baked crisp. Puff or flaky pastry is the richest pastry; it takes longer to make and also takes a little practice to get perfect. It rises spectacularly into lots of flaky layers and is used for such recipes as vol-au-vents or *millefeuilles* – 'thousand leaves'. That said, I strongly recommend you use a good commercial variety, which when well baked gives good results, rather than laboriously making your own.

Choux pastry uses a completely different method: first cooking on the hob before shaping (piping) and baking. It is used for such cakes as éclairs and profiteroles.

Here are some guidelines for successful pastry.

* When possible, make the pastry in a cool, dry atmosphere.
* Handle the pastry as little as possible, using only your fingertips if you are rubbing the fats in by hand; or use a wire pastry blender or food processor.
* Use ice-cold water for mixing.
* In all cases, you are aiming to *surround* particles of fat with flour. This gives the pastry its shortness. When a 'heavy hand' is used, or the pastry is overworked by machine, or has too much water added to it, it toughens.
* Water encourages the gluten content of the flour to develop, causing elasticity. So, particularly when making pastry in a food processor, take care to use the specified amount of water.
* Use a lightly floured work surface to roll out on. Roll the pastry lightly, rotating it regularly to keep an even shape; try to use even pressure with both hands and avoid stretching the pastry unnecessarily as it will only shrink back whilst baking, thus spoiling the finished shape.
* Bake pastry in a hot oven (Gas 7/425°F/220°C) to start with, then lower the temperature to Gas 4/350°F/180°C to dry out.
* Whenever possible, chill the pastry between making and rolling out. This allows the gluten content of the flour to relax.
* For most recipes it is better to bake the pastry blind.

Shortcrust Pastry

8 oz plain flour
½ tsp salt
3 oz lard

2 oz unsalted butter
3 tbsps water

Sieve the flour and salt into a large bowl. With your fingertips or a pastry blender, rub in the fats until the mixture resembles fine breadcrumbs.

Sprinkle the water over the flour and stir together with a fork. Gather into a ball with floured fingertips and knead lightly for a few seconds to give a firm, smooth dough. Slip the pastry into a plastic bag and chill for at least 30 minutes.

Roll out on a lightly floured board, rolling evenly in one direction only, turning the pastry round occasionally but not turning it over. Avoid unnecessary pulling or stretching. Roll to about ⅛-inch thickness.

Rich Shortcrust Pastry

8 oz plain flour
½ tsp salt
6 oz unsalted butter

3 tbsps icing sugar
1 egg plus 1 egg yolk

Sieve the flour, sugar and salt into a large bowl. With your fingertips or a pastry blender, rub in the butter until the mixture resembles fine breadcrumbs.

Beat together the egg and the yolk, then stir into the flour mixture with a fork. With floured fingers collect into a ball and very lightly knead to give a smooth, firm dough.

Slip the pastry into a floured plastic bag and chill for 30 minutes before rolling out thinly.

Pre-baked Pastry Cases

1 batch of rich shortcrust pastry (see
above) will make two 9-inch
pastry cases

Chill the pastry for 30 minutes after lining pie-plates or flan rings. Line the pastry cases with greaseproof paper and fill with dried peas or crushed aluminium foil. Bake at Gas 7/425°F/220°C for 10 minutes. Reduce the temperature to Gas 5/375°F/200°C and remove the peas and paper.

Continue to bake for a further 20–25 minutes or until the pastry looks dry and appetisingly brown. Cool before filling. Baked pastry cases freeze well, in which case defrost before adding a filling.

Flaky or Puff Pastry

The minimum viable amount when making flaky pastry is 1 lb flour and 1 lb butter. Flaky pastry can be stored successfully, and almost indefinitely, in the freezer in ½lb pieces.

1 lb plain flour	**7 fl. oz** cold water
½ **tsp** salt	**1 tsp** lemon juice
1 lb unsalted butter	

Sieve the flour and salt into a bowl. With the fingers or a pastry cutter, cut or rub in 4 oz of the butter. Stir in the water and lemon juice with a fork.

Turn the dough on to a floured board and knead it until it is pliable. Form this into an oblong. Put it into a floured plastic bag and leave to rest in the refrigerator for 2 hours. (This will help the elasticity – gluten – to become more workable.)

Using a rolling pin and with the butter between two sheets of plastic film, work the remainder of the butter into a rectangle roughly 7×4 inches. The butter should be workable but not too soft: if it is too soft, put it back into the fridge.

Now roll the dough into a rectangle 13–14 inches long and 7–8 inches wide. Keep the work surface lightly dredged with flour, but use a pastry brush continually to remove any excess flour from the pastry as you roll.

Set the block of butter centrally on the rolled pastry. Roll out the sides where the butter is by an inch or so; fold these two flaps over the ends of the butter block. Now fold the top of the pastry over to the bottom edge of the butter. Brush away any flour. Then bring the bottom edge of the pastry up and over to the top edge, forming a neat parcel.

Turn the pastry clockwise so that the flaps are like a book. Gently press the open side, top edge and bottom edge with the rolling pin. Then, starting at the top, press very gently with both hands at ½-inch intervals down the block of pastry, using light, even pressure and watching carefully that you don't press it out of line or push the butter through.

Gradually start *rolling* the pastry until you have a rectangle the same size as the one you started with: 7–8×13–14 inches. Brush the surface of the pastry again, dredging the work surface if necessary.

Fold the pastry as before and roll again, folding in exactly the same way. You have now given the pastry a double turn. Slide the block of pastry into a floured plastic bag and put it to set in the refrigerator for an hour. This will also harden up the butter again.

Repeat the process again – rolling, folding, turning twice, *gently* pressing at ½-inch intervals before gradually changing to a light, rolling movement over the whole surface of the pastry. Take care at all times that the butter never bursts through the pastry. (If there are any signs of this happening, return the pastry to the fridge to set the butter.)

Return the pastry, in the floured plastic bag, to the refrigerator for another hour. When you are ready to use it, roll and fold it twice as before. You now have hundreds (486 to be exact) of layers of pastry and butter which, when baked in a hot oven, Gas 7/425°F/220°C, will puff up into delicate, butter-crisp layers. If you remember that you are aiming to have the two media, butter and dough, at the same consistency so that you are not forcing one against the other, you won't go wrong.

Choux Pastry

This is a light crisp pastry which trebles in size when cooked because of the air trapped inside it. Here are a few guidelines for success.

* Add all the flour at one fell swoop.
* Beat the mixture over the heat until it leaves the sides of the pan cleanly and forms a ball.
* The eggs should be added gradually and beaten in very thoroughly until the mixture has a good sheen.
* The mixture will handle more easily if it is chilled in the refrigerator in the piping bag for 30 minutes or so.
* Do not open the oven door during baking.
* Split open the baked pastry shells to let out any steam.
* Dampening the baking trays with cold water before piping helps to prevent sticking.

3 oz unsalted butter
4 fl. oz water
3¾ **oz** plain flour, sieved

3 medium eggs, beaten
a pinch of salt

Put the butter and water into a heavy-bottomed pan and heat gently until the butter has melted, then bring to the boil. Remove the pan from the heat.

Tip in the flour and the salt and beat thoroughly with a wooden spatula. Return the pan to a low heat and beat until the mixture forms a ball. Remove from the heat again and leave to cool for a minute or two.

Gradually beat in the eggs to give a piping consistency. Beat vigorously to trap in as much air as possible and until the mixture is shiny. If the mixture stops 'peaking', stop adding the beaten egg.

Spoon the mixture into a piping bag fitted with a ½-inch plain nozzle. Chill for 30 minutes.

Pre-heat the oven to Gas 6/400°F/200°C. Dampen a large baking tray. Pipe fingers for éclairs or small mounds for cream puffs (see below), cutting off the pastry with a wet knife.

Bake for 35 minutes or until well risen and golden brown. Slit to allow the steam to escape. Remove from the baking tray to a wire cooling rack.

Cream Puffs

Makes 20 puffs

Allow 3–4 inches between each piped mound of choux pastry.

Lightly butter some 2½-inch diameter dariole tins, and place over each mound. Bake as instructed for choux pastry. Do not be tempted to lift the tins for the first 25 minutes.

When they are ready, the 'puffs' should be quite dried out. They will have cracked tops.

Split and fill each puff with one of the cream fillings given below. Dredge well with icing sugar.

Chocolate Éclairs

Makes 12–16 éclairs

Pipe the choux pastry into 3-inch 'tubes'. Bake as instructed. Cool.

Split open and fill with either of the following creams and top with an icing.

Cream Filling I

1 pint double cream
1½ oz caster sugar

2 **fl. oz** liqueur of your choice
(Cointreau, Drambuie, apricot brandy) or 2 tsps vanilla essence

Whip together all the ingredients to piping consistency. Fill some of the cream into a piping bag fitted with a ½-inch star nozzle. Pipe a thick band of cream on the base of the split éclair. Dip each top into the icing and place it on top of the cream-filled half, icing uppermost.

Cream Filling II (English Custard Cream)

6 large egg yolks   **½ pint** single cream
2 oz caster sugar   **2 oz** unsalted butter, softened
1 heaped tsp cornflour   **1 tsp** vanilla essence
½ pint milk

In a bowl, cream the egg yolks and sugar until light and fluffy. Add the vanilla essence. Gradually beat in the cornflour.

Bring the milk and cream to the boil, remove from the heat and pour slowly over the creamed mixture, stirring (slowly at first) with a wire balloon whisk. As you add the milk, change to a more rapid whisking movement and whisk until smooth.

Return the pan to a low heat and, whisking all the time, allow the custard cream to boil. It should be thick enough to pipe, but not rigidly stiff. Remove from the heat and whisk in the softened butter. Allow to cool – when it will appear to thicken further.

Cover with plastic film to prevent a skin forming. When cold, pipe into the éclairs or choux buns.

Chocolate Icing I

6 oz plain chocolate, broken up   **¼ pint** thick cream

Melt the chocolate with the cream in a bowl over simmering water. Allow to cool, then beat until all is smooth.

Chocolate Icing II

6 oz icing sugar   2 drops of vanilla essence
2 oz cocoa powder   a little boiling water

Sieve the two dry ingredients into a bowl. Add the vanilla essence and spoonfuls of boiling water until you have a spreading consistency, beating well after each addition.

Mini Mocha Éclairs: *see p. 177*

Lardy Cake

'Shaley cake', as it is known in Wiltshire, is a flaky, rich, spicy fruit cake which can also be eaten hot as a pudding. If it has lost its freshness, refresh it in a medium oven for 10 minutes. Hampshire and Wiltshire are renowned for their lardy cakes.

1 tbsp dried or ½ oz fresh yeast	**2 oz** unsalted butter
½ pint warm water	**4 oz** caster sugar
1 tbsp caster sugar	**1 tsp** mixed spice
15 oz strong white flour	**3 oz** sultanas
2 tsps salt	**2 oz** lard
1 tbsp soya oil	a little extra oil

Grease a 10×8-inch loaf tin.

Mix the yeast, sugar and water in a small bowl and leave in a warm place for 10 minutes until frothy.

Sieve the flour and salt into a large bowl, stir in the yeast liquid and the oil. Mix to a soft dough. Knead on a lightly floured surface for 5 minutes.

Place the dough in a lightly oiled plastic bag and leave in a warm place for 1–1½ hours until it has doubled in size. Knock back the dough and knead again for 5 minutes.

Roll out the dough into an oblong ¼ inch thick. Cover two-thirds of the dough with flakes of the butter and sprinkle over 3 tablespoons of sugar, half the spice and some of the fruit. Fold and roll out as for puff pastry (see pp. 186–7); repeat with the lard, 3 tablespoons of sugar, and the remaining spice and fruit.

Fold and roll again. Fold again, to incorporate the fruit, and place in the prepared tin. Return to the oiled plastic bag and leave to rise in a warm place until doubled in size – about 1 hour.

Pre-heat the oven to Gas 7/425°F/220°C.

Brush the top with a little oil and sprinkle with the remaining sugar. With a sharp knife, mark a criss-cross pattern on the top. Bake for about 30 minutes or until a rich golden brown.

Turn out and cool on a wire rack. Serve warm or cold.

Shoofly Pie

Whether Shoofly Pie is from the stoves of America's Deep South, where it is said flies descended on this sweet, sticky pie and had to be shooed away, or from the Pennsylvanian Dutch, is open to conjecture. Whatever its origin, it's good. My youngest sister makes the pie with chopped figs or dates soaked in rum.

Serves 6–8

4 oz shortcrust pastry (see p. 185)

Filling

4 oz muscatel raisins
2 oz soft brown sugar
¼ tsp bicarbonate of soda
2 tbsps rum, whisky or water

Topping

4 oz plain flour
½ tsp cinnamon
¼ tsp nutmeg
¼ tsp ground ginger
2 oz unsalted butter
2 oz soft brown sugar

Soak the raisins, brown sugar and bicarbonate of soda in the alcohol overnight to plump up the fruit.

Pre-heat the oven to Gas 7/425°F/220°C.

Sieve the flour and spices for the topping. Rub in the butter.

Line a loose-bottomed 7-inch fluted pie tin with the pastry. Spoon in the soaked raisins. Spread the sieved flour and spices over and sprinkle the brown sugar on top. Bake for 15 minutes, then lower the heat to Gas 5/375°F/190°C for 20 minutes.

Serve warm or cold with thick cream, soured cream or ice-cream.

Wilfra Apple Cake

An ancient recipe from the North Yorkshire market town of Ripon, best served warm but almost as good cold. No custard or cream is needed.

Serves 9–12

Pastry

4 oz unsalted butter, cut into cubes
2 oz lard
8 oz plain flour
1 egg yolk

Filling

1 tsp vanilla essence

grated zest and juice of a lemon
4 large Bramley apples
2 tbsps golden syrup
4 oz caster sugar
6 oz Wensleydale cheese, crumbled, or cottage cheese
cream or top of the milk
caster sugar for dredging
icing sugar for dredging

To make the pastry case. Rub the fats into the flour. Beat the egg with 2 tablespoons iced water, add to the fats and flour, and gather the mixture into a pliable dough (don't knead too much). Leave to rest for an hour.

Pre-heat the oven to Gas 6/400°F/200°C.

Butter a Swiss roll tin measuring about 14×9 inches. Roll out half the pastry to line the tin. Prick all over. Bake blind for 15 minutes. Leave to cool.

To make the filling. Put the vanilla essence and the lemon zest and juice into a large glass or china bowl. Peel, core and slice the apples very thinly, tossing them in the juice mixture as you do so to keep them white.

Lay the apple slices evenly in the pastry case. Dribble the golden syrup over the top. Dredge with caster sugar. Pour over any remaining lemon juice. Crumble or spread the cheese over the top.

Reheat the oven to Gas 6/400°F/200°C.

To make the pastry lid. Roll out the remaining pastry. Brush the edges of the baked pastry case with cream or top of the milk. Fit the lid and decorate as liked. Brush the lid with cream or top of the milk and dredge with caster sugar.

Bake for 20 minutes. Reduce the heat to Gas 5/375°F/190°C for a further 20–25 minutes until the crust is crisp and golden brown.

Dredge with icing sugar and serve warm or cold, cut into 3–4-inch squares.

Apple Turnovers

Makes approximately 20 turnovers

12 oz shortcrust or rich shortcrust pastry (see p. 185)
1½ lb Cox's Orange Pippins

2 tbsps caster sugar
juice of a lemon, strained
1 egg, lightly beaten

Pre-heat the oven to Gas 6/400°F/200°C.

Cut the pastry into circles about 3 inches in diameter – use a large cutter, or a saucer as a template – then elongate into ovals.

In a lidded, non-stick pan, toss together the apples, sugar and lemon juice until the juices draw. Simmer until fallen. Cool, then mash with a fork, leaving some texture.

Spoon fruit pie-filling or mincemeat on to one half of the pastry. Brush the edges with lightly beaten egg and fold the second half over the first. Pinch the edges together and place on a baking tray.

Brush with a little beaten egg, or with cream, and sprinkle with sugar. Slash the tops two or three times with a sharp knife to allow steam to escape.

Bake for about 15–20 minutes or until a rich golden brown.

Currant and Mint and Apple Pasties

No self-respecting country tea-table would be complete without a Mint Pasty or an Apple Pasty. The quantities for *each* filling are for the amount of pastry given.

Serves 8–12

Pastry

8 oz plain flour
3 oz lard
2 oz unsalted butter
1 oz caster sugar
3–4 tbsps water to mix

Currant and Mint filling

3 oz unsalted butter
3 oz caster sugar

5 oz currants
3 oz sultanas
4 tbsps mint, freshly chopped

Apple filling

1 lb Cox's Orange Pippins, peeled, cored and thinly sliced
strained juice of a large lemon
2 oz unsalted butter
1–2 oz caster sugar

Make up the pastry in the usual way.

To make the currant and mint filling. Cream the butter and sugar together until light and fluffy. Mix in the fruits and mint.

To make the apple filling. Toss all the ingredients together in a non-stick pan until the juices start to draw. Cover and simmer for 10–15 minutes until the apples are soft. Cool, then mash roughly with a fork.

Pre-heat the oven to Gas 7/425°F/220°C.

On a floured work surface roll out the pastry to a rectangle no more than ¼ inch thick. Spoon and spread the chosen filling over one half of the pastry. Double over the other half. Damp the edges with water and pinch them together.

Slide the pasty on to a buttered baking tray. Sprinkle the top with a little extra sugar. Bake for 15–20 minutes.

Serve warm or cold, cut into 1½-inch squares.

New Lemon Cheese Tarts

I find it ironical that today, in the 1980s, we are paying lip-service to the French *tarte au citron* as it makes an appearance on almost every *nouvelle cuisine* menu, when our very own lemon cheese tarts, baked with a filling of home-made lemon cheese, are not only just as good but, if made by the hands of a pastrymaker in her own kitchen, are far superior.

Makes 12–18 tarts

¾ **lb** rich shortcrust pastry
  (see p. 185)
finely grated zest and juice of 2 large
  lemons

6 **oz** caster sugar
4 large eggs, beaten
¼ **pint** double cream
icing sugar for dredging

Pre-heat the oven to Gas 5/375°F/190°C. Make the pastry and line 12–18 well-buttered shallow 2–2½-inch tart tins. Bake blind for 10 minutes. Allow to cool.

Beat the eggs with the sugar in a heatproof bowl until the sugar is dissolved. Stir in the cream, then the lemon juice and zest.

Arrange the bowl over a pan of simmering water and stir the mixture until it is as thick as custard. Allow to cool.

Reheat the oven to Gas 3/325°F/170°C. Spoon the filling into the tartlet shells. Bake until set. Cool on a wire cooling tray.

Dredge with icing sugar before serving, or for added luxury and richness ice with a little icing made by sieving 4 oz icing sugar into a bowl and mixing with enough lemon juice to give a flowing icing.

Individual Red Fruit Tarts

Makes 12 tarts

Pastry

½ **lb** rich shortcrust pastry
  (see p. 185)
½ **lb** redcurrant jelly

Suitable fruits for filling

12 **oz** raspberries
72 grapes, skinned, seeded and
  halved
12 **oz** strawberries, hulled and
  quartered
12 **oz** redcurrants, picked

Pre-heat the oven to Gas 6/400°F/200°C.

Lightly butter twelve shallow tart tins 2–2½ inches in diameter. Line with thinly rolled pastry, and bake these blind until golden brown and completely crisp through – this can take 15 minutes, but take care you don't burn the pastry. Lift on to a cooling tray.

Melt the redcurrant jelly in a small pan over a minimal heat, stirring slowly all the time with a small wooden spoon. The jelly should not be allowed to boil, as this will darken it. Keep the jelly hot and melted by standing the pan in a second pan of simmering water.

Brush the inside of each baked tart shell with the melted jelly, then pile your chosen fruit elegantly into each one, and dab or drizzle jelly over the top of the fruit. If desired, top with a blob of double cream beaten with icing sugar and Kirsch. Serve the same day.

Mini Chocolate Apricot Tartlets

Makes 36 tarts

Pastry	Filling
4 oz unsalted butter	**6 fl. oz** single cream
5 oz plain flour	**6 oz** plain chocolate
1 oz cocoa powder	**1 heaped tbsp** apricot jam, sieved
2 oz caster sugar	
1 egg yolk	
1 tsp vanilla essence	
2 tbsps cold water	

Pre-heat the oven to Gas 6/400°F/200°C.

Sieve together the flour and cocoa powder, then rub in the butter. Toss in the sugar. Mix to a dough with the egg yolk, vanilla essence and cold water. Chill for 30 minutes.

Roll out the dough thinly. Line two dozen mini tartlet tins with the pastry. Prick the base of each tartlet and bake blind for 12–15 minutes until really crisp. Remove to a wire cooling rack.

Meanwhile make the filling. Break the chocolate into squares and, in a bowl over hot water, melt the chocolate and the cream. Allow to cool. When quite cold, gently beat until stiff.

Put a blob of apricot jam into the bottom of each of the tartlets. Put the chocolate cream into a piping bag and pipe rosettes into the tartlets to fill them.

Jam Tarts

Makes approximately 30 tarts

½ **lb** shortcrust pastry (see p. 185)   jam

Pre-heat the oven to Gas 6/400°F/200°C.

Roll out the pastry on a lightly floured board to approximately ⅛ inch thick. Using a 2¾-inch fluted cutter, cut the pastry into circles and place these in lightly buttered shallow tart tins. Spoon two-thirds full with jam (or use lemon curd).

Bake for approximately 15 minutes or until golden brown. Lift the tarts carefully from the tins, using a fork to 'cradle' the crisp, crumbling pastry. Cool on a wire rack.

Bakewell Tart

Serves 6–8

1 pre-baked pastry case (see
  pp. 185–6)
6 oz unsalted butter
6 oz caster sugar
finely grated zest and strained juice
  of 4 lemons

4 eggs, beaten
3 oz fresh white breadcrumbs
2 oz ground almonds

Pre-heat the oven to Gas 4/350°F/180°C.

Beat together the butter and sugar until soft and fluffy. Beat in the lemon zest, then the eggs, a little at a time. Gradually beat in the lemon juice and fold in the breadcrumbs and ground almonds. The mixture will be quite soft. Spoon into a pastry case and smooth the top. Stand on a baking tray to cope with possible spillage when baking.

Bake for about 1 hour or until the filling is firm and a rich golden brown. Serve at room temperature with whipped cream, if desired.

Chocolate Bakewell Tart

These ingredients are sufficient to make a 10-inch diameter, 2-inch deep tart.

Serves 8–10

Pastry

3 **oz** unsalted butter
5 **oz** plain flour
1 **oz** caster sugar
1 egg yolk
2 **tbsps** water

Filling

3 **oz** self-raising flour
2 **tbsps** cocoa

4 **oz** unsalted butter
4 **oz** caster sugar
2 medium-sized eggs, lightly beaten
1 **tsp** vanilla essence
4 **oz** ground almonds, rubbed
   through a sieve
finely grated zest of a lemon
2 **tbsps** lemon juice
4 **heaped tbsps** seedless raspberry
   jam
icing sugar, to decorate

Butter a loose-bottomed tart tin or flan ring well. (If you are a crinkle dish addict, then this pastry must first be baked blind or you'll have a soggy base.) Rub the butter into the flour, then toss in the sugar. Beat the egg yolk and 2 tablespoons of water together and add to the flour mixture using a fork. Work everything into a loose dough and form into a round pad.

Leave the pastry to rest for 30 minutes. Roll it out evenly and line the tin. Put it to rest again (or bake it blind if using a crinkle dish).

Pre-heat the oven to Gas 7/425°F/220°C.

Sieve the flour and cocoa together. Cream the butter and sugar until light and fluffy. Gradually add the beaten eggs and vanilla essence. Fold in the flour and cocoa, ground almonds and lemon zest. Mix to a dropping consistency with the lemon juice.

Spread the jam liberally over the base of the pastry shell. Spoon in the mixture and level the top. Bake for 15 minutes, then lower the heat to Gas 4/350°F/180°C for a further 15 minutes or until the tart is cooked.

Serve warm or cold. Dredge the top with icing sugar just before serving.

Rich Eccles Cakes

Eccles Cakes should always be served warm with clotted cream or rum butter. And that is advice from a Northerner! If you have great patience, Eccles Cakes, like mince pies, are extra special when made small – 2 inches in diameter when finished.

Makes 10–14

Pastry
1 lb flaky pastry (ideally, home-
  made; see pp. 186–7)

Filling
4 oz sultanas
4 oz currants
3 tbsps rum or whisky
2 oz ground almonds

2 oz unsalted butter, softened
2 oz Demerara or caster sugar
grated zest and juice of a lemon
½ tsp cinnamon

Sugar glaze
2 oz caster sugar ⎫
2 tbsps water   ⎬ to glaze
                 ⎭

Soak the fruits in the alcohol for 2 hours or overnight. Mix with the rest of the ingredients for the filling.

Make a sugar glaze by bringing to the boil the water and caster sugar. (It should be clear and *sticky*.) Leave to cool.

Pre-heat the oven to Gas 7/425°F/220°C.

Roll out the pastry evenly into one vast sheet. Using a saucer as a template, cut out 4–5-inch circles. (Just how many you get depends on how adeptly you roll the pastry.)

Put large teaspoonfuls of the mixture into the centre of each circle. Gather the pastry over the mixture and pinch together to seal the edges. Place the cakes on a buttered baking tray. Lightly press them flat, but don't squash them totally. Brush with a little of the sugar glaze.

Bake for 15 minutes, then reduce the temperature to Gas 4/350°F/180°C and bake for a further 20 minutes or until crisp and browned.

Glaze the cakes with more syrup when baked.

Coventry Godcakes

Godparents in Coventry gave their godchildren these cakes for good luck at New Year.

Makes 12 cakes

1 12-oz packet frozen puff pastry,
  thawed
8 oz home-made mincemeat
  (see p. 252)

sugar for sprinkling

Pre-heat the oven to Gas 7/425°F/220°C.

Roll out half the pastry to an oblong 12×8 inches, then cut it into 4-inch squares. Repeat with the other piece of pastry, then cut all the squares in half to form triangles.

Place a teaspoonful of mincemeat in the centre of half the triangles. Dampen the edges of the pastry and place the remaining triangles on top, pressing to seal.

Brush the tops of the triangles with water and sprinkle with sugar. Make three slits in the top of each cake. Place on damp baking trays and bake for 15–20 minutes until golden brown and risen. Cool on a wire rack.

Maid-of-Honour Tarts

These famous cheesecakes, a speciality of Kew, Surrey, are made from a sixteenth-century recipe. This one is from Hampton Court Palace. They were said to have been a favourite delicacy of Anne Boleyn, the name being given to them by Henry VIII when he saw her eating them while she was a maid-of-honour to Catharine of Aragon, his first wife.

Makes 12 tarts

8 oz puff pastry (see pp. 186–7)
1 pint *fresh* milk (not pasteurised)
1 tsp rennet
a pinch of salt
4 oz unsalted butter
2 egg yolks

2 tsps brandy
½ **oz** sweet nibbed almonds
a little sugar
a little ground cinnamon
zest and juice of half a lemon
currants to decorate

Make the pastry and refrigerate it until you are ready to use it. The next day, warm the milk to blood heat. Add the rennet and the salt. When the curds have set, drain through a fine muslin overnight.

Rub the curds through a sieve with the butter. Beat the yolks of the eggs to a froth with the brandy. Add to the curds.

Pre-heat the oven to Gas 7/425°F/220°C.

Blanch and nib the almonds, then add them to the curds with a little sugar and cinnamon. Add the zest and juice of the lemon.

Line patty tins with the pastry. Fill them with the mixture and sprinkle in the currants. Bake for 20–25 minutes or until well risen and golden brown.

Raspberry Coconut Slice

Makes 20–24 small pieces

Pastry
7 oz flour
4 oz lard
1 oz unsalted butter

Filling
6 oz unsalted butter

6 oz caster sugar
finely grated zest of a lemon
3 large eggs, lightly beaten
1 tbsp flour
10 oz desiccated coconut
12 oz raspberry jam

Pre-heat the oven to Gas 5/375°F/190°C.

Line with pastry a Swiss roll tin approximately 14×9 inches, and leave enough pastry to make lattice strips to decorate the top of the slice.

Cream the butter and sugar with the lemon zest. Beat in the eggs slowly and then the flour. Mix in the coconut.

Spread the jam evenly over the bottom of the pastry-lined tin. Spoon the coconut mixture over, spreading evenly. Arrange lattice strips of pastry over the top. Bake for 35–40 minutes. Leave to cool.

Cut into 2–2½-inch squares or 1×2-inch fingers and store in layers in an air-tight tin with greaseproof paper between the layers.

Almond and Quince Slices

Makes 16–18 slices

Pâte frollé
6 oz plain flour
3 oz unsalted butter, slightly chilled
3 oz caster sugar
1 level tsp lemon zest
1 egg, size 4
3 oz ground almonds, sieved
2–3 tbsps quince or apricot jam

Frangipane
3 oz unsalted butter, softened
5 oz caster sugar

2 eggs, size 4, at room temperature
5 oz ground almonds
1 oz plain flour
1–2 oz flaked almonds, blanched

Choice of flavourings
1 tbsp Jamaica rum
1 tbsp triple-strength orange-flower water
1 heaped tsp grated orange zest
1 tbsp lemon juice
1 tsp lemon zest

To make the pâte frollé. Sieve the flour on to a work surface. Make a well in the centre and add the butter (in small lumps), sugar, lemon zest and egg. Sprinkle the ground almonds over the top. 'Peck' and combine to a smooth paste. Chill well before using to line a buttered rectangular tin, 12×8×½ inch. Chill again, then spread the quince or apricot jam over the top.

Pre-heat the oven to Gas 4/350°F/180°C.

To make the frangipane. Cream the butter and sugar. Lightly beat the eggs, then beat them into the creamed mixture by degrees. Add any of the flavourings listed, or leave the mixture plain, and fold in the ground almonds and flour. Spread the mixture evenly over the jam base, and sprinkle thickly with blanched, flaked almonds.

Bake in the centre of the oven for 45 minutes. Allow to cool.

Individual Pecan Pies

This recipe was given to me by a lady living in Madison, the old capital of Georgia, when I lunched with her a few years ago.

Makes 12 small pies

rich shortcrust pastry (see p. 185)
4 oz caster sugar
6 oz maple syrup

3 small eggs, well beaten
3 oz unsalted butter, melted but cool
4 oz pecan nuts, roughly crushed

Line twelve 2½–3-inch tart tins, ¾ inch deep, with rich shortcrust pastry.

Pre-heat the oven to Gas 7/425°F/220°C.

Over a minimal heat, dissolve the sugar and syrup together in a pan. Allow to cool slightly. Have the eggs ready beaten in a bowl and dribble them into the warm syrup mixture, beating as you do so.

Mix in first the melted butter, then the crushed pecans. Fill to within ¼ inch of the top of the tart shells. Bake for 5 minutes. Reduce the temperature to Gas 4/350°F/180°C for a further 15 minutes or until the filling is set.

If you do not serve the pies on the day of baking, dredge them with icing sugar.

Cheshire Souling Cake

Souling cake was traditionally made for the custom of 'Hodening', which took place on All Souls' Day, 2 or 3 November. A band went round the streets accompanied by the 'Soulers', and children went from house to house singing this song:

> Soul! Soul! for a Soul Cake!
> I pray you good missis, a Soul Cake,
> An apple, a plum, a pear or cherry,
> Or any good thing to make us all merry.
> One for Peter and two for Paul,
> Three for Him that made us all.

Makes 20–24 cakes

12 oz plain flour	**6 oz** caster sugar
½ **tsp** cinnamon	**6 oz** margarine or unsalted butter
½ **tsp** mixed spice	**1** egg
a pinch of nutmeg	1½ **tsps** vinegar

Pre-heat the oven to Gas 4/350°F/180°C.

Mix the dry ingredients, rub in the fat, drop in the egg and vinegar, and knead until soft.

Roll out to ¼ inch thick, cut into rounds with a 3–4-inch cutter and bake for 15–20 minutes until the cake is slightly coloured. Cool on a wire rack.

BISCUITS

BISCUITS

Melting Moments

Everyone has his or her favourite recipe for a version of this type of biscuit, the sort we all enjoy with morning coffee or afternoon tea. They're certainly not slimming, not so much because of their calorific count – for *one* would add precious little to the daily intake – but because they are 'more-ish' and we don't stop at one!

This recipe was introduced by my French-born wife to The Kitchen, an intimate little restaurant in Albion Street in Leeds, which I owned back in the 1960s. We recently totted up and estimated that between us and our various cooks we must have made over half a million Melting Moments in the years we spent in Yorkshire!

Makes 40–50 biscuits

5 oz lard	**1** egg, beaten
3 oz unsalted butter	**12 oz** plain flour
6 oz caster sugar	

Pre-heat the oven to Gas 5/375°F/190°C.

Rub the two fats into the flour until you have a sand-like texture. Stir in the sugar and mix to a soft dough with the beaten egg.

Lightly butter a baking tray. Scoop out teaspoonfuls of the mixture, roll them deftly into small balls, place them on the tray and press them flat with three fingers (or use a fork). Decorate the top of each one with a glacé cherry or half a walnut.

Bake for 15 minutes. Leave to set before lifting carefully on to a wire cooling tray. As they are so fragile store in layers with soft kitchen paper between each layer.

For a chocolate version, substitute 2 oz cocoa powder for 2 oz of the flour. Sieve the powder and flour on to a paper before rubbing in the fats. Add a chocolate button in place of the cherry or walnut.

Caraway Seed Biscuits

Makes 35–40 biscuits

12 oz plain flour
6 oz unsalted butter, cubed
2 oz lard
6 oz caster sugar

1 level tbsp caraway seeds
1 egg plus 2 egg yolks, mixed with
   1 tbsp water
juice of half a lemon, strained

Pre-heat the oven to Gas 5/375°F/190°C.

Rub the butter and lard into the flour. Mix in the sugar thoroughly, then the caraway seeds and lemon juice. Mix to a biscuit dough with the egg mixture.

Roll out on a floured work surface to $\frac{1}{8}$–$\frac{1}{4}$ inch thick. Cut out with a biscuit cutter. Lightly brush two baking trays with melted butter and arrange the biscuits on them in rows.

Bake for 12–15 minutes or until golden and crisp. Leave to set before removing to a wire cooling rack.

Almond Tuiles

So called because of their curved Provençal-tile shape. These delicious crisp biscuits also go well with ice-cream. I suggest you have a production line going for your first attempt, baking six at a time until you get used to what is happening.

Makes approximately 36 biscuits

2 egg whites
4 oz caster sugar
2 oz plain flour

2 oz unsalted butter, melted but
   cooled
2 oz flaked almonds

Pre-heat the oven to Gas 5/375°F/190°C.

Beat the egg whites until quite slack. Mix in the sugar. Sieve in the flour. Mix well. Mix in the melted butter and then the almonds.

Butter two baking trays. Spoon the mixture into tiny pools (1 small teaspoonful each) 2–3 inches apart, as the biscuits spread when cooking.

Bake for 7–8 minutes or until brown at the edges and just cooked in the centre.

Remove with a palette-knife to a cooling tray; the biscuits will crisp up in seconds. Or lay each one over a rolling pin to get the *tuile* curve. Then remove to a wire rack.

Store in a dry place in an air-tight container. Handle carefully as the biscuits are fragile.

Lemon Tile Biscuits

Makes 16–20 biscuits

2 **oz** unsalted butter
2 **oz** caster sugar
2 egg whites
2 **oz** plain flour

a pinch of salt
grated zest of half a lemon or vanilla
   essence

Pre-heat the oven to Gas 5/375°F/190°C.

Soften the butter in a bowl over hot water but do not let it get oily. Beat lightly with a fork, gradually adding the sugar, until very light and fluffy. Beat in the unwhisked egg whites a little at a time.

Sieve the flour with the salt into a bowl and fold it gently into the butter mixture. Flavour with lemon zest or vanilla essence.

Put the mixture into a piping bag fitted with a ½-inch nozzle and pipe 2-inch lengths on to baking trays lined with buttered greaseproof paper, allowing room for the biscuits to spread. Bake for 10 minutes until golden brown around the edges.

While the 'tiles' are still warm, remove them carefully from the baking trays and lay them over a greased rolling pin to make them curl. Leave them until cold.

Sablés I

These are also known as Sand Biscuits.

Makes 24–30 biscuits

4 **oz** unsalted butter
5 **oz** caster sugar
2 egg yolks
8 **oz** plain flour

1 **tsp** vanilla essence
1 egg yolk, mixed with 2 tsps cold
   water, to glaze

In a food processor, cream the butter and sugar. Add the egg yolks and vanilla essence, and mix well. Add half the flour and allow it to mix in. Add the remaining flour, stopping the machine as soon as it is incorporated.

Lightly flour a sheet of non-stick plastic film. Form the dough into one or two 3-inch pipes, rolling it to an even shape. Wrap these in the film and chill for an hour. Pre-heat the oven to Gas 4/350°F/180°C.

Cut the dough into ⅛-inch discs and arrange them on a lightly but well-buttered baking tray or trays. Brush each biscuit with a little of the glaze and bake for 8–10 minutes. Remove to a wire cooling rack.

Sablés II

This is an old French recipe for Sablés. Make sure the biscuits are well baked so that there is no streak uncooked in the middle.

Makes 36–40 biscuits

4 **oz** unsalted butter
8 **oz** plain flour
5 **oz** caster sugar
4 hardboiled egg yolks, sieved

grated zest of 2 lemons
3 raw egg yolks, mixed with the
  juice of a lemon

Pre-heat the oven to Gas 4/350°F/180°C.

Rub the butter into the flour until crumb-like. With a fork mix in the sugar, sieved yolks and grated zest. Mix to a soft dough with the lemon and egg-yolk mixture.

Turn on to a floured work surface, press and roll gently until ⅓ inch thick. Cut into circles or sticks.

Bake for 20–25 minutes or until golden and crisp. Test one for shortness throughout. Remove to a wire cooling rack.

Pecan Nut Biscuits

Stored in an air-tight container, these biscuits will keep for weeks.

Makes 24–30 biscuits

4 **oz** unsalted butter or margarine
4 **oz** soft light brown sugar
3 **tbsps** golden syrup
3 **tbsps** black treacle
1 large egg, beaten
4 **oz** wholemeal flour

2 **oz** Quaker oats
2 **oz** pecan nuts, roughly crushed
2 **oz** extra nuts, for topping (optional
  luxury for high days)
1 **oz** raisins or sultanas

Pre-heat the oven to Gas 4/350°F/180°C.

Place the butter, sugar, syrup and treacle in a bowl and beat until light in texture, using a hand electric mixer. Beat in the egg. Mix in the flour, oats, pecan nuts and raisins until evenly dispersed.

Lightly butter a baking tray and put on it teaspoonfuls of the mixture, spaced well apart. Sprinkle the surface of each biscuit with chopped nuts if used.

Bake until the biscuits have risen, spread and are golden brown. Cool to set before moving to a wire cooling rack.

Orange Biscuits

Makes 30–40 biscuits

8 oz caster sugar
4 oz unsalted butter
2 egg yolks
1 tbsp orange juice

grated zest of half an orange
12 oz plain flour
1 tsp baking powder
¼ tsp salt

Cream the butter. Beat in the sugar, egg yolks, orange juice and grated zest. Sieve together the flour, salt and baking powder, and add to the sugar and egg mixture. Mix well. Chill in the refrigerator for 3–4 hours.

Pre-heat the oven to Gas 5/375°F/190°C.

Take up teaspoonfuls of the mixture and roll them into small balls. Place these on a greased baking tray, flatten slightly and cook for 8–10 minutes.

Brush the biscuits lightly with melted butter while they are still warm.

Coconut Biscuits

Makes 20–24 biscuits

2 oz unsalted butter
3 oz caster sugar
1 egg, beaten

3 oz plain flour
1 oz desiccated coconut

Pre-heat the oven to Gas 3/325°F/160°C.

Cream the butter and sugar together until light and fluffy. Fold the egg into the mixture, followed by the flour and the coconut.

Put teaspoonfuls of the mixture on to greased baking trays and bake for 10–15 minutes. Cool on a wire rack.

Ginger Biscuits

Makes 20–30 biscuits

4 oz self-raising flour
½ tsp bicarbonate of soda
1½–2 tsps ground ginger
1 tsp cinnamon

1 oz caster sugar
2 oz unsalted butter
3 oz golden syrup

Sieve the dry ingredients together. Warm the syrup over a low heat until hot and runny. Add the butter and mix until just melted. Scrape into a bowl. Mix in the dry ingredients to form a dough. Put to chill for an hour.

Roll out the dough in manageable batches to $\frac{1}{4}$ inch thick. Cut out with a round or fluted biscuit cutter.

Pre-heat the oven to Gas 5/375°F/190°C.

Lightly butter a baking tray and lay the biscuits on it. Bake for 10–12 minutes. Cool the biscuits before removing them to a wire cooling rack.

Ginger Snaps

Makes 24–30 biscuits

4 oz unsalted butter	**4 oz** caster sugar
4 tbsps golden syrup or maple syrup	1 egg yolk, beaten
8 oz plain flour	$\frac{1}{2}$ **tsp** bicarbonate of soda
a pinch of salt	a little milk
1 tsp ground ginger	caster sugar

Pre-heat the oven to Gas 5/375°F/190°C.

Melt the butter and syrup together in a pan. Sieve the flour, salt and ginger into a bowl and stir in the sugar. Blend in the melted butter and syrup and the beaten egg yolk. Dissolve the bicarbonate of soda in a little warm milk and add to the mixture.

Turn the dough on to a floured work surface and knead until smooth. Roll out thinly on a sugared work surface and cut into rounds about $2\frac{1}{2}$ inches in diameter. Place on greased and floured baking trays and bake for 15–20 minutes.

Allow the biscuits to set on the baking trays, then remove to a wire rack and leave to cool.

Almond Macaroons

Makes 18–20 macaroons

8 oz caster sugar	2 egg whites
4 oz ground almonds, sieved	rice paper
2 heaped tsps ground rice	split almonds, to decorate

Pre-heat the oven to Gas 2–3/300–325°F/150–170°C.

Mix together the sugar, ground almonds and ground rice. Stir in the *unbeaten* egg whites.

Line a baking tray with rice paper, then either spoon or pipe dessert-spoonfuls of the mixture on to the paper. Place a split almond in the centre of each macaroon. Bake for 20–25 minutes.

Flapjacks

Makes 16 flapjacks

4 oz unsalted butter	**8 oz** rolled oats
1 oz caster sugar	a pinch of salt
2½ tbsps golden syrup	

Pre-heat the oven to Gas 5/375°F/190°C.

Put the butter and sugar into a bowl and beat until smooth. Heat the syrup in a saucepan, stir it into the butter and sugar, then add the oats and a pinch of salt, and mix well.

Spread the mixture into a well-greased shallow tin, approximately 8 inches square, pressing well into the corners and flattening the top. Bake for 30–40 minutes until crisp and golden brown.

Mark into bars immediately on removal from oven. Leave in the tin to cool before removing and breaking into bars.

Avola Sticks

Avola, in southern Sicily, produces the best almonds – hence the name of these biscuits.

Makes 30–40 biscuits

7 oz plain flour	**8 oz** caster sugar
6 oz unsalted butter	**2 eggs**, size 4, lightly beaten
7 oz ground almonds, sieved	

Pre-heat the oven to Gas 2–3/300–325°F/150–170°C.

Rub the butter into the flour. Toss in the ground almonds and sugar, mixing thoroughly. Mix in the eggs and gather to a soft paste.

Butter a baking sheet. Fit an 8-point 'rope' nozzle or a ½-inch plain nozzle into a piping bag. Pipe out 'sticks' about 3 inches long. Bake for 30 minutes. Cool on a wire rack.

Shortbread

Makes 12–16 fingers

4 oz unsalted butter   **2 oz** ground rice or semolina
2 oz caster sugar   **6 oz** plain flour

Pre-heat the oven to Gas 5/375°F/190°C.

Cream the butter and sugar until light and fluffy. Sieve the semolina with the flour and mix in with a fork, then change to a kneading action. Knead until smooth.

Form the dough into an 8×3-inch oblong. Prick it all over at ½-inch intervals with a fork, pinch the edges between finger and thumb, and mark it into 1-inch sticks.

Place on a lightly buttered baking tray and bake for 10 minutes, then reduce the temperature to Gas 3/325°F/160°C and bake for a further 25–30 minutes.

Dredge with caster sugar while hot, and cut the 'fingers' through.

Note: If you want to freeze shortbread, freeze it uncooked.

Almond Petticoat Tails

Makes 8 pieces

4 oz plain flour   **1** egg white, beaten (see method)
2 oz ground rice   extra caster sugar
2 oz caster sugar   **2 oz** flaked or nibbed almonds
4 oz unsalted butter

Pre-heat the oven to Gas 2/300°F/150°C.

Sieve the flour, ground rice and sugar together on to a work surface. Cut the butter into cubes and rub in. Knead lightly, form into a ball, press and roll lightly into an 8-inch circle. Place on a buttered baking tray.

Using a knife, divide the dough into eight even segments without cutting right through. Brush each with beaten egg white and sprinkle with a little caster sugar and the flaked or nibbed almonds. Press lightly with the palm of your hand.

Bake for 40–45 minutes. Cool for a little while before cutting right through the petticoat markings. Store, as with other biscuits and macaroons, in an air-tight tin. (If you want to freeze the shortbread, freeze it uncooked.)

Apricot Shortcakes

Makes 16–20 biscuits

6 oz plain flour
4 oz unsalted butter
2 oz ground rice
2 oz caster sugar

1½ oz apricot jam
extra jam for decoration
extra caster sugar, for dredging

Pre-heat the oven to Gas 4–5/350–375°F/180–190°C.

Sieve the flour into a bowl and rub in the butter until the mixture resembles fine breadcrumbs. Add the ground rice and sugar, and mix together. Put the jam in the centre of the mixture and work into a smooth dough.

Roll out the dough on a floured board to about ¾ inch thick and cut it into fancy shapes. Place these on greased baking trays. Make a small hollow in the centre of each biscuit with a thimble and put a little jam in the hole.

Bake for about 20 minutes. Cool on a wire rack and when the biscuits are cold, dredge them with caster sugar.

Walnut Shortbread Biscuits

This dough is soft and must be handled with care.

Makes 24–30 biscuits

7 oz plain flour
4 oz walnuts, finely crushed
8 oz unsalted butter, softened
4 oz icing sugar

2 small egg yolks
½ tsp vanilla essence
1 egg white, beaten ⎫
caster sugar ⎬ to glaze (optional)
⎭

Pre-heat the oven to Gas 6/400°F/200°C.

This dough can be made by the 'pecking' method. Mix the flour and walnuts together, then make a well in the centre. Mix the butter to a soft paste with the icing sugar and egg yolks, and place in the well. Then gradually draw the flour from the sides and 'peck' it in. Alternatively, it can be made in a food processor using the all-in-one method.

Roll out the dough on a lightly floured work surface to ⅛–¼ inch thick. Cut out with 2–2½-inch round cutters.

If you wish to glaze, brush the tops of the biscuits with beaten egg white and dredge lightly with sugar *before* placing the biscuits on the baking tray.

Lift the biscuits with a palette-knife on to a lightly buttered baking tray and bake for 8–10 minutes. Leave to set before lifting to cool on a wire rack.

Palmiers

Simple and easy to make, these traditional pastry *petits fours* are different when given an optional dredge of cinnamon. For the novice, I suggest you bake these biscuits no more than eight at a time: this will make it easier to remove them to your cooling rack.

Makes 30–36 biscuits

1 8-oz packet puff pastry, thawed   extra caster sugar, for rolling
2–3 oz caster sugar

Dredge your work surface with caster sugar. Pre-heat the oven to Gas 5/ 375°F/190°C.

Roll out the pastry into an oblong roughly 12×8 inches. Dredge it evenly with plenty of the sugar. Fold the pastry long sides to middle, then long sides together.

Dredge the whole work surface again with sugar. Roll out the pastry again to the same size as before. Dredge with the remaining sugar and press well in. Fold the long sides to the middle, then long sides to middle again. Press well together with the rolling pin. You should have a long, flat sausage, approximately 12×1½ inches. Cut it into ⅓-inch pieces.

Bake for 20–25 minutes on a dry baking tray, placing the pieces flat, 1½ inches or more apart. They will spread into sticky heart-shaped palmiers.

If you have difficulty removing the palmiers (the caramel sets as they cool), return the tray to the oven for a few seconds to soften the sugar. They should be crisp, glossy and chestnut brown. Store in a dry place.

Pin-wheels

Proceed as for Palmiers, but after the first pastry rolling, sugaring and folding, roll out again to a 12×8-inch oblong and sugar well, pressing the sugar into the pastry. *Roll* up the pastry and cut into ¼-inch discs. Bake as before.

Cinnamon Sticks

Proceed as for Palmiers, but after rolling and sugaring the pastry once, dredge with sugar and cinnamon. Fold over once. Roll or press together. Cut into ⅓×6-inch strips. Twist these carefully and bake as above.

Note: Do not be tempted to touch the caramelised surfaces of these biscuits with your fingers while they are still hot and sticky; wait until they are cool and crisp.

Cornish Fairings

At one time 'fairings' were gifts bought at the local fair for your loved one. Over the years the word came to mean a token biscuit – made from a recipe peculiar to the district or county – and eaten at the fairground.

Makes 30–40 biscuits

1 **lb** plain flour
½ **tsp** ground mace
1 **tsp** ground ginger
5 **oz** unsalted butter
2 **oz** lard
8 **oz** Muscovado or other soft brown sugar

4 **oz** mixed chopped candied peel
8 **oz** golden syrup
1 **level tbsp** bicarbonate of soda
1 **level tbsp** cream of tartar

Pre-heat the oven to Gas 4/350°F/180°C.

Sift the flour with the spices. Rub in the butter and lard to a sand-like texture. Mix in the sugar with a fork, adding the peel as you go along.

Warm the syrup in a small bowl, standing this in a pan of simmering water. Stir in the cream of tartar and the bicarbonate of soda.

Make a well in the flour mixture, pour in the syrup and mix to a soft dough.

Lightly flour a work surface and roll out the dough to ¾ inch thick. Cut into 2-inch circles or 2-inch strips.

Place on a lightly buttered baking tray and bake for 30 minutes or until nicely browned, risen somewhat and short.

Shrewsbury Biscuits

Makes 30–40 biscuits

8 oz unsalted butter	**1 tbsp** Amontillado sherry
8 oz caster sugar	**1 level tsp** caraway seeds
1 egg, beaten	**2 oz** currants (optional)
2 fl. oz double cream	**8 oz** plain flour

Pre-heat the oven to Gas 4/350°F/180°C.

Cream the butter and sugar until light and fluffy. Beat in the egg. Mix in the cream and sherry. Stir in the currants, if used, and the caraway seeds. Work in the flour and knead to a soft dough.

Roll out on a floured work surface to less than ¼ inch thick. Cut out with a 2½-inch fluted cutter.

Bake on a buttered baking tray for 20–25 minutes or until crisp and golden brown.

Funeral Biscuits

This is my family recipe, first published in the Women's Institute's *A Cook's Tour of Britain*.

Two kinds of funeral biscuit or cake were common in the north of England. The first had a spongy texture and was usually made by a local baker and sold in the village shop. The second type was more like a shortbread, and this was made by the deceased's family and relations. Both were round in shape and, when cold, were cut in half, one half being placed on top of the other. Each pair of halves was then wrapped up in a special way in waxed white paper, and sealed with black sealing wax. While the mourners were waiting for the cortège to come out of the house, two women dressed in deepest black would go round distributing the funeral cakes along with glasses of wine.

Makes 20–24 biscuits

8 oz plain flour	**1 oz** currants
6 oz unsalted butter	**1** egg, beaten
6 oz caster sugar	

Pre-heat the oven to Gas 4/350°F/180°C.

Rub the butter into the flour. Add the sugar and currants. Mix to a stiffish dough with the beaten egg.

Knead a little and roll out. Cut into circles about the size of a small saucer. Bake until golden brown.

Arrowroot Biscuits

If you have never tasted home-made Arrowroot Biscuits, then I urge you to do so. These plain biscuits are ideal for family tea.

Makes 40–50 biscuits

8 oz unsalted butter, softened
8 oz plain flour
6 oz arrowroot (available from
  chemists)

8 oz caster sugar
4 large eggs, beaten

Pre-heat the oven to Gas 5/375°F/190°C.

Sieve the arrowroot and flour together twice on to a paper.

Cream the butter and sugar until light and fluffy. Dribble in the eggs and beat.

Combine the two mediums to a soft dough-like mixture.

Brush two baking trays lightly with melted butter. Scoop or drop teaspoonfuls of the mixture on to them, leaving a 1-inch space between rows. Press to flatten slightly.

Bake in batches for 12–15 minutes or until crisp and golden brown. Cool for a minute or so to set before lifting on to a wire cooling rack.

Oatmeal Biscuits

Stilton or my favourite Blue Cheshire cheese are at their best served with home-made oatmeal biscuits, spread liberally with walnut and raisin butter (see p. 241) for a special treat. This is my adaptation of a recipe from Jean Butterworth of White Moss House, Rydal Water, Cumbria.

Makes approximately 24 biscuits

$\frac{1}{2}$ lb wholemeal flour
$\frac{1}{2}$ tsp salt
$\frac{1}{2}$ tsp bicarbonate of soda
3 oz unsalted butter, cold and cut
  into cubes

3 oz lard, cold and cut into cubes
$\frac{1}{2}$ lb rolled oats
3 oz caster sugar
milk

Pre-heat the oven to Gas 6/400°F/200°C.

Sieve the flour, salt and bicarbonate of soda into a bowl. Rub in the cold fats. Toss in the oats. Add the sugar and mix with a little milk to a firmish dough.

Roll out on a floured board to $\frac{1}{8}$ inch thick. Cut into rounds and bake on a lightly buttered baking tray for about 10 minutes or until cooked.

Quaker Oat Biscuits

Makes 30–36 biscuits

4 oz Quaker oats
2 oz wholemeal flour
3 oz soft brown sugar
2 oz desiccated coconut

1 tsp baking powder
4 oz unsalted butter, melted but cool
1 egg, beaten

Pre-heat the oven to Gas 4/350°F/180°C.

In a bowl mix all the dry ingredients together. Mix to a dough with the melted butter and beaten egg. Knead well.

Flour a work surface and roll out the mixture to ¼ inch thick. Cut out with a plain cutter 2–2½ inches in diameter.

Bake on a lightly buttered baking tray for 15–20 minutes or until brown and crisp. Cool on a wire rack.

Queen Mary's Cheese Biscuits

These biscuits will melt in your mouth.

Makes 16–20 biscuits

4 oz plain flour
3 oz good unsalted butter
2 oz fresh Parmesan cheese, grated

1 egg yolk
a little salt
tip of a teaspoon of nutmeg

Rub the butter into the flour. Add the grated cheese and seasonings, then bind with the egg yolk. Do not add any additional water. Leave to rest.

Pre-heat the oven to Gas 5/375°F/190°C.

Roll out to ¼ inch thick, then cut into 1½-inch circles (the pastry is too fragile for larger biscuits). Bake for 7–10 minutes.

Jill Watt's Cheese Shortbreads

Makes 50–60 biscuits

8 oz unsalted butter
8 oz plain flour

8 oz mature Cheddar cheese
½ tsp salt

Pre-heat the oven to Gas 5/375°F/190°C.

Sieve the flour with the salt. Rub in the butter with your fingertips until you have a moist, sand-like texture.

Mix in the grated cheese. Knead to a soft pliable dough. Place 1-inch knobs of the dough on to a buttered baking tray and press out with the floured tines of a fork.

Bake for 8–10 minutes or until crisp. Cool to set a little before moving to a wire rack.

These small biscuits keep well (warm them through before serving) and are ideal when people pop in unexpectedly for a glass of sherry.

FRUITS,
ICES,
CUSTARDS
AND
JELLIES

Summer Fruits

It was customary in Georgian England to go to the Assembly Rooms in Bath, York or Norwich, or to London's pleasure-gardens at Vauxhall, Ranelagh or Marylebone not only in the evenings when a 'rout' might be taking place, but also in the morning, after visiting your milliner, haberdasher, or glovemaker. People went there to parade, promenade and pirouette; to see and be seen; and to indulge in that wonderful social habit – gossip!

'Subtleties' and 'conceited' dishes such as rich creams, exotic jellies and aromatic ices would be served. Special glasses were made to receive these delicacies: the V-shaped syllabub glass, the handleless jelly glass and the miniature squat custard cup with its tiny looped handle, for example. All would be displayed on flat, broad, round, single-footed glass syllabub stands or 'tazzas', today sometimes mistaken for cakestands. (Sherry glasses or small wine glasses, or even Christening or coffee cups, make perfect substitutes today.)

The delightful habit of partaking of these delicacies eventually transferred to the afternoon-tea table. Next time you give a tea-party, present a selection of them on silver salvers or glass plates – they will surprise and delight your guests.

Strawberries and Cream

Where in the world do you get such fine, luscious, piquant-flavoured strawberries as you find in England? Strawberries and cream are *de rigueur* at Wimbledon, Glyndebourne, Ascot, Stratford-upon-Avon, Putney and Henley. They appear at every tea-party in the land, from a church social to a lazy afternoon in your own back garden.

There are endless arguments as to what to serve with them. Let us take the 'original' way first – the way in which many people still enjoy eating strawberries to this day.

In bygone times, when leisure and money were plentiful, unhulled strawberries were delicately arranged on silver-gilt strawberry dishes, each green stalk pointing outwards for ease of picking up. Alongside would be a handsome silver jug containing that rich, thick, buttery yellow cream found only in our country. A woven silver basket, lined in blue Bristol glass, would hold sugar, or, in fashionable households, an elegant silver caster with its pierced domed top might well have made an appearance.

Each person took some strawberries on to a glass or painted china dessert plate, together with a spoonful of cream and a dredging of sugar, then, taking hold of a strawberry by the hull, dipped it first into the rich thick cream, then into the sugar, before popping it, whole, into the mouth where with an elegant sucking action the hull was pulled away and discarded at the side of the plate. There you have it – and I can assure you that this is the most sensual way of eating strawberries and cream, once tried, never abandoned!

For those unsure of pulling off the feat with elegant aplomb, using small crystal bowls is the next best thing, with a finely wrought dessert-spoon and fork as a means of transporting fruit, sugar and cream to their resting place in the mouth with some semblance of dignity!

Then there are those – like me – who like pepper on strawberries, and no cream. Try it from time to time, if only to ring the changes: the complement is wonderful, particularly with the added squeeze of a little lemon juice. And again, some strange people take a little salt – each to his own!

An exotic and pretty wonderful way of serving strawberries on a hot summer's afternoon, while sipping a glass of chilled champagne, is to serve them halved and quartered, their cut faces bathed in Kirsch before masking them in a fresh, tangy raspberry purée: our two great garden berries shown off in the best possible way.

Raspberry Sauce

Serves 6

8 oz fresh raspberries   juice of half a lemon
4 tbsps icing sugar

Mix all the ingredients together, then press and rub the mixture through a fine-meshed wire sieve. Chill well.

Raspberries and Cream

Many people rate raspberries above strawberries for excellence of flavour. At one time they had a very short season, but today in Britain they are available for longer periods from the raspberry gardens in Scotland. They also freeze well.

For their first appearance of the year, raspberries should be served traditionally, with thick fresh cream and sugar. Then you can ring the changes, either by complementing them with their own purée (see above) or by bathing them in the following redcurrant liqueur sauce. However you serve them, you can choose to accompany them with cool heavy cream or not.

Raspberries with Redcurrant Sauce

Serves 4–6

1½ **lb** raspberries (frozen ones are
  almost perfect)
12 oz redcurrants, picked over
2 **tbsps** sugar (or to taste)

2 **tbsps** cold water
1 measure Kirsch or eau de vie de
  framboise
2–3 **oz** flaked sweet almonds

Do *not* rinse the raspberries: just pick them over.

Put the redcurrants, sugar and water into a heavy-bottomed saucepan.
Shake and stir over a low heat until the juices draw, then simmer for 3–4
minutes until tender. Cool a little before pressing and rubbing through a
fine-meshed wire sieve. Chill well before stirring in the liqueur.

Dribble the sauce over the raspberries an hour before serving. Serve well
chilled, scattered with the flaked almonds.

ICE-CREAMS

Delicious ices are often served for afternoon tea, particularly when the occasion is an extra special one like an afternoon wedding, a christening, or when guests are here from abroad. Here are some traditional ice-creams, plus one or two new ones.

Basic Vanilla Ice-cream (Custard Ice-cream)

Makes 3–4 pints (enough for 24 servings)

5 eggs, beaten
up to 4 oz vanilla sugar or ordinary sugar plus 1 vanilla pod or 1 tbsp vanilla essence

1 pint rich milk
1 pint double cream

Cream the eggs and sugar together until white and fluffy.

In a non-stick pan, bring the milk to boiling point with the vanilla pod or vanilla essence if used; pour it over the egg mixture, stirring all the time. Remove the pod.

Return the pan to a low heat and stir with a straight-edged wooden spatula until the mixture thickens enough to coat the back of the spatula and an obvious trail is left when the finger is drawn across the coated spatula. *Do not allow to boil.* Cool and then chill for 30 minutes.

Whip the cream to soft peaks and lightly but thoroughly fold it into the custard.

Pour into an ice-cream maker, following the directions for freezing pertaining to your particular machine. (You may have to churn it in batches.)

Store in plastic-lidded containers.

Brown Bread Ice-cream

To each 2 pints of basic custard ice-cream (see above) add the following mixture.

Serves 12–16

2 tbsps sweet Madeira or sherry
6 oz soft white breadcrumbs
2 oz salted butter

2 oz caster sugar
1 tsp vanilla essence

Melt the butter, without browning, in a wide, heavy-bottomed frying pan. Stir in the breadcrumbs, and sprinkle in the sugar. Splash with the wine as the crumbs begin to crisp, add the vanilla essence and allow the whole mass to caramelise and crisp over a low heat, stirring the crumbs around all the while to prevent scorching and to ensure even colouring.

When crisp, tip the crumbs on to a baking tray to cool, then crush them with the end of a rolling pin or in a liquidiser.

Add the crumbs to the ice-cream while it is in the ice-cream maker.

Ginger Ice-cream

To each 2 pints of basic custard ice-cream (see p. 223) add the following mixture.

2 tsps ground ginger
8 oz stem ginger, finely blended to a
  purée

Add the ground ginger while creaming the eggs and sugar, then mix in the stem ginger.

Gooseberry and Rosemary Ice-cream

Makes approximately 1½ pints (enough for 12 servings)

1 lb gooseberries, rinsed, topped
  and tailed
⅛ pint cold water
4 oz caster sugar

pared zest of half a lemon
a good sprig of rosemary or 1 tsp
  ground rosemary
½ pint double cream, half whipped

Put the first five ingredients into a pan, cover and simmer over a low heat until pulped. Allow to cool, then make a purée in a liquidiser or food processor. Rub the purée through a fine-meshed sieve to remove seeds and skins.

Cut and fold in the half-whipped cream. Churn in an ice-cream maker and freeze.

Fruit Salad Ice-cream

This ice-cream, which can be made with or without the double cream, is tangy and very refreshing. It can be served moulded or scooped.

Serves 6–8

Stock syrup
1¼ **lb** caster sugar
1½ **pints** water
3½ **fl. oz** glucose syrup

½ **pint** fresh lemon juice, strained
  (approx. 5 lemons)
½ small egg white, beaten to slacken
¼ **pint** double cream, whipped to soft
  peaks

Make the stock syrup by boiling together the caster sugar, water and glucose syrup until the liquid is clear.

Mix all the ingredients together and pour them into an ice-cream maker. As soon as the mixture gets to the ribbon stage where the paddles are leaving a distinct trail, add half the following fruit mixture, then continue churning until frozen to your liking.

½ fresh pineapple, peeled, cored and
  cut into 1-inch pieces
2 kiwi fruits, peeled and diced
1 orange, peeled, segmented and cut
  into 1-inch pieces
¼ **lb** seedless grapes, halved

¼ **lb** small wine grapes or black
  grapes, halved and seeded
6 strawberries, quartered
zest of one orange and half a lemon
3 **tbsps** Kirsch/Cointreau ⎫ ⎮for the
3 **tbsps** lemon juice ⎭ marinade

Peel the fruits and dice them. Strain those which go into the ice-cream, leaving the juices to be served with the remaining fruits to be eaten alongside.

Apple and Rose Petal Ice-cream

This creamy ice is evocative of an English garden; it would be perfect served at an afternoon wedding reception.

Serves 8–10

1 **pint** stock syrup (see above)
1 **pint** concentrated apple juice
½ egg white, lightly beaten
3 **tsps** triple-strength rose flower
  water

3 drops of red colouring
¾ **pint** double cream, whipped to soft
  peaks
sugared rose petals, to garnish (see
  below)

Put all the ingredients except the cream and sugared rose petals into an ice-cream maker. When the ice-cream is ribboning, spoon in the half-whipped cream and churn until you reach a soft set.

Store in the freezer, or spoon into ice glasses and serve freshly made. Decorate with sugared rose petals.

To sugar rose petals. Pick old-fashioned, blowsy, scented red or pink roses and remove the petals (use only perfect petals). Beat an egg white until light and frothy, and with a clean paint-brush, brush each petal completely on both sides with the egg white. Arrange the petals on a sheet of kitchen paper laid on a tray. Dredge on both sides with caster sugar. Any bald patches will go mouldy, so take care to cover each petal meticulously. Leave to dry overnight, or for as long as it takes. (When the atmosphere is very humid you may have difficulty in drying them, so perhaps you might do this in the airing cupboard.) Store in an air-tight container.

Three-nut Ice-cream

Serves 10–12

4 oz caster sugar
2 tbsps cold water
4 oz flaked almonds
2 pints basic custard ice-cream,
  freshly made (see p. 223)

4 oz walnut halves
2 oz hazelnuts
crystallised chestnuts (optional)

Put 2 oz of the caster sugar with the cold water into a heavy-bottomed pan and bring to the boil. Boil fairly rapidly until a caramel starts to form. Lower the heat and tip in the flaked almonds. Stir them round with a fork and leave the mixture to cook until the nuts are brown.

Turn the almonds on to a piece of lightly oiled foil or a non-stick baking tray. Leave to cool. Crush the nuts to a fine powder, using either a rolling pin or a liquidiser or food processor.

Repeat this process with the remaining 2 oz sugar and the walnut halves, taking care not to burn the walnuts as, being dark in colour, it is difficult to see when they are crisp. Roughly crush the walnuts. *Never touch the caramel mixture with your bare fingers.*

Toast the hazelnuts in a hot oven, Gas 9/475°F/240°C, and rub off the skins with a damp cloth. Cool and crush roughly.

Add all the nuts to the basic custard ice-cream as it is beginning to set.

A few of the walnuts and hazelnuts can be reserved as a garnish, if desired. Likewise, the ice-cream can be garnished by adding a crystallised chestnut or two to each serving.

CUSTARDS, JELLIES AND CREAMS

Syllabub (Sillebube)

Syllabub is England's answer to the Italian *zabaglione* and the French *sabayon*. The name is derived from the Old French for champagne: *sille*. The Tudors and Hanoverians must have actually *drunk* it, and what we class as syllabub today is really a first cousin of the frothing affair served in its own glass and elegantly placed on its syllabub stand.

'Receipts' abound in old cookery books for 'A *Sillebub* to last a Week', as well as for 'A *Syllabube* under the cow' – for this latter we are instructed to pour the warm milk 'from a great height' when 'no cow is to hand'!

This is one of our great national sweets and has made an early return to favour; already there are many versions of it. It slots ideally into an afternoon-tea menu for a special occasion.

Serves 8

1 orange
4 tbsps caster sugar
3 fl. oz medium dry Madeira or
   Amontillado sherry
1 fl. oz brandy

1 pint thick double cream
pieces of candied fruits or
   crystallised flower petals
   (optional)

Finely grate the zest and squeeze the juice from the orange. Put the zest, juice, sugar and liquors into a bowl. Cover it and leave for a few hours to let the oils from the zest impregnate the liquor.

Strain the liquid into a clean bowl and stir in the cream, then beat the mixture until it ribbons and nearly stands in peaks. (Take it to 'peak' stage only if you want to serve the syllabubs immediately, as cream gets thicker as it chills.)

Pour it into the most attractive glasses you have – use custard cups or, if you are lucky, real syllabub glasses. Chill for 4 hours or overnight. Decorate with small strips of candied fruits or crystallised flower petals.

Custard Cups

Custard, which even the French have the grace to call *crème anglaise*, is as old as The Conqueror! It makes a delightful tea-time 'subtlety', as such confections were called in eighteenth-century England, when they were often aromatised delicately with rose or orange flower water, cowslips or violets.

Serves 8–10

½ **pint** double cream
¾ **pint** single cream
2 oz caster sugar
1 tsp cornflour

8 large egg yolks
2 tbsps orange or rose flower water,
   brandy or Madeira
edible rose petals

Cream the egg yolks, cornflour and sugar until light and fluffy. In a non-stick pan, bring the two creams to the boil and, using a wire balloon whisk, whisk this into the egg mixture.

Return the pan to the lowest possible heat and stir continually, using a straight-edged wooden spatula, until the mixture has thickened. Remove from the heat, still stirring.

Have an ice-cube ready to pop into the mixture to remove any residual heat, which may curdle the custard. Keep on stirring while you pour in the flower water, brandy or Madeira. Allow the custard to cool.

Pour into custard cups and chill well.

Sprinkle the custard with icing sugar, or cover with small pieces of plastic film to prevent a skin forming. Decorate with an edible rose petal.

Petits Pots de Crème au Mocha

Serves 4–6

2 tbsps strong liquid coffee
2 oz plain chocolate
½ **pint** single cream

2 egg yolks
1½ **oz** caster sugar

Pre-heat the oven to Gas 4/350°F/180°C.

Break the chocolate into pieces and put it into a small bowl with the coffee. Arrange the bowl over a pan of simmering water. When the chocolate has softened, stir that and the coffee together.

In a non-stick pan, bring the cream just to boiling point, stirring from time to time. Mix it in to the chocolate mixture away from the heat.

Cream the egg yolks and sugar together. Pour the hot chocolate and cream mixture on to the egg and sugar mixture, whisking all the time.

Pour into ramekins and stand these in an oven dish with enough hot water to come halfway or two-thirds up the sides of the ramekins. Bake for 20–25 minutes or until set. Cool, then chill well.

Sack Creams

'Sack' was the old English word for sherry. Proceed as for Custard Cups (see pp. 227–8), substituting ¼ pint of cream sherry or Amontillado sherry for some of the single cream. Omit the flower waters.

Orange Jellies

Serves 6–8

1 **pint** fresh orange juice, strained
   (6–8 oranges; ruby oranges are
   excellent)
zest of 2 oranges
3 **tbsps** orange curaçao

1½ **tsps** gelatine crystals
2 drops of orange liqueur or
   Angostura bitters (optional)
12–16 orange segments, to decorate

Put the orange zest with the juice into a pan and bring to the boil slowly in order to extract the oils from the zest. Turn off the heat.

Sprinkle the gelatine crystals into the liquid and stir until fully dissolved. (The gelatine gives a smooth, spoonable set.) Cool completely. Add the liqueurs.

Strain into individual glasses and put to set. Cover with plastic film. Before serving, decorate each glass with 2 orange segments.

Port and Claret Jelly

Serves 8, or 6 if made in a mould

zest of 2 oranges
1 **oz** caster sugar
1 packet blackcurrant jelly, broken
   into cubes

½ **pint** ruby port
½ **pint** claret-type wine
whipped cream, to decorate
   (optional)

Remove the zest of the oranges with a potato-peeler – this eliminates getting much of the bitter white pith on the flavoursome orange peel. Finely shred this zest and place it in a bowl together with the sugar and the jelly cubes.

Combine the wine and port and bring to just under boiling point. Pour into the bowl, stirring until all the jelly is dissolved. Allow to cool, then pour into eight small, stemmed sherry glasses or a wetted mould and leave to set.

Decorate with lots of unsweetened whipped cream, if desired.

Wine Jelly

The very word 'jelly' smacks of nursery food and school meals, but a wine jelly is a long step from this and makes a most refreshing finish to any meal. For those of you with endless patience in your kitchens, it can be made with ½ pint of fresh blackcurrant juice when these berries are in season, but the following recipe using a packet jelly is a very good substitute and will convert many jelly-loathers!

Serves 8

1 packet blackcurrant or other dark
  or red fruit jelly, broken into cubes
1 pint claret-type wine
zest of 1 orange

2 good tbsps caster sugar
½ **pint** unsweetened double cream,
  whipped, to decorate (optional)

Finely shred the orange zest and place it in a bowl, together with the sugar and jelly cubes.

Bring the claret to just under boiling point and pour it into the bowl, stirring until all the jelly is dissolved. Allow to cool, then pour into a glass bowl or individual glasses and put to set.

Decorate with lots of unsweetened whipped cream, if desired.

Special Fools and Ices

Here are five 'modern' conceits to serve when next you have an elaborate tea-party.

Kiwi Fruit and Chartreuse Fool

If you cannot readily obtain miniature bottles of green Chartreuse, use gin.

Serves 4

4 kiwi fruits, peeled
2 tbsps green Chartreuse

¼ **pint** double cream
1 oz caster sugar

Make a purée of the kiwi fruit flesh and 1 tablespoon of the liqueur. Press through a fine-meshed sieve to remove all the black seeds.

Whip the cream with the sugar and remaining Chartreuse until it stands in firm peaks. Combine the purée and cream.

Spoon into small glasses. Chill well. Decorate with slices of kiwi fruit.

Lemon Ice-cream

Serves 5–6

8 egg yolks
2 oz caster sugar
grated zest of 2 lemons

¼ **pint** lemon juice
½ **pint** double cream

Whisk the egg yolks, sugar and lemon zest until very light and fluffy. Stir in the lemon juice.

Half whip the cream until it ribbons well but does not peak. Stir it thoroughly into the lemon mixture.

Use a home ice-cream maker to freeze the mixture.

Mango and Coconut Fool

If no coconut liqueur is available, use Grand Marnier and add 1 teaspoon of grated orange zest to the mixture.

Serves 4

2 mangoes, peeled
1 sherry glass of coconut cream liqueur

1 tsp lemon juice
½ **pint** double cream

Cut the flesh of the mangoes away from the stone. Make a purée of the flesh, the coconut liqueur and the lemon juice. Reserve 4 tablespoons of the purée.

Whip the cream to stiff peaks. Cut and fold the remaining purée into it.

Spoon into glasses and float a layer of the mango purée on the top of each fool. Chill well.

'Foulade' of Parfait d'Amour

Parfait d'Amour is a liqueur of violets.

Serves 4

12 fl. oz double cream
4 tbsps Parfait d'Amour
2 tbsps caster sugar

1 drop of violet colouring (optional)
1 oz crystallised violets, crushed
extra violets for garnish

Whip the cream, liqueur, sugar and violet colouring to a soft peak. Fold in the crushed crystallised violets. (The violets will 'bleed' if the mixture is left for a long time, but this doesn't affect the delicate flavour.)

Spoon into small glasses. Chill well and decorate with extra violets.

Raspberry Fool with Framboise

This produces a delicious pink fool topped with a layer of raspberries.

Serves 6

1 lb raspberries, fresh or frozen
2 oz caster sugar
juice of half a lemon
½ **pint** double cream

2 tbsps eau de vie de framboise
extra raspberries, to garnish
(optional)

Put the raspberries, sugar and lemon juice into a pan with 1 tablespoon of water. Toss or stir the fruit over a low heat until cooked and fallen.

Press or rub the mixture through a fine-meshed sieve until only the seeds remain in the sieve. Cool then chill the purée.

Stir and whisk in the cream and liqueur until the mixture just ribbons. Pour into a bowl or six glasses. Cover with plastic film and chill well.

Serve covered with a layer of raspberries, if desired.

BUTTERS

Butters

Any sandwich is improved by having a goodly amount of well-flavoured butter spread on it, no matter which bread or biscuit is used. Butters can be sweet or savoury, and made up in flavours to complement the particular filling used. As well as enriching the sandwich, butter keeps the bread moist, at the same time preventing any wetness from the filling making it soggy. So make sure you 'Spread to the Edge' – a motto which should be engraved on your cutting board!

Other spreads, such as flavoured cream cheese or herb-tinted and lemon-spiked mayonnaise, can be used instead of butter. Even fine vegetable purées made in a liquidiser have their place: mushroom, celeriac or even carrot or pea purée, for example. You might enjoy spreading the bread with a cushion of cold, well-seasoned creamed celeriac when next you make a chicken sandwich; and a fine purée of mushroom has a place with a crisp bacon filling.

There are absolutely no rules as to what to put with what – the choice is yours. Here are some ideas for butter spreads to start your mind ticking over and get the gastronomic juices flowing.

Note: Many of these butters have a 'second life' and can be used as an accompaniment to grilled fish, chicken or meat, should you have any left unused. Simply shape any leftover butter into a small roll or into individual pots and wrap it in aluminium foil or plastic film and store it in the freezer.

Using Butter

Half a pound of butter is enough to spread 20–24 slices of bread measuring 4×4 inches.

Unsalted butter is called for in all my recipes and certainly for all sweet recipes: you can add salt; you cannot take it out.

I also advise all trainee cooks who have occasion to come under my wing to practise *melting* butter. This may sound prosaic, but butter is used not only to enrich dishes with its fat content, but also to impart flavour to them. One of these flavours is that delicious almond aroma emanating from 'nut' butter (*beurre noisette*), where butter is melted carefully and evenly – by this I mean where the pan is tilted and turned over a moderate heat so that the butter melts and colours without burning at the edges – before other ingredients are added. The 'nut' stage is reached when the butter, after sizzling and spluttering a little, goes 'quiet' and looks a delicate tan colour, giving off an exotic almond smell.

To Clarify Butter

Top chefs use clarified butter all the time. It eliminates both the salt in salted butter and any excess moisture when used for frying. The amateur cook may not wish to use it all the time, but he or she does need to use clarified butter for sealing potted meats or fish and for pan-fried bananas or pineapple, in which any sediments are unsightly, and, in the case of potted foods, the impurities impair the life of the butter. For the diet-conscious, the coating of clarified butter can be eliminated, in which case cover the containers with plastic film.

There is little reason to clarify unsalted butter, but margarine fanatics might like to clarify that, as margarine contains a good deal of water – almost one-third of the content in some brands – and its flavour is improved when clarified.

The easiest way to clarify butter or margarine is to cut half a pound into cubes and bring it to the boil in ½ pint of water. Pour it into a bowl, let it cool, and then put it to set in the refrigerator. Lift off the set fat and scrape off any sediment from the under surface before patting it dry with paper towels. Re-melt the butter over a low heat and pass it through a fine muslin before use.

To Soften and Cream Butter

In certain recipes where butter is used for enriching and supporting other ingredients, such as some savoury mousses and pâtés, it is essential that the butter is properly softened and creamed in order to obtain a velvety texture in the finished dish.

Ideally you should start with the butter at room temperature. If you have forgotten to take it from the refrigerator, cut it into squares, put it into a bowl and stand this in the microwave for a second or two or in a regular oven at Gas ½/150°F/66°C for a minute or so (taking care that it doesn't oil) until it is soft enough to beat. Use a wooden spatula to beat the butter until it is lump-free, white and light-textured.

An alternative way is to turn the butter on to a clean work surface and cut and squash it with a palette-knife before transferring it back to the bowl for creaming as above.

For any soup or sauce recipe which is intended for serving either cold or chilled, you should use a flavourless oil instead of butter as oiled butter becomes 'grainy' when set.

Savoury Butters

Tomato Butter

12 oz unsalted butter, softened
2 tbsps tomato purée
½ tsp ground mace or dried rosemary
   or nutmeg
1 tsp brown sugar

1 tsp salt
¼ tsp freshly ground black pepper
1 tbsp dry sherry, warmed in cold
   weather

Make a fine purée of all the ingredients. Pack and serve as above.

Tomato Curry and Orange Butter

12 oz unsalted butter, softened
1 level tsp salt
2 tbsps good tomato purée

1 tsp finely grated orange zest
1 heaped tsp mild Madras curry
   powder or paste

Mix all the ingredients together in a liquidiser. Rub through a fine-meshed sieve and put them into wax or plastic cartons. Chill until required in either the freezer or the refrigerator. When ready to use, take the butter out of the freezer or refrigerator and allow it to come to room temperature.

Lemon Butter

12 oz unsalted butter, softened
1 level tsp salt
ground white pepper

juice and finely grated zest of a
lemon

Make a paste of all the ingredients in a liquidiser. Rub through a fine-meshed sieve. Pack and store as above.

Lemon and Parsley Butter

Make up one batch of Lemon Butter as above. After sieving, add 1 teacup of very finely chopped, freshly picked parsley.

Foie Gras and Artichoke Butter

6 oz unsalted butter, softened
1 4-oz tin of Mousse de Foie Gras or
  'Parfait' de Foie Gras
1 scant tsp salt

freshly ground white pepper
2 tsps orange juice
1 4-oz tin artichoke bottoms,
  drained, rinsed and drained again

Chop the artichoke bottoms very finely. In a liquidiser, make a fine purée of the remaining ingredients. Scrape them into a bowl and mix in the chopped artichoke. Pack and store as above.

Mint Butter

12 oz unsalted butter, softened
20–24 large mint leaves, picked and
  rinsed

2 tsps lemon juice
1 level tsp salt
1 level tsp sugar

Make a fine purée of all the ingredients in a liquidiser. Rub through a fine-meshed sieve. Pack and store as above.

Garlic Butter

12 oz unsalted butter, softened
8 large cloves of garlic, peeled

1 level tsp salt
2 tsps lemon juice

For sandwiches, the garlic aroma must be soft and gentle. So, blanch the garlic in boiling water for 2 minutes. Drain and cool. Push through a garlic press and beat into the softened butter along with the salt and lemon juice. Pack and store as above.

Mixed Herb Butter

12 oz unsalted butter, softened
4 tbsps each of the following fresh
  herbs:
  parsley, fennel fronds, chervil and
    chives or basil or tarragon,
    chives and flat-leaf parsley

½ clove of garlic, crushed
1 tsp lemon juice
1 tsp salt
freshly ground pepper to taste

Finely chop the herbs and blend together all the ingredients.

Basil Butter

12 oz unsalted butter, softened
1 tbsp tomato purée
1 tsp lemon juice
1 tsp caster sugar
1 tsp salt
1 packed teacup basil leaves, freshly picked and rinsed

Make a fine purée of the first five ingredients, adding the basil leaves towards the end so that some texture is left. Store and pack as above.

Tarragon Butter

12 oz unsalted butter, softened
1 packed teacup French tarragon leaves, freshly picked and rinsed
1 tbsp tarragon vinegar, warmed
1 tsp salt
freshly ground pepper

In a liquidiser make a fine purée of the ingredients. (The vinegar is warmed to help it emulsify in cold weather.) Rub through a fine-meshed sieve. Pack and store as above.

Chive Butter

12 oz unsalted butter, softened
1 teacup chives, very finely snipped
1 tsp lemon juice
ground white pepper

Beat the butter with the pepper and lemon juice. Mix in the snipped chives. Pack and store as above.

Watercress Butter

4 bunches crisp dark-leaf watercress
10 oz unsalted butter, softened
1 tsp caster sugar
1 tsp salt

Pick all the leaves from the watercress and discard the stalks. Drop the leaves into a pan of lightly salted boiling water for 30 seconds only. Drain, rinse under cold water and drain again. Squeeze out excess water. In a liquidiser, make a purée of the leaves, the softened butter, the sugar and salt. Pack and store as above.

Anchovy Butter

12 **oz** unsalted butter, softened
2 cloves of garlic, crushed
24 anchovy fillets (tinned variety)
2 **tsps** lemon juice

tip of a tsp cayenne or 6–8 drops of
   Tabasco
½ **tsp** freshly ground black pepper

In a liquidiser, make a purée of all the ingredients, then rub the mixture through a fine-meshed sieve. Pack and store as above.

Note: There is no added salt in this recipe.

Mustard Butter

12 **oz** unsalted butter, softened
2 **tbsps** mild French mustard

1 **tbsp** lemon juice

Beat everything to a smooth paste. Pack and store as above.

Horseradish Butter

12 **oz** unsalted butter, softened
2 **tbsps** freshly scraped horseradish
   root, finely grated

2 **tsps** lemon juice
2 **tsps** caster sugar
1 **tsp** salt

In a liquidiser, make a fine purée of all the ingredients.

Hazelnut Butter

12 oz unsalted butter, softened
6 oz hazelnuts, toasted and skins
   rubbed off

2 tsps soft brown sugar
½ tsp ground cinnamon
1 tbsp brandy

In a liquidiser, make a purée of all the above ingredients, adding the nuts a few at a time in order to leave some nutty texture. Store and pack as above.

Cinnamon Butter

12 oz unsalted butter, softened
4 oz soft brown sugar

2 tsps ground cinnamon
1 tsp finely grated orange zest

In a liquidiser, make a fine purée of all the ingredients. Pack and store as above.

Cumberland Rum Butter

12 oz unsalted butter, softened
4 oz Muscovado sugar
2 fl. oz Jamaican rum, warm in cold
   weather

½ tsp ground nutmeg

In a liquidiser, make a purée of all the ingredients, dribbling the warm rum so that it emulsifies. Pack and store as above.

Orange Butter

12 oz unsalted butter, softened
2 tsps finely grated orange zest

¼ tsp ground mace

In a liquidiser, make a fine purée of all the ingredients. Pack and store as above.

Brandy Butter

12 oz unsalted butter, softened
6 oz caster sugar
3 fl. oz brandy, warmed

1 tsp lemon zest
juice of half a small lemon, strained

In a liquidiser, make a purée of all the ingredients, dribbling in the warmed brandy to help make a smooth emulsion. Pack and store as above.

Honey Butter

12 oz unsalted butter, softened
4 oz flower-scented honey
  (Hymettus, Acacia or Orange
  Blossom)

1 tbsp orange or rose flower water

In a liquidiser, make a fine purée of all the ingredients. Pack and store as above.

Walnut Butter

12 oz unsalted butter, softened
2 tsps soft brown sugar
1 tbsp brandy

$\frac{1}{4}$ **tsp** ground nutmeg or mace
2 tsps lemon juice
4 oz walnuts, finely ground

Make a purée of the first five ingredients in a liquidiser. Fold in the crushed walnuts. Pack and store as above.

Walnut and Raisin Butter

$\frac{1}{2}$ **lb** best unsalted butter, softened
juice of half a lemon
a pinch of salt
8–10 grindings of pepper

4 oz seedless Muscatel raisins,
  chopped
4 oz walnuts, roughly crushed

Beat together the butter, lemon juice and seasonings until fluffy. Fold in the raisins and walnuts. Pack into a container and chill.

JAMS,
FRUIT BUTTERS
AND CHUTNEYS

JAMS

Commercial products such as Tiptree and Elsenham are readily available in the better stores, and are almost as good as home-made jams. However, there are a few which may have escaped the manufacturers' attention: most of those here are from my Edwardian mother's own recipe book.

Marrow and Ginger Jam

Makes 12 lb

6 lb prepared marrow (two smaller marrows will yield a better texture than one huge coarse one)

juice and zest of 4 lemons
3 oz root ginger
6 lb preserving sugar

Peel, seed, and remove the pith from the marrow before weighing the flesh. Cut the flesh into even ½-inch cubes, and steam these (in batches, if necessary) over boiling water until tender. Put the cooked marrow into a bowl with the lemon zest and juice.

Mix the sugar with the marrow, and leave in a cool place overnight.

Peel the ginger, slice it roughly and bruise it with the end of a rolling pin. Tie the ginger loosely in a piece of muslin cloth with a string long enough to attach it to the handle of the jam pan.

Put everything into a pan and stir over a medium heat until the sugar is quite dissolved. Continue cooking gently until the marrow is transparent and the syrup thick. Remove the ginger and drain it by pressing with a wooden spoon against the side of the pan. Discard the ginger.

Pour into hot jam jars. Cover and seal in the usual way.

English Summer Jam with Rose Petals

As with Summer Pudding – surely our best national dish – this jam can be made only during that short time when the four fruits are available together.
　　Only 'blowsy', velvety, heavily scented, old-fashioned roses should be used.

Makes 8 lb

1 lb blackcurrants	**4 lb** preserving sugar
1 lb redcurrants	$\frac{1}{4}$ **pint** water
1 lb raspberries	1 large, blowsy red rose
1 lb strawberries	

Rinse and pick the currants, using the tines of a large dinner fork to facilitate the job. Rinse, hull and quarter the strawberries. Pick over but do not rinse the raspberries.

Remove the petals from the rose and rinse them, discarding the 'green' inner ones.

Simmer the blackcurrants in the water until tender. Add all the remaining fruits and simmer until they too are tender.

Stir in the sugar until dissolved. During the final 10 minutes, stir in the rose petals. Boil hard to setting point.

Pour into hot jars. Cover and seal in the usual way.

Rhubarb and Raspberry Jam

Makes 12 lb

3 lb raspberries	$\frac{1}{2}$ **pint** water
3 lb rhubarb	**6 lb** preserving sugar

Pick over the raspberries and rinse them with a water spray. Trim, wash and cut the rhubarb into 1-inch pieces.

Over a low heat, simmer the rhubarb in the water until soft. Add the raspberries, stir them in and continue cooking until they too are soft.

Stir in the sugar, and continue stirring until dissolved. Boil hard to setting point.

Pour into hot jars. Cover and seal in the usual way.

Apricot Jam

Makes 12 lb

6 lb fresh apricots	**6 lb** preserving sugar
1$\frac{1}{4}$ pints water	**1 tsp** vanilla essence
juice of a lemon	

Wash, split and 'pit' the apricots. Crack the 'pits' or stones. Take out the kernels and blanch these in boiling water for 2–3 minutes. Rinse, cool and roughly crush them.

Meanwhile, cook the apricots with the lemon juice and water until quite soft. Add the kernels when they are ready. Add the sugar, stirring until dissolved. Boil hard to setting point, then stir in the vanilla essence.

Pour into hot jars. Cover and seal in the usual way.

Gooseberry and Elderflower Jam

These two typical English flavours make a very good marriage, particularly when spread on toasted crumpets or used as a layer in chocolate cake.

Makes 12 lb

6 lb under-ripe gooseberries	**10 heads** of elderflowers
2 pints water	**6 lb** preserving sugar

Wash, top and tail the gooseberries. Pick the elderflowers off the stalks; discard the stalks and roughly chop the flowers.

Simmer the fruit and flowers in the water until pulped, mashing them as they cook. Stir in the sugar until dissolved. Boil briskly to setting point.

Pour into hot jam jars. Cover and seal in the usual way.

Note: Fast boiling produces a green jam; prolonged boiling a darker, almost red jam.

Blackcurrant Jam

Makes 10 lb

4 lb blackcurrants	**6 lb** preserving sugar
3¼ pints water	

Rinse the blackcurrants and remove them from their stalks with the tines of a fork. Put them into a jam pan with the water and simmer until soft.

Over a medium heat, stir in the sugar until dissolved, then boil hard to setting point.

Pour into hot jars. Cover and seal in the usual way.

Greengage Jam

Makes 12 lb

6 lb greengages   **6 lb** preserving sugar
1 pint water

Wash the greengages. Cut them in half, removing the stones.

Crack the stones and remove the kernels. Blanch the kernels for 2 minutes in boiling water and split or cut them in half.

Put the greengages, kernels and water in a jam pan and simmer until soft. Add the sugar, stirring until dissolved, and boil hard to setting point.

Pour into hot jam jars. Cover and seal in the usual way.

Damson Jam

At home my mother never removed the stones when making damson jam, telling us children to make up a game by counting them on our plate edges. It was her way of getting us to eat this jam!

Makes 6 lb

3 lb damsons   **3 lb** preserving sugar
1¼ pints water

Wash the damsons and simmer them in the water until soft, skimming off any stones that come to the surface. Mix in the sugar, stirring until dissolved, and boil well to setting point.

Pour into hot jam jars. Cover and seal in the usual way.

FRUIT BUTTER AND FRUIT CHEESE

Both fruit butter and fruit cheese are old fashioned and still very desirable ways of preserving fruits. The difference between them is in the consistency. Fruit butter is soft and spreadable, and should be used on crumpets, muffins or on plain buttered brown toast, whereas fruit cheese is set in straight-sided jars, turned out and cut into slices, and can be served with a crumbly cheese or eaten in small amounts with a fork. In the eighteenth century fruit cheese was eaten – alone – with a fork or served with cold meats, rather as you would serve cranberry sauce or chutney nowadays. Today it is a nice novelty to serve a fruit cheese at tea-time.

Blackberry Cheese

This is wonderful served with mature Cheddar or a crumbly Wensleydale cheese.

Makes approximately 7 lb

4 lb blackberries   preserving sugar (see method)
2 tsps tartaric acid

Pick over and rinse the fruit. Put into a pan with the tartaric acid and barely enough water to cover. Simmer until the fruit is soft. Press and rub through a fine-meshed sieve. Strain. Weigh the pulp.

Add 1 lb sugar to 1 lb pulp. Stir over a low heat until the sugar has dissolved.

Boil gently until very thick, stirring almost continuously.

Pour into hot, small, straight-sided containers. Cover and seal as for jam.

To serve, run a hot palette-knife around the sides of the jam in the jars. Turn out and slice with a hot knife.

Lemon Cheese

In some parts of England this is called Lemon Curd. Use it in tarts, as a spread on tea-breads, or as an accompaniment to ice-cream.

Makes 3 lb

4 large lemons   1 lb preserving sugar
6 oz unsalted butter, softened   4 large eggs, well beaten

Grate just the zest from the lemons, avoiding the bitter white pith (use a potato-peeler to do this). Squeeze the juice and strain it, pressing the debris well.

In a double pan, or in a heatproof bowl over a pan of simmering water, melt the butter. Add the lemon juice, zest and sugar, and stir with a wire balloon whisk until the sugar is dissolved.

Gradually incorporate the well-beaten eggs and stir slowly but thoroughly until the mixture is thick and ribbons or trails well when the whisk is drawn through the mixture.

Pour into smallish hot jars. Cover and seal as for jam.

Apple and Plum Butter

Makes approximately 7 lb

3 lb apples, peeled, cored and
   roughly cut up
1 lb red plums, stoned and cut up

¼ **pint** water
juice of a lemon, strained
preserving sugar (see method)

Over a low heat, cook both the fruits in the water until pulped. Add the lemon juice. Stir well during this process. Pass through a food processor, then rub the fruit pulp through a fine-meshed sieve.

Weigh the pulp, put into a clean pan, and add 12 oz sugar to each 1 lb pulp. Stir the mixture until the sugar is dissolved, then boil until thick.

Pour into hot jars. Cover and seal as for jam.

Chutney

Chutney is an integral part of Indian meals. The word has its roots in Imperial India, deriving from the Hindu *chatni*. In Britain – during and following the Raj – chutney became popular as an accompaniment to cold cuts. The belly-burning curries so sought after today as a result of the rise in popularity of ethnic restaurants were not known in England before the Second World War. However, chutney was and still is an excellent addition to many sandwich fillings.

English-made chutneys are milder and, I think, often more subtle than their 'mother' chutneys. I give you my three favourites to try as an introduction to this relish, though I'm sure in the better stores you will find good commercial brands, such as Sarsons, Tiptree and Elsenham.

Apple Chutney

Makes 10 lb

5 lb apples, peeled, cored and diced
1 pint malt or red wine vinegar
1 lb Demerara sugar
1 tbsp salt
1 tbsp ground ginger
3 chillies or 1 oz mustard seeds

8 oz onions, peeled and finely chopped
8 oz Muscatel raisins, chopped
8 oz sultanas
juice and grated zest of a lemon

In a preserving pan bring to the boil the vinegar, salt, sugar and chillies or mustard seeds. Add all the remaining ingredients and simmer for 1 hour or more. The type of apples used will very much determine how much juice they yield (I use Cox's Orange Pippins). The chutney should be simmered until of a jam-like consistency. Stir from time to time to prevent scorching.

Pour into hot jars. Cover and seal as for jam.

Tomato Chutney

Makes 4 lb

1 lb ripe tomatoes, skinned only, then chopped
2 eating apples, cored and chopped
8 oz onions, skinned and finely chopped
1 lb sultanas
8 oz soft brown sugar

1 pint malt or red wine vinegar
2 tsps salt
1 oz mustard seeds, tied in a bag
2 tsps ground ginger
tip of a tsp cayenne pepper or $\frac{1}{4}$ tsp Tabasco

250

Put all the ingredients into a preserving pan. Bring to the boil and simmer, stirring from time to time, until thick and a good reddish-brown colour.

Pour into hot jars. Cover and seal as for jam.

Gooseberry Chutney

Makes 6–7 lb

3 lb green gooseberries
1½ lb preserving or granulated sugar
8 oz Muscatel raisins
1 lb redskin onions, skinned and
  finely chopped

2 tsps salt
½ oz mustard seeds
¼ tsp cayenne pepper
1¼ pints red wine vinegar

Tie the mustard seeds loosely in muslin. Put all the ingredients into a preserving pan. Bring to the boil, lower the heat, and simmer gently for 1¾–2 hours, stirring from time to time to prevent burning. The chutney should be the consistency of jam.

Ladle into hot jars. Cover and seal as for jam.

MINCEMEAT

Christmas Mincemeat with Rum

Although any spirit may be used (it is there to preserve and mature the ingredients), rum is perhaps the one most associated with Christmas in England. Make the mincemeat at least a month in advance to give it time to mature properly. Use a 5 fl. oz teacup as a measure.

Makes approximately 7 lb

2 lb green cooking apples
3 **teacups** shredded beef suet
(commercial brand)
3 **teacups** Muscatel raisins, roughly
chopped
2 **teacups** sultanas
3 **teacups** currants
2 **teacups** finely chopped mixed peel
juice and grated zest of a large
lemon

juice and grated zest of an orange
1 **tsp** ground cinnamon
1 **tsp** ground mace
½ **tsp** ground nutmeg
4 **teacups** moist unrefined brown
sugar
1 **tsp** salt
1½ **teacups** Demerara rum or brandy

Core, seed and grind the unpeeled apples (or use the coarse side of a grater). Roughly chop all the dried fruits. Resist the temptation to grind these, as a rough texture is preferable.

Using your clean hand and a large bowl, mix all the ingredients very well together. Leave for 24 hours in a cool place, covered with plastic film.

All the juices should now be absorbed. Stir well again and pack into cold jars. Seal with plastic film, or use old-fashioned screwtop jars with rubber ring seals.

Leave to mature in a cool place for at least a month.

OTHER
SAVOURY
ITEMS

Patties

The name for small vol-au-vents, 1 inch in diameter, is not to be confused with the French *pâté*. (That said, the word derives from the word 'patty', which in turn came out of 'pastry', which (of course!) came from the French *pâte* or paste.)

Patties are an essential item on an afternoon-tea menu for a party, and are served warm with a variety of fillings based on a rich, creamy white sauce. Fill them cold, then warm them through in the oven at a low temperature before serving.

Patty Cases

(Patty Shells or Bouchées)

Makes approximately 20–24 patties

1 lb puff pastry (bought variety or see pp. 186–7)   beaten egg, to glaze

Pre-heat the oven to Gas 8/450°F/230°C. Use two cutters, one of them 1½ inches in diameter, and the other a centre cutter 1 inch in diameter.

Roll out the puff pastry evenly to ⅓ inch thick. Thrust the larger cutter through the pastry without twisting it, as this can seal the edges and impede the rising of the pastry.

With the second cutter, cut halfway through each circle of pastry you have just made.

With a palette-knife, lift the patties on to a wetted baking tray, placing them 1 inch apart. Brush the tops with beaten egg, avoiding getting any on the cut edges.

Bake for 10 minutes, then lower the temperature to Gas 4/350°F/180°C for a further 7–10 minutes or until the shells are risen, golden brown and totally crisp. Leave to cool.

With a pointed knife, carefully cut round and remove the centre ring. This will reveal some soft dough in the cavity. Using the rounded end of a teaspoon handle, or something similar, carefully scrape out as much of this as will readily come without piercing the base.

Either re-heat the shells and lids and fill with a hot filling or leave to cool, fill with a cold filling, put on their lids, and re-heat as instructed above.

For variation, patties can be cut 1½ inches square.

Heavy Rich Cream Sauce for Patties

1 pint fills 24–30 cocktail-size (1–1½ inch diameter) and 16–20 tea-size (2–2¼ inch diameter) patty cases

2 oz unsalted butter
1½ oz plain flour
¾ pint milk
¼ pint single cream

1 tsp salt
¼ tsp ground mace
a little freshly ground pepper
1 tsp lemon juice

In a non-stick saucepan melt the butter and stir in the flour.

Using a wire balloon whisk, whisk in the milk and, stirring, allow the sauce to come to the boil. Lower the heat and bubble for 2 minutes. Stir in the cream, seasonings and lemon juice. Cover with a buttered circle of paper to prevent a skin forming. Leave to cool.

When ready for use, pre-heat the oven to Gas 3/325°F/170°C, stir the chosen filling (see following recipes) into the sauce, spoon into empty patty cases, and stand these on a baking tray. Heat through for 20 minutes.

Serve the patties on a silver dish lined with a folded white napkin.

Mushroom Patties

To each pint of cold, rich white sauce (see above) add:

8 oz white-cap mushrooms, finely chopped

4 fl. oz dry Madeira
1 tsp mild French mustard

Simmer and toss the mushrooms in the Madeira. Strain, then reduce the liquor to 2 tablespoonsful. Mix in the mustard, then mix the whole lot into the white sauce.

Shrimp Patties

To each pint of cold sauce add:

8 oz cooked shrimps or prawns, finely chopped
1 tsp paprika and salt and freshly ground pepper

a good squeeze of lemon juice

Chicken Patties

To each pint of cold sauce add:

2 8-oz chicken breasts, finely diced
(¼ inch)
1 oz unsalted butter

1 tsp ground mace
salt and freshly ground pepper
2 fl. oz dry sherry

Melt the butter in a heavy skillet until foaming. Over a high heat, seal and fry the diced chicken, seasoning with salt, pepper and mace as you go along.

Pour in the sherry and bubble until syrupy, when the chicken will be cooked but still moist. Cool before stirring into the sauce.

Salmon Patties

To each pint of cold sauce add:

12 oz cold poached salmon, flaked
or minced
a good squeeze of lemon juice

salt and freshly ground pepper to
taste

Sausage Rolls

These little meat-filled pastry rolls have done much to earn British food a bad name. They appear everywhere from station buffets and tea-shops to school lunch-boxes and vending machines in factory canteens.

Yet there was a time when afternoon tea without a sausage roll was unthinkable. They were made small with a melt-in-the-mouth crust and a tasty sausage-meat filling.

I urge you to try my recipe, where the filling is of two different home-made sausages: pork, and chicken and ham. I think you'll agree they deserve to regain their good reputation.

Sausage Roll Pastry

Makes approximately 30 small rolls of each filling

1 lb plain flour	**1 egg** plus 1 egg yolk
1 tsp salt	**2 tbsps** single cream or milk, to
6 oz unsalted butter	glaze
2 oz lard	

Sieve the flour and salt into a large bowl. With your fingertips or a pastry blender rub in the butter and lard until you have a moist sand-like texture.

Whisk together the egg, egg yolk and cream. Using a fork, mix this into the dry ingredients to form a soft dough. With your fingers, draw the dough into a ball, then wrap it in plastic film and refrigerate for at least an hour.

Chicken and Ham Filling

1 lb raw chicken breast, boned, skinned and diced	**1 tsp** salt
	1 tsp freshly ground pepper
8 oz raw ham	**1 egg**, beaten with 4 tbsps double
4 oz streaky bacon	cream
2 teacups fresh white breadcrumbs	**4 tbsps** parsley, finely chopped
1 tsp ground mace	

In a food processor, blend the chicken, ham and bacon until fine. Add the breadcrumbs, seasonings and the egg mixture. Blend thoroughly, finally quickly adding the parsley.

Turn on to a floured board or work surface and divide into two equal parts. Form each half into a sausage approximately 20 inches long.

Pork Filling

1¼ **lb** boneless pork loin, diced
1 eating apple (preferably a Cox's
  Orange Pippin), quartered and
  cored but not peeled
2 **teacups** fresh white breadcrumbs
2 **tsps** rubbed sage

½ **tsp** ground mace
1 **tsp** each salt and freshly ground
  pepper
1 egg, beaten with 1 tbsp double
  cream

In a food processor, blend the pork until finely cut. Slice in the apple and blend for 1 minute. Add the remaining ingredients and continue to process until evenly mixed together.

Turn on to a floured board or work surface. Divide into two equal pieces and shape each half into a sausage approximately 20 inches long.

To Fill Sausage Rolls

Pre-heat the oven to Gas 5/375°F/190°C.

Cut the pastry into two. Roll one half into a rectangle 20×10 inches. Cut this in half lengthwise to give two oblongs 10×5 inches.

Place the two rolls of chicken filling down the centre of each pastry oblong, brush the edges with beaten egg, and fold them over to enclose the filling. Press and pinch the edges together. Cut each roll in half and place all four rolls on a lightly greased baking tray. Brush the rolls all over with beaten egg and make cuts three-quarters through the pastry at approximately 1-inch intervals.

Repeat with the other half of the pastry and the pork filling.

Bake for 20–25 minutes or until golden brown. Allow to cool slightly before completely cutting through.

These sausage rolls freeze well after they are cooked. Thaw and gently re-heat them. They may also be frozen shaped but uncooked. Thaw, brush with beaten egg, then cook as above. Sausage rolls should always be eaten hot or warm.

POTTED MEATS AND FISH

As a means of preserving foods, potting has gone on for hundreds of years throughout Europe. Cooked fish, meat or poultry is sealed under a thick layer of butter or lard, giving it an extended storage life. Revealing the natural flavours of the food almost unhampered, it is understandable that potted foods have stayed popular.

Originally these coarse-textured potted fish, meats and game were eaten for breakfast, or as part of a high tea. Potted foods moved gradually towards the afternoon-tea table in the nineteenth century, becoming more refined as they did so, and eventually joined the band of sandwich fillings.

Today, they are regaining their popularity as an alternative, and often a better one, to the ubiquitous French pâtés. They are excellent spread on small crackers at cocktail time, and better still if attractively displayed in their own handsome 'pots' for guests to spread on to mini-muffins or biscuits.

Potted foods also make excellent starters for a lunch or dinner party, again served in their pot, and eaten with crusty bread, dry brown toast or fingers of hot buttered toast.

Some people like to use their portion of the film of clarified butter from the top of the pot to spread on to their toast; others do not choose to add to their cholesterol intake in this way and leave it on the side of their plate.

The all-essential ingredient is, of course, this sealing butter. Today clarified butter (see pp. 234–5) is used, as it is free of any sediments which might otherwise allow the fat to become rancid. Clarifying also drives out the air from the butter, giving it a 'hard' set. For added interest, I sometimes add a smidge of ground mace, nutmeg or thyme, and a little grated lemon zest to the clarified butter before spooning it over the food to be potted.

When the pots have been prepared, they can be kept in the refrigerator for up to two weeks, and they freeze well for up to six months. Always allow the potted product to come to room temperature before serving; this will bring out the flavour.

In most country towns, potted beef and salmon 'paste' can be purchased from any good family grocer, though these are not nearly so good as the home-made variety.

Potted Meat: see pp. 75–6.

Potted Tongue

Makes $\frac{3}{4}$ lb

$\frac{1}{2}$ **lb** ox or lamb's tongue, cooked
2 oz unsalted butter
1 tbsp dark rum

1 tsp mild French mustard
3 oz clarified butter (see pp. 234–5)
1 extra $\frac{1}{4}$-inch slice of ox tongue

Cut the slice of tongue into very small ($\frac{1}{4}$-inch) dice and put these on one side.

Put the first four ingredients into a liquidiser or food processor and make a fine paste. Scrape this into a bowl and mix in the diced tongue.

Put into a dish or individual ramekins. Spoon a thin film of clarified butter over the top. Refrigerate until ready for use.

Potted Devilled Ham

Makes $\frac{3}{4}$ lb

8 oz cooked lean *smoked* ham, de-rinded and diced, and including its fat
3 oz unsalted butter
1 good tsp mild mustard

3–4 drops of Tabasco
2–3 pinches cayenne pepper
salt, if required
1 tbsp Worcestershire sauce
3 oz clarified butter (see pp. 234–5)

In a food processor or liquidiser, make a fine purée of all the ingredients except the clarified butter.

Put the purée into a pot or individual ramekins. Spoon a thin film of clarified butter over the top. Refrigerate until ready for use.

Potted Duck

Makes $1\frac{1}{2}$–2 lb

1 small (3–4lb) duck
1 oz unsalted butter, softened
1 tsp ground mace

1 tsp salt
1 tsp freshly ground pepper

Pre-heat the oven to Gas 5/375°F/190°C.

Make a paste of the butter, mace, salt and pepper. Rub this well into the skin of the duck.

Stand the duck on a wire trivet and roast for 1¼ hours, by which time the duck will be fairly well done. Allow it to cool enough to handle it. Remove the skin and discard this (or see below).

Strip the meat from the carcass, discarding any bits of sinew there might be in the legs.

Using two forks, drag and pull the meat into fine shreds. Chop any of the longer shreds so that all is of a similar texture.

Choose a pot large enough to contain the duck meat. Lay a few freshly picked sage leaves in the bottom of the pot. Layer the meat, dribbling between the layers enough of the cool duck fats to hold things together. Ensure that the meat is just covered with the fats before putting to set in the refrigerator.

This can be used as a rich sandwich filling, in which case spread brown bread with a little duck fat and cover with thin strips of the crisp duck skin and a film of sage and apple jelly before spreading the potted duck on top.

Potted Salmon

Makes 1¼–1½ lb

1 lb fresh salmon, in a single piece
1 tsp ground mace
1 slice of lemon
¼ tsp ground cloves or 2 cloves
¼ tsp ground bay or 1 bay leaf
    broken into bits

salt and freshly ground pepper
2–3 oz unsalted butter
3 oz clarified butter (see pp. 234–5)

Pre-heat the oven to Gas 6/400°F/200°C.

Skin and slice the salmon into thinnish pieces. Put these into an earthenware pot just large enough to contain them, seasoning well with the herbs and spices as you arrange the pieces and dispersing the butter amongst the pieces. Put a lid on the pot and stand it in a container of hot water.

Bake until the fish is cooked (about 45 minutes). Cool completely.

Purée the fish in a food processor or liquidiser. Adjust the seasoning if necessary, and pack the purée into an attractive china container. Spoon a thin film of clarified butter over the top. Chill well.

Serve like a pâté, or use as a sandwich filling.

Potted Smoked Trout

Makes 1 lb

10 oz smoked trout, skinned and
  boned
2 oz unsalted butter
2 oz Philadelphia cream cheese
2 tbsps soured cream

juice of half a small lemon
2–3 drops of Tabasco
½ tsp ground mace
salt and freshly ground pepper
3 oz clarified butter (see pp. 234–5)

Purée the fish flesh in a liquidiser or food processor. Mix in all the remaining ingredients, except the clarified butter.

Spoon into a pretty pot or individual ramekins. Pour a thin film of clarified butter over the top. Refrigerate to set. Remove from the refrigerator an hour before use.

Potted Kippers

Smoked haddock can be used as an alternative, but is not so robust and smoky as a good Loch Fyne or Manx kipper. Salt is not added in this recipe, as the smoked fish is probably salty enough.

Makes 1 lb

8 oz cooked kipper or smoked
  haddock
2 oz unsalted butter
2 oz Philadelphia cream cheese

2 tbsps double cream
freshly ground pepper
1 tbsp whisky
3 oz clarified butter (see pp. 234–5)

Purée the kipper or haddock in a liquidiser. Mix in the remaining ingredients, except the clarified butter, in short, sharp bursts.

Spoon into a pretty pot or individual ramekins and pour a film of clarified butter on top. Leave to set.

Take out of the refrigerator at least 1 hour before serving. Serve with hot, dry brown toast, or use as a sandwich filling.

Potted Crab

This is my recipe from *New English Cookery*, which is itself an 'update' on my recipe for Potted Crab in *Fine English Cookery*, concocted some fifteen years ago. Here I have refined things even more and aromatised it with a touch of orange.

Makes 1 lb

8 oz dressed crab, both light and
  dark meats
5 oz unsalted butter, softened
2 tbsps dry Madeira or Amontillado
  sherry
finely grated zest and juice of a small
  orange

¼ tsp salt
¼ tsp freshly ground pepper
¼ tsp ground mace
1 tsp finely grated orange zest
2 tbsps water
1½ oz unsalted butter

Cut the 5 oz butter into ½-inch cubes and leave to soften at room temperature. Bring the wine and orange juice to the boil in a small pan. Reduce this liquid to 1 tablespoon by boiling rapidly. Remove the pan from the heat.

Vigorously beat in the cubes of butter a little at a time, using a small balloon whisk. When you have a creamy consistency and all the butter is incorporated, beat in the crab meat, using a wooden spatula or spoon. Season well with salt, pepper and mace as you go along.

For a fine purée, the fish can now be laboriously rubbed through a fine-meshed wire sieve; or it can be left somewhat coarse in texture.

Spoon the purée into a pot just large enough to contain it and pour a thin film of the clarified orange butter on top (see below).

To make the clarified orange butter. Put the 1½ oz butter together with the 2 tablespoons of water and the orange zest into a small pan, and gently melt it over a low heat. Remove from the heat and strain the butter through a fine-meshed sieve into a teacup, pressing through all the oils from the zest. Put to set in the refrigerator. Remove the 'circle' of set butter, and pat and wipe the underside clean. Clean the cup and re-melt the orange-flavoured clarified butter by standing the cup in a pan of simmering water. Allow the butter to cool before spooning over the potted crab.

If you are making the potted crab for use in sandwiches there is no need to use this clarified butter, which is there to seal the top of the pot or pots when the fish is intended for use as a starter at dinner.

Beef and Ham Mould

Ideal as a sandwich filling when sliced thinly.

Serves 12–14

1½ **lb** best steak, trimmed of all
  excess fat
1½ **lb** ham, with fat
6 **oz** pork fat
1 sachet of gelatine
¼ **pint** cold water

2 **oz** white breadcrumbs
2 eggs, beaten
grated zest of half a lemon
4 **tbsps** parsley or 2 tbsps chives,
  freshly chopped
1½ **tsps** salt

Pass the meats and fats through a mincer once, or chop them in a food processor. Dissolve the gelatine in the cold water. Combine all the ingredients and season well.

Pack the mixture into a 2½–3-pint well-buttered basin or mould. Cover with buttered foil, making a 2-inch pleat in the foil. Tie it down firmly, using a slip knot. Steam or boil for 2 hours. Cool, then refrigerate.

Serve cut into thin slices, accompanied by a herb salad and home-made pickle or chutney.

Patum Peperium (Gentleman's Relish)

This extraordinary and uniquely English stuff is sold in flat white china pots, not dissimilar to pomade jars. It is a very strong pâté with a heavy anchovy base (anyone who has ever tasted Tapénade in the south of France will be thinking along the right lines!). Served spread on Bath Oliver biscuits or fingers of hot buttered toast, it certainly induces a thirst!

It is still to be found in some of the gentlemen's clubs of London's St James's. A sophisticated hostess might have a pot to hand at afternoon tea for any gentleman present – the minuscule sandwiches perhaps being considered too effete for the visiting country squire or clubland gentleman!

Elsenham produce Gentleman's Relish, and it is certainly available from specialist food shops.

TEA-PUNCHES
AND
WINE-CUPS

TEA-PUNCHES

The best results for a cold tea base for chilled tea-punches is to infuse the leaves of a good quality tea such as Ceylon, Yunnan, Darjeeling or Keemun overnight in the refrigerator; the result will be a crystal-clear liquid. A hot infusion, although quicker, often produces a cloudy liquid.

It is also easier to use a sugar syrup for sweetening cold teas; this can be prepared and stored indefinitely in the refrigerator.

Iced Tea

Serves 4–6

5 tsps tea, Darjeeling, Orange Pekoe or Yunnan
1 pint cold water

3–4 tsps sugar or to taste, or use sugar syrup (see below)

Put everything into a glass jug. Stir well and refrigerate for 12 hours or overnight.

Stir well before going to bed, and again when you get up. Some leaves will sink, others will float.

Strain – first through a fine-meshed sieve, then through a sieve lined with kitchen paper or a clean muslin. Chill again.

Sugar Syrup

20 oz caster sugar
2 pints cold water

pared zest of a lemon

Bring all the ingredients slowly to the boil. Simmer until clear. Cool. Store refrigerated in a screw-top glass jar.

Champagne Tea Fizz

Serves 8–10

1 pint Yunnan, Darjeeling or Keemun tea, made with 1 oz tea
1 bottle 'party' champagne, well chilled
sugar syrup to taste (see above)

a curl of pared orange zest for each glass
1 'stick' of pineapple for each glass
1 'tot' Cointreau

Have ready chilled glasses containing the orange zest, pineapple stick, Cointreau and 1 teaspoon of syrup. Half fill these with the chilled tea. Top up with champagne as you serve.

Simple Chilled Tea-punch

Serves 6

5 tsps Keemun or Ceylon tea
1 pint cold water

sugar syrup to taste (see p. 266)

Pour the tea over cracked ice with sprigs of apple-mint (which should first be bruised), a slice of lemon and sugar syrup to taste. Serve in small, elegant glasses.

Hot Tea-punch

Serves 12–14

2 pints hot tea of your choice
sugar syrup to taste
1 pint freshly squeezed orange juice,
   strained

$\frac{1}{4}$ **pint** freshly squeezed lemon juice,
   strained

Serve with slices of lemon and orange in heatproof tea-glasses. This punch is excellent when served chilled with the addition of cucumber sticks and the odd borage flower.

Tea Toddy

Serves 8

1 pint hot Lapsang Souchong tea
juice of 2 lemons, strained
zest of a small lemon

sugar syrup to taste (see p. 266)
$\frac{1}{4}$ **pint** Irish whiskey

Iced Strawberry Tea-punch

Serves 6

1 **pint** Earl Grey tea, chilled
Grenadine or sugar syrup (see
  p. 266), to taste

2 strawberries, quartered, per glass
2 mint leaves, bruised, per glass
crushed ice or ice cubes

Put the fruit and mint in glasses and cool in the refrigerator. Pour the chilled tea over. Add a little ice. Sweeten to taste with Grenadine or sugar syrup.

Afternoon Wine-cups

On special occasions, such as afternoon weddings, a wine-cup should be served.

Claret Cup

This is a very simple and effective afternoon drink. Pour equal quantities of any claret-type wine and dry ginger ale over crushed ice. Add a sprig of mint to each glass.

Pimm's Cup

There is a strange connection between tea- and coffee-drinking and Pimm's Cup. Back in the early nineteenth century, one James Pimm had an oyster bar in the City, right in the heart of the area where all the tea- and coffee-merchants had their warehouses and offices, and where the tea- and coffee-shops first saw the light of day. He concocted what we now know was the world's first 'gin sling' (which is not an American drink as many might imagine). His customers enjoyed his secret recipe very much. In 1896, a later generation of the Pimm family bottled this delicious cooler for retail sale, and the drink enjoyed great commercial success at such places as Henley, the Oxbridge May Balls, and other fashionable events.

Today there is a big rebirth of Pimm's drinking – not just because it is an excellent drink, but because it has a low alcohol content and can be drunk without too much fear of inebriation: if you don't over-pour, that is! If you can't get hold of a bottle, then you might like to try the Smith version, which I concocted during Pimm's decline in popularity.

½ **pint** gin
½ **pint** sweet vermouth
¼ **pint** 1-part dry vermouth
4 drops of Angostura bitters

A Pimm's Cup is traditionally served chilled in small silver, pewter or glass tankards, into each of which should be put:

ice cubes
1 2-inch stick peeled cucumber
1 wedge Cox's Orange Pippin
½ slice of orange
½ slice of lemon
1 cocktail cherry on a stick
a sprig of borage or mint

Top up with chilled sparkling lemonade. Just how much of the base mixture you use depends very much on how strong you like your drinks. I suggest you start with 2 fl. oz per ½-pint tankard or glass.

Rum Tea-punch

Serves 6–8

1 **pint** hot Yunnan, Darjeeling or
  Ceylon tea, made with 1 oz tea
sugar syrup to taste (see p. 266)

1 stick cinnamon, broken up
zest of a small orange
¼ **pint** Demerara rum

Infuse the tea with the cinnamon and orange zest. Sweeten to taste. Strain into a warm punch bowl, then add the rum. Serve in small quantities!

Pimm's Royale Cup

Follow the recipe for Pimm's Cup, using champagne or sparkling wine in place of the lemonade.

Buck's Fizz

Combine equal proportions of freshly squeezed chilled orange juice and chilled champagne.

Red Buck's Fizz

Use ruby or blood oranges for an interesting effect.

Strawberry Champagne Cup

1 bottle pink champagne, well
  chilled
1 sugar cube, rubbed over an
  orange to absorb the oils, per
  glass, plus 1 drop of Angostura
  bitters
1 small tot orange curaçao per glass

small twists of orange zest
1 strawberry, quartered, per glass
1 well-shaped berry, nicked with a
  knife and slipped over the rim of
  the glass
extra unhulled strawberries for
  dunking

Sparkling Cider Cup

Serves 12

1 2-pint bottle sparkling cider
2 fl. oz sugar syrup (see p. 266)
2 fl. oz brandy
2 fl. oz orange curaçao
1 pint weak China tea, made with
  1 oz Yunnan or I-Chang tea

juice of 2 oranges, squeezed and
  strained
slices of fruit, to garnish

Put ice cubes into a punch bowl or jug. Pour over all the ingredients, adding the sparkling cider just before you serve the cup.

Freshly Made Lemonade

Serves 12

6 large lemons
5–6 oz sugar
2½ **pints** boiling water

Cut the lemons in half; squeeze and strain the juice. Put the juice and skins into a china jug, add the sugar, pour the boiling water over and stir well. Leave to cool, then chill overnight.

Strain off the liquid, squeezing the skins well, then add the liquid again. Chill again until ready for use. Serve topped up with sparkling water.

Claret Cup for a Winter's Day

Serves 24

2 bottles claret
¼ **pint** dry sherry
¼ **pint** brandy

¼ **pint** Maraschino
zest of a lemon and an orange
sugar syrup, to taste (see p. 266)

Serve cold, and in small tots as it is fairly potent! An alternative is to serve it in larger glasses, and top it up with sparkling water to taste.

Wedding Champagne Punch

Serves 12

1 bottle dry champagne, chilled
1 bottle Sauternes, chilled
¼ bottle Cointreau, chilled

ice-cubes
slices of orange
slivers of orange zest

Half fill a punch bowl with ice-cubes (crushed ice melts too readily). Pour all the ingredients over. Float orange slices in the punch bowl, and twists of orange zest in each glass.

When orange blossoms are in bloom, it is pretty to scatter a few of the scented flowers in the punch bowl.

Badminton Cup

This is a Victorian red-wine 'Spritz' or 'Seltz'.

Serves 12–16

1 bottle Burgundy or Beaujolais
2 75cl bottles soda water

zest of an orange and a lemon
¼ bottle orange curaçao

Put all the ingredients except the soda water into a punch bowl or glass jug. Chill very well. Serve in small glasses, topped up with soda water: about one-third wine-base to two-thirds soda.

White Wine 'Seltz'

This drink was considered elegant, refreshing and quite proper for Victorian and Edwardian ladies to partake of in the afternoon without their getting tipsy!

Serves 10–12

1 bottle dry Moselle or Rhine wine,
   chilled

a twist of lemon zest
soda water, chilled

One-third fill each glass with wine, fill up with soda water and squeeze a twist of lemon oils over the surface.

Loving Cup

To serve as a toast at weddings.

Serves 18

1 bottle champagne	**4 oz** sugar cubes
½ bottle Madeira	2 lemons
¼ bottle brandy	sprigs of borage or apple-mint
1½ **pints** sparkling water	

Rub the sugar cubes over the lemon zest until saturated in the lemon oils. Slice the lemons. Knife-peel the lemon slices thinly. Put all the ingredients except the champagne and sparkling water into a punch bowl. Chill well.

When ready to serve, stir until the sugar is dissolved. Fill up with the wine and water.

Moselle Cup

Serves 10–12

1 bottle Moselle wine	1–2 **oz** sugar, to taste
4 **fl. oz** orange curaçao	soda water
strained juice and thinly pared zest of a lemon	

Mix the first five ingredients and chill well. Half fill glasses and top up with soda or other sparkling water.

Cranberry Ruby Fizz

The glowing red colour of this sparkling drink would be ideal for a Ruby Wedding celebration.

Makes 8–10 large glasses

1 bottle dry sparkling wine or pink champagne	½ **pint** ruby or blood orange juice
1 **pint** cranberry–raspberry fruit juice (see p. 274)	fresh raspberries, to garnish (optional)

Half fill tall, 10-fl. oz glasses with crushed ice. Fill with one-quarter cranberry–raspberry juice, one-quarter orange juice and top up with sparkling wine. Garnish each drink with two or three fresh raspberries.

Cranberry Cooler

The slightly bitter aftertaste of the cranberry juice makes this an excellent adult non-alcoholic drink: perfect for drivers.

Cranberry juice is now commercially available in this country, but is mixed with either raspberry or apple juice to make it a more palatable drink – though some of us enjoy it straight! I can heartily recommend it as a drink at any time of the day, and at party-time it makes a welcome change from the ubiquitous orange squash or cola.

Serves 4–6

1 bottle cranberry–apple fruit juice, chilled
ice-cubes made by freezing apple juice

thin wedges of red-skinned apple for garnish
thin lemon wedges

Pour the juice over two or three apple ice-cubes. Slip an apple wedge and a lemon slice over the rim of each glass, and serve.

Café Brûlot

Non tea-drinkers, try this for a change. As far as I am concerned, after-dinner coffee should be hot, black and with *white* sugar. Brown sugar changes the flavour totally. If you must play around, then go the whole hog – and why not, for you will pay dearly in restaurant, hotel or local pub for this delicious and aromatic way of serving coffee.

Serves 2

1 tbsp coffee beans (after-dinner type), crushed
2 fl. oz Cognac or Armagnac
6 sugar cubes
1 2-inch strip each of orange and lemon zest

2 cloves
1 2-inch stick of cinnamon
1 2-inch piece of vanilla pod
2 *demi-tasses* well-made hot black coffee (after-dinner type)

In a small enamel or stainless steel pan, roast the crushed beans until the aroma rises. Remove the pan from the heat.

Add the rest of the ingredients except the made-up coffee. Stir until the sugar is dissolved. Leave to infuse for 10 minutes.

Re-heat gently and ignite. Extinguish the flames by pouring in the hot coffee. Stir well and leave to settle. Decant into *demi-tasses*, using a tea-strainer. *No cream please!*

MENUS
FOR
SPECIAL
OCCASIONS

A Movable Feast – A Picnic Tea

BACON AND AVOCADO SANDWICHES
LETTUCE SANDWICHES
SARDINE AND EGG SANDWICHES

*   *   *

FINGERS OF HERB AND CHEESE BREAD
WITH POTTED SALMON

*   *   *

WHOLEMEAL SCONES
RHUBARB AND RASPBERRY JAM

*   *   *

RASPBERRY AND COCONUT SLICE
DARK COFFEE CAKE
CURRANT AND MINT PASTY

*   *   *

ICED UVA TEA

An Elegant Ladies' Tea-party

CUCUMBER SANDWICHES

CRAB SANDWICHES

*   *   *

SLIVERS OF BUTTERED BROWN BREAD

GREENGAGE JAM

*   *   *

SAND CAKE

*   *   *

ROSE PETAL ICE-CREAM

*   *   *

ICED EARL GREY TEA

Wetting the Baby's Head

A Christening Tea

SPARKLING CIDER CUP

*   *   *

CHICKEN PATTIES

*   *   *

STIR-FRIED SALMON AND GINGER SANDWICHES

QUEEN ALEXANDRA'S SANDWICHES

EGG AND CURRY SANDWICHES

*   *   *

BUTTERED LEMON TEA-BREAD

*   *   *

MINI MOCHA ÉCLAIRS

COCONUT KIRSCH ROLL

WALNUT CAKE

*   *   *

RICH DARK PLUM CHRISTENING CAKE

*   *   *

ICED KEEMUN TEA

A Summer Wedding
at Home in the Afternoon

LOVING CUP
JILL WATT'S CHEESE BISCUITS

*   *   *

MUSHROOM PATTIES
CHICKEN AND HAM ROLLS

*   *   *

ASPARAGUS AND HOLLANDAISE PIN-WHEEL
SANDWICHES
SALMON CREAM CHEESE AND CHIVE PÂTÉ
SANDWICHES
SMOKED CHICKEN AND BELGIAN ENDIVE SANDWICHES
PÂTÉ, PICKLED WALNUT AND PEANUT SANDWICHES

*   *   *

WALNUT AND PINEAPPLE MERINGUE CAKE
ORANGE ALMOND LIQUEUR CAKE

*   *   *

RASPBERRIES WITH REDCURRANT SAUCE

*   *   *

ICED YUNNAN TEA

*   *   *

MARZIPAN STRAWBERRIES

*   *   *

WEDDING CAKE

*   *   *

VINTAGE CHAMPAGNE

Easter Day Tea-party

HOME-MADE SAUSAGE ROLLS

*   *   *

SMOKED SALMON, CREAM CHEESE AND PISTACHIO
NUT SANDWICHES

CHICKEN AND ALMOND SANDWICHES

*   *   *

DROP SCONES WITH FRUIT

*   *   *

PALM BISCUITS

SIMNEL CAKE

SPONGE CAKE

*   *   *

HOT TEA-PUNCH

A Traditional Summer Tea-party in the Garden

CUCUMBER SANDWICHES

SALMON SANDWICHES

POTTED MEAT SANDWICHES

TOMATO SANDWICHES

and they don't come more traditional than that!

*   *   *

FRESHLY BAKED WARM SCONES WITH GOOSEBERRY
AND ELDERFLOWER JAM

*   *   *

BUTTERED FINGERS OF DATE AND WALNUT BREAD

*   *   *

CHOCOLATE SHERRY CAKE

SYLLABUBS

STRAWBERRIES

*   *   *

CHILLED TEA-PUNCH

Christmas Day Afternoon

CRISPLY TOASTED HOME-MADE CRUMPETS
WITH FOIE GRAS AND ARTICHOKE BUTTER

* * *

FINGERS OF HARVO BREAD

* * *

PLAIN CHRISTMAS CAKE
WITH NUGGETS OF WENSLEYDALE CHEESE

GINGER ICE-CREAM

* * *

LAPSANG SOUCHONG TEA TODDY

A Nursery Tea-party

A party tree holding:

EGG SANDWICHES

HONEY SANDWICHES

COLD SAUSAGES

CRISPS

*　　*　　*

GINGER BISCUITS

COCONUT MACAROONS

ROCK CAKES

*　　*　　*

FRESHLY MADE LEMONADE

Hands Across the Water
An American Tea

Smoked Salmon and Cream Cheese Sandwiches

*   *   *

Toasted Muffins with Maple Syrup

*   *   *

Brownies

*   *   *

George Washington Cake

*   *   *

(Boston) Tea-punch

Michael Smith's Own Favourite Afternoon Tea

HOME-MADE SAUSAGE ROLLS

*   *   *

TOASTED CRUMPETS WITH POTTED CRAB

*   *   *

POTTED MEAT SANDWICHES

*   *   *

FINGERS OF BUTTERED BARA BRITH

*   *   *

CHOCOLATE AND GOOSEBERRY CAKE

COCONUT CAKE

ALMOND AND QUINCE SLICE

*   *   *

CLARET JELLIES

*   *   *

HOT TEA-PUNCH

List of Establishments

offering a set afternoon tea or a well-made cup of tea

Reprinted by kind permission of Mr Egon Ronay

Egon Ronay is Britain's top hotel and restaurant critic. Each year he publishes a very comprehensive Guide pointing readers to establishments of reasonable excellence. The Guide is positive in its attitude, never condemnatory – except in his introduction and his summing up of any places falling below his high standards. He pulls no punches in saying why so many places don't make the grade.

In 1985, he published the fourth edition of *Just a Bite: Guide for Gourmets on a Family Budget*. In this guide, among budget restaurants, he lists tea-rooms and cafés. I suggest you obtain a copy and keep it handy.

This list, which I give with his blessing but without his comments – and which should be seen as a list and not as my personal recommendations – will at least help you to find somewhere offering afternoon tea when next you are out for a drive in the country.

THE TEA PLACE OF THE YEAR

When we first introduced our good tea symbol (a teapot) four years ago, very few caterers were serving a quality tea graded by the Tea Council. Today 3-star quality teas – the same quality as most people drink at home – dominate the catering market. The exotic-sounding speciality teas like Darjeeling, Orange Pekoe and Lapsang Souchong are also in great demand.

Yet, in spite of this encouraging move towards quality graded teas, our inspectors report that a good cup of tea is still hard to find.

Sadly, it appears that caterers do not take as much care in brewing tea as they do in baking the cakes, scones and pastries many so temptingly offer with it. Freshly boiled water, a warm pot and time for infusion are as important as the quality of tea used. And adding the right *quantity* of tea makes all the difference too. One tea bag dropped into a pot, regardless of size, is just not enough to produce the required strength. The old rule of one per person and one for the pot is often forgotten.

Tea quality for caterers is graded by the Tea Council, and nothing less than their 3-star quality grade should be used in an establishment in this Guide.

For choosing the Tea Place of the Year, we asked the Tea Council to invite professional tea-tasters to see whether they agreed with our inspectors' choice. They did and we are happy to announce the winner for its all-round excellence:

POLLY
MARLBOROUGH, WILTSHIRE

Previous winners –

1982 Claris, Biddenden, Kent
1983 Original Maids of Honour Shop, Kew, Surrey
1984 Hyatt Carlton Tower, Chinoiserie, London SW1

The search for good cups of tea will continue.

Afternoon Teas

Here is a list of establishments offering set afternoon tea, including a good cup of tea. Up to date in 1986.

London

Athenaeum Hotel, Windsor Lounge, London W1
Le Bistroquet, London W1
Brown's Hotel Lounge, London W1
Connaught Hotel Lounge, London W1
The Dorchester, Promenade, London W1
Goring Hotel Lounge, London SW1
Harrods Georgian Restaurant, London SW1
The Heal's Restaurant, London W1
Hyatt Carlton Tower, Chinoiserie, London SW1
Hyde Park Hotel, Park Room, London SW1
Inn on the Park Lounge, London W1
Inter-Continental Hotel, Coffee House, London W1
Muffin Man, London W8
Richoux, London SW3 and W1
The Savoy, Thames Foyer, London WC2
Sheraton Park Tower Restaurant, London SW1
Tea Time, London SW4
Westbury Hotel Lounge, London W1
The White House Garden Café, London NW1

Southern England

Alfriston, E. Sussex	Singing Kettle
Arundel, W. Sussex	Café Violette
Biddenden, Kent	Claris's Tea Shop
Billingshurst, W. Sussex	Burdock Provender
Bishop's Waltham, Hampshire	Casey's
Brighton, E. Sussex	Mock Turtle
Brook, Isle of Wight	Hanover House
Burley, Hampshire	Forest Tea House

Canterbury, Kent	Paradise Café
	Sweet Heart Pâtisserie
Collier Street, Kent	Butcher's More
Dorking, Surrey	Burford Bridge Hotel Lounge (Sunday only)
Hailsham, E. Sussex	Homely Maid
Haslemere, Surrey	Sue's Coffee Shop
Henfield, W. Sussex	Norton House
Herstmonceux, E. Sussex	Cleavers Lyng
Kew, Surrey	Original Maids of Honour
Lamberhurst, Kent	The Down
Luccombe Chine, Isle of Wight	Dunnose Cottage
Midhurst, W. Sussex	Shelly's
Newport, Isle of Wight	God's Providence House
Penshurst, Kent	Quaintways Tea Rooms
Pulborough, W. Sussex	Chequers Hotel
Richmond, Surrey	Richmond Gate Hotel, Terrace Restaurant
Ringmer, E. Sussex	Coffee House
Romsey, Hampshire	Cobweb Tea Rooms
St Margaret's at Cliffe, Kent	Country Fayre
Sevenoaks, Kent	Old Coffee House
Shoreham-by-Sea, W. Sussex	Cuckoo Clock
Southampton, Hampshire	Bountiful Goodness
Stockbridge, Hampshire	Old Dairy
Sutton Scotney, Hampshire	Riverside Tea Garden
Tenterden, Kent	Peggy's Tea Shop
Warlingham, Surrey	Botley Hill Farm House
Winchelsea, E. Sussex	Finch of Winchelsea
	Winchelsea Tea Rooms
Winchester, Hampshire	Wessex Hotel Coffee Shop
Wye, Kent	Wye Hill Caffee
Yarmouth, Isle of Wight	Jireh House

Thames Valley and Chilterns

Berkhamsted, Hertfordshire	Cook's Delight
Blewbury, Oxfordshire	Lantern Cottage
Burford, Oxfordshire	Jackie's Tea Rooms
Henley-on-Thames, Oxfordshire	Copper Kettle
	Henley Tea Shop
Oxford, Oxfordshire	Browns
Woodstock, Oxfordshire	Blenheim
	Marney's Kitchen
	Tiffany's of Woodstock

West Country

Abbotsbury, Dorset	Flower Bowl
Ashburton, Devon	Ashburton Coffee House
	Old Saddlery
Avebury, Wiltshire	Stones
Bath, Avon	Canary
	Francis Hotel Lounge
	Pump Room
Bossington, Somerset	Old Bakehouse
Bournemouth, Dorset	Carlton Hotel Lounge
Bourton-on-the-Water, Gloucestershire	Mad Hatter
	Small Talk Tea Room
Bradford on Avon, Wiltshire	Corner Stones
Bridport, Dorset	Pedlar
Broad Chalke, Wiltshire	Cottage House
Castle Cary, Somerset	Old Bakehouse
Castle Combe, Wiltshire	Manor House Hotel
Cheddar, Somerset	Wishing Well Tea Rooms
Chipping Camden, Gloucestershire	Bantam Tea Rooms
Compton Abbas, Dorset	Milestones
Crewkerne, Somerset	Pantry
Dorchester, Dorset	Potter In
Dunster, Somerset	Tea Shoppe
East Budleigh, Devon	Grasshopper's
Lechlade, Gloucestershire	Katie's Marlborough House
Lustleigh, Devon	Primrose Cottage
Marlborough, Wiltshire	Polly
Milton Abbas, Dorset	Tea Clipper
Minchinhampton, Gloucestershire	Coffee Bean
Nether Stowey, Somerset	Castle Coffee House
Oakford, Devon	Higher Western Restaurant
Painswick, Gloucestershire	Cup House
Poundsgate, Devon	Leusdon Lodge
Selworthy, Somerset	Periwinkle Cottage
Sidbury, Devon	Old Bakery
	Old Clock House
Spetisbury, Dorset	Marigold Cottage Tea Rooms
Stow-on-the-Wold, Gloucestershire	Ingram's
Tarr Steps, Somerset	Tarr Farm
Tewkesbury, Gloucestershire	Ancient Grudge
	Wintor House
Trebarwith Strand, Cornwall	Mill Floor
Warminster, Wiltshire	Vincents

Williton, Somerset	Blackmore's Bookshop Coffee Room
Wilton, Wiltshire	Wilton House Restaurant
Woodbury, Devon	Tea Bungalow

East Anglia

Binham, Norfolk	Binham Tea Shop
Castle Hedingham, Essex	Trading Post
Clacton-on-Sea, Essex	Montagu Hill China Cup Café
Clare, Suffolk	Ship Stores
Framlingham, Suffolk	Tiffin's
Frinton-on-Sea, Essex	Anne's
Southwold, Suffolk	Friar's Restaurant
	Sutherland House
Sudbury, Suffolk	Friar's Restaurant
Swaffham, Norfolk	Red Door
Wansford, Cambridgeshire	Haycock Hotel Lounge
Wickham Market, Suffolk	Taylor's Wine Cellar

East Midlands

Ashbourne, Derbyshire	Spencers Coffee House
Ashford-in-the-Water, Derbyshire	Cottage Tea Room
Bakewell, Derbyshire	Country Kitchen
Castleton, Derbyshire	Rose Cottage Café
Chesterfield, Derbyshire	Mr C's
Edensor, Derbyshire	Stable Tea Rooms
Hathersage, Derbyshire	Country Fayre Tea Room
Oakham, Leicestershire	David Weston Gallery, Rutland Room
Stamford, Lincolnshire	Bay Tree
	George of Stamford
Tissington, Derbyshire	Old School Tea Rooms

West Midlands

Abbots Bromley, Staffordshire	Marsh Farm Tea Room
Alstonefield, Staffordshire	Old Post Office Tea Rooms
Broadway, Hereford and Worcester	Coffee Pot
Lyonshall, Hereford and Worcester	Church House
Ombersley, Hereford and Worcester	Ombersley Gallery Tea Room
Ross-on-Wye, Hereford and Worcester	Walford House Hotel
Shipston-on-Stour, Warwickshire	Kerry House Tea Rooms

Tutbury, Staffordshire	Old Mill Tea Room
Uttoxeter, Staffordshire	Ye Olde Pantry
Worcester, Hereford and Worcester	Inglenooks Restaurant

North East

Aldborough, N. Yorkshire	Museum Tea Rooms
Alnwick, Northumbria	Maxine's Kitchen
Barden, N. Yorkshire	Howgill Lodge
	Low House Farm
Blanchland, Northumbria	White Monk Tea Room
Bolton Abbey, N. Yorkshire	Tea Cottage
Castleton, N. Yorkshire	Castleton Tea Rooms
Easingwold, N. Yorkshire	Truffles
Edlingham, Northumbria	New Moor House
Harrogate, N. Yorkshire	Betty's
Ilkley, W. Yorkshire	Betty's
Lastingham, N. Yorkshire	Lastingham Lodge
Northallerton, N. Yorkshire	Betty's
Pateley Bridge, N. Yorkshire	The Willow
Scunthorpe, Humberside	Bees Garden
Settle, N. Yorkshire	Car & Kitchen
Sheffield, S. Yorkshire	Toffs Restaurant & Coffee House
Soyland, W. Yorkshire	Far Flat Head Farm
Whitby, N. Yorkshire	Magpie Café
Yarm, Cleveland	Coffee Shop
York, N. Yorkshire	Betty's
	Taylors Tea Rooms

North West and Lake District

Alston, Cumbria	Brownside Coach House
Ambleside, Cumbria	Rothay Manor
Barrow-in-Furness, Cumbria	Ambassador Coffee Lounge
Bleasdale, Lancashire	Bleasdale Post Office Tea Room
Boot, Cumbria	Brook House Restaurant
Bowness on Windermere, Cumbria	Laurel Cottage
Brampton, Cumbria	Tarn End
Caldbeck, Cumbria	Swaledale Watch
Carlisle, Cumbria	Dundas Coffee House
Chester, Cheshire	Chester Grosvenor Lounge
Grasmere, Cumbria	Rowan Tree
Hawkshead, Cumbria	Minstrels Gallery
Loweswater, Cumbria	Kirkstile Inn, Verandah & Vintage Room
Melmerby, Cumbria	Village Bakery

Ullswater, Cumbria	Sharrow Bay Country House Hotel
Windermere, Cumbria	Langdale Chase Hotel
	Miller Howe Hotel

Scotland

Dryburgh Abbey, Borders	Orchard Tearoom
Falkland, Fife	Kind Kyttock's Kitchen
Isle of Gigha, Strathclyde	Gigha Hotel
Moffat, Dumfries and Galloway	Beechwood Country House Hotel

Wales

Bala, Gwynedd	Sospan Fach
Hay-on-Wye, Powys	Granary
	Polly's Tea Rooms
Llanrwst, Gwynedd	Tu-Hwnt-i'-r-Bont
Tay-nant, Clwyd	Bronnant Tea Shop

Channel Islands

St Anne's, Alderney	The Gossip
Gorey, Jersey	Jersey Pottery Restaurant
Portinfer, Jersey	L'Assembliée
St Brelade's Bay, Jersey	Hotel l'Horizon

To Test for 'Doneness'

Bread

After its stated baking time, test for doneness by tapping the base of the baked loaf with the knuckle: it should sound hollow, and the loaf should be crisp and a good brown colour.

Cakes

After the stated baking time, the cake will shrink somewhat from the sides of the pan and will be resistant to light pressure from your forefinger when pressed in the centre.

A second test is to insert a *wooden* skewer or cocktail stick into the centre of the cake. This will come out 'clean' when the cake is baked.

A third test is that the cake will be 'quiet' if you listen to it – this is a good test for rich fruit cakes.

Biscuits

Many biscuits, when baked, are soft until cooled – so you have to rely on your eye. Watch for a nice, rich, golden-brown colour, with no soft uncooked mixture in the centre.

Note: Anything with syrup, caramel, a sugar-glazed topping or jam must not be touched with the finger, as it will be hot enough to cause blistering.

Conversion Tables

SOLID MEASURES

British	*Metric*
16 oz=1 lb	1000 grammes (g)=1 kilogramme (kilo)

Approximate equivalents

BRITISH	METRIC	METRIC	BRITISH
1 lb (16 oz)	450g	1 kilo (1000g)	2 lb 3 oz
½ lb (8 oz)	225g	½ kilo (500g)	1 lb 2 oz
¼ lb (4 oz)	100g	¼ kilo (250g)	9 oz
1 oz	25g	100g	4 oz

LIQUID MEASURES

British

1 quart	= 2 pints	= 40 fl. oz
1 pint	= 4 gills	= 20 fl. oz
½ pint	= 2 gills	
	or 1 cup	= 10 fl. oz
¼ pint	= 8 tablespoons	= 5 fl. oz
	1 tablespoon	= just over ½ fl. oz
	1 dessertspoon	= ⅓ fl. oz
	1 teaspoon	= ⅛ fl. oz

Metric

1 litre=10 decilitres (dl)=100 centilitres (cl)=1000 millilitres (ml)

Approximate equivalents

BRITISH	METRIC	METRIC	BRITISH
1 quart	1.1 litres	1 litre	35 fl. oz
1 pint	6dl	½ litre (5dl)	18 fl. oz
½ pint	3dl	¼ litre (2.5dl)	9 fl. oz
¼ pint (1 gill)	1.5dl	1dl	4 fl. oz
1 tablespoon	15ml		
1 dessertspoon	10ml		
1 teaspoon	5ml		

American

1 quart	= 2 pints	= 32 fl. oz
1 pint	= 2 cups	= 16 fl. oz
	1 cup	= 8 fl. oz
	1 tablespoon	= ⅓ fl. oz
	1 teaspoon	= ⅙ fl. oz

Approximate equivalents

BRITISH	AMERICAN	AMERICAN	BRITISH
1 quart	2½ pints	1 quart	1½ pints+3 tablespoons (32 fl. oz)
1 pint	1¼ pints		
½ pint	10 fl. oz (1¼ cups)	1 pint	¾ pint+2 tablespoons (16 fl. oz)
¼ pint (1 gill)	5 fl. oz		
1 tablespoon	1½ tablespoons	1 cup	½ pint−2 tablespoons (8 fl. oz)
1 dessertspoon	1 tablespoon		
1 teaspoon	⅓ fl. oz		

INDEX

Quaker oat biscuits, 217
Queen Adelaide's sandwiches, 82–3
Queen Alexandra's sandwiches, 82
Queen Mary's cheese biscuits, 217
quince: almond and quince slices, 200–1

rainbow or marble cake, 152–3
raisins: chocolate and raisin roll, 146–7
    Dales cut-and-come-again cake, 138
    rolled muscatel raisin and rum pin-
        wheels, 90
    shoofly pie, 191
    walnut and raisin butter, 241
raspberries: fresh raspberry cake, 160
    hazelnut cake, 165
    hazelnut, raspberry and redcurrant
        Swiss roll, 144–5
    raspberries and cream, 221
    raspberries with redcurrant sauce, 222
    raspberry coconut slice, 200
    raspberry cream layer cake, 161–2
    raspberry fool with framboise, 232
    raspberry sauce, 221
    rhubarb and raspberry jam, 245
red buck's fizz, 270
redcurrants: hazelnut, raspberry and
        redcurrant Swiss roll, 144–5
    raspberries with redcurrant sauce, 222
rhubarb and raspberry jam, 245
rice cake, lemon, 130
rich dark plum cake or Christmas cake,
    132
rich Eccles cakes, 197–8
rich shortcrust pastry, 185
rolled muscatel raisin and rum pin-
    wheels, 90
rolled sandwiches, 89–90
rolls: bridge rolls, 63
    croissants, 66–7
rose petals: apple and rose petal ice-
        cream, 225
    English summer jam with, 244–5
    to sugar, 226
Rosee, Pasqua, 16–17
rosemary: gooseberry and rosemary ice-
    cream, 224
Rosie's wedding cake, 132–4
roulades see sponge rolls
royal icing, 134
rum: Christmas mincemeat with rum, 252
    Cumberland rum butter, 240
    rolled muscatel raisin and rum pin-
        wheels, 90
    rum tea-punch, 270
Russian caravan tea, 38
Russian sandwiches, 77
rye bread, 61–2

sablés, 206–7
sack creams, 229
saffron cake, 117–19
salami special sandwiches, 92

Sally Lunn cakes, 119–20
salmon: devilled salmon sandwiches, 76
    potted salmon, 261
    salmon and cucumber sandwiches, 84
    salmon patties, 256
    salmon season sandwiches, 93
    stir-fried salmon and ginger
        sandwiches, 87
    see also smoked salmon
samovars, 45
sand biscuits, 206–7
sand cake, 128–9
sandwiches, 70–95
    asparagus rolls with hollandaise sauce,
        89
    bacon and avocado, 85–6
    banana and jam, 95
    banger special, 91
    beetroot and sour cream, 88
    breakfast buttie, 91
    brown sugar and chocolate, 95
    caviare, 81–2
    celery, 82
    cheese 'n' apple, 92
    chicken and almond, 77
    choc full o' nuts, 94
    Christmas cheese, 78
    Christmas special, 92
    Christmas turkey, 78
    corny cake, 94
    crab and artichoke, 84
    cream cheese, 95
    cream cheese and pineapple, 80
    cream cheese and shrimp 80–1
    cream cheese and walnut, 80
    cream cheese, chive and almond, 81
    cream cheese, date and pecan nut, 84
    cream cheese, olive and walnut, 86
    cream cheese, orange and hazelnut, 81
    creamy chicken licken', 91
    creamy tomato and anchovy, 76
    crowd o' shrimps, 93
    cucumber, 74
    Delhi, 77
    devilled fish, 78
    devilled salmon, 76
    egg, 75, 95
    egg and cress, 74–5, 93
    egg and curry, 84
    fillet o' fish, 92
    fresh crab, 83
    ham 'n' nut, 93
    Hawaiian bite, 93
    honey, 95
    kipper tie-break, 92
    lettuce, 79
    lobster, 78
    make-a-date, 91
    mangetout and shrimp, 85
    mock crab, 80
    'new' English sandwiches, 91–4
    nursery tea, 95–6

301